KADDISH
WOMEN'S VOICES

KADDISH
WOMEN'S VOICES

Edited by MICHAL SMART
Conceived by BARBARA ASHKENAS

URIM PUBLICATIONS
Jerusalem • New York

Kaddish, Women's Voices

Edited by Michal Smart
Conceived by Barbara Ashkenas

Poems: Michal Smart

Copyright © 2013 by Michal Smart and Barbara Ashkenas

Typeset by Ariel Walden

Printed in Israel

First Edition

ISBN: 978-965-524-150-1

Library of Congress Cataloging-in-Publication Data

Kaddish , women's voices / edited by Michal Smart ; conceived by Barbara Ashkenas.
    pages   cm
Includes bibliographical references.
    ISBN 978-965-524-150-1 (hardcover : alk. paper) 1. Kaddish. 2. Jewish
mourning customs. 3. Women in Judaism. 4. Feminism—Religious
aspects—Judaism. I. Smart, Michal, 1965– editor. II. Ashkenas, Barbara.
    BM670.K3K33 2013
    296.4'45—dc23   2013023087

Urim Publications, P.O. Box 52287, Jerusalem 91521 Israel

www.UrimPublications.com

In Loving Memory
לעילוי נשמת

לעילוי נשמות הורינו

לויה בת מרדכי ושיינה

יוסף דוד בן אברהם וזיסה

רבקה לאה בת זלמן וחנה

אליעזר בן מרדכי ופריידה

❧

We dedicate this book, with love, to our Parents

May their memory be for a blessing

Louise Weiss Fox

David Joseph Fox

Evelyn Weinberger

Edward Weinberger

Contents

Two

Three

Four

Contents

Seven

Eight

Nine

Ten

Eleven

Contents

Twelve

Preface

BARBARA ASHKENAS

There is nothing so whole as a broken heart.
The Kotzker Rebbe

WHILE SAYING KADDISH for my Mom in 2007, a half dozen other women in my community happened to also be saying Kaddish. Together we became a warm and supportive group. Jointly we embraced our sadness and quenched our thirst for intimacy and kindred spirituality. Over the years, while raising my children in Stamford, CT, I had befriended many women, but I must admit the "Kaddish bond" was rare and special.

But what did Kaddish mean to us? How was saying Kaddish as a woman different than the experiences recounted by men? While in mourning, I turned to Jewish literature for guidance and insight. Yet none of these were written from a woman's perspective. I began to imagine a book about women saying Kaddish; one that shared our experiences and could serve as a guidepost to others. I shared my vision with my Kaddish friends and family. They all encouraged me to make this journey.

I was introduced to Michal Smart in April 2010. Mid-conversation, Frank Sinatra's "My Way" came over the Starbucks speakers. When we discovered that this song had been played at both my mother's and her father's funerals, we knew that we were meant to collaborate on this project. Michal took the reins as lead editor, and my vision would never have become a reality without her.

The conversation continued in my living room in May. A dozen women who had recently experienced a loss and said Kaddish came together to begin a new project: the creation of the book *Kaddish, Women's Voices*. Loss was the currency of intimacy, and through listening to one another, a community was created. The room filled with a sense of poignant and powerful possibility.

This book is a continuation of those conversations. It is part of a growing conversation, where women's voices can be heard through the heartstrings of Kaddish.

It is interesting to note that in the first edition of Rabbi Maurice Lamm's classic "purple book," *The Jewish Way in Death and Mourning*, written in 1969, he states that "the obligation to recite Kaddish is placed upon the son, not the daughter." Thirty years later, however, in the second edition of his book, Rabbi Lamm notes that ". . . today, reciting the Kaddish is open to all women who want to express their grief in this manner and speak to the Almighty on behalf of their beloved departed relatives. . . . All Jewish people stand to benefit from a woman's holy resolve in saying Kaddish."

I believe women who commit to saying Kaddish do indeed have a holy resolve – that shines through in these pages. Some resolve to hold onto their loved one a little longer. Some need to resolve issues with the departed, and use Kaddish to reflect and bring closure. Still others resolve to renew their commitment to Jewish life. I hope this book will serve as a companion to others, spark many meaningful conversations, and open the possibilities for women to choose how to mourn and remember a loved one.

Through Kaddish, may our broken hearts indeed become whole again, and in the words of Rabbi Yosef Eliyahu Henkin (quoted by Rabbi Lamm), may we be blessed ". . . with *kedusha*, lives filled with holiness of purpose, instead of Kaddish."

Introduction

MICHAL SMART

J UDAISM TAKES A NEW MOURNER by the hand, and guides him or
her through the initial period of life after loss. At a time of aloneness,
the mourner is drawn out and supported by a caring community.
Amidst tumult and change, there is also time to reflect and to feel. In the
face, perhaps, of anger or a sense of abandonment, the mourner is forced
to confront and communicate with God. When a key relationship has
come to an end, there is an opportunity for continued involvement, and
closure. And the cornerstone of this process is the recitation of Kaddish.

The grieving heart is torn open. And that openness is an opportunity
to grow spiritually and to reorient one's life. As Jewish women, we inherit
a legacy of strength and resilience in difficult times. In the Book of Ruth,
when Naomi's husband and both her sons die, she is left in a strange
land, bereft and alone. Yet the very next thing we read is "*vatakam hi,*
and she (Naomi) rose up." She was not defeated. In fact, it is only at this
point that we first see Naomi take life into her own hands, and begin her
long journey home. Childless, the Bible's Chana is so distraught that she
weeps at the holiday table and cannot eat or drink. Yet here, too, we read
"*vatakam Chana.*" She rose out of her despair and turned her life around.
And how did she do it? Through prayer.

This book explores what the recitation of Kaddish meant to different
women, most of whom made a daily commitment to say it. Did they
find the community and the consolation they were seeking? How did
saying Kaddish affect their relationships with God, with prayer, with
the deceased, and with the living? With courage and generosity, authors
of diverse backgrounds and ages reflect upon their experience of *aveilut*

15

(mourning). They share their relationships with the family members they lost and what it meant to move on, how they struggled to balance the competing demands of childrearing, work, and grief, what they learned about tradition and themselves, and the disappointments and particular challenges they confronted as women.

This book does not seek to provide simplistic or uniform answers to complex and personal questions, or to force any one conclusion on the many points for discussion raised within its pages. Rather, through fifty-two honest and personal essays, the book invites the reader into the intimate experience of a woman in mourning, and reveals the multiplicity of women's experiences, seen through the prism of Kaddish. Authors recount experiences across the globe, including all parts of the United States and Israel, Canada, England, India and Australia. The collection shares viewpoints from diverse denominations and perspectives, and explores what it means to heal from loss and to honor memory in family relationships both loving and fraught with pain.

Kaddish is a responsive prayer that can only be recited in the presence of a *minyan* (quorum for public prayer). It is not a mitzvah, a formal commandment, for anyone to say Kaddish. Nonetheless, many commonly regard it as such, undertaking a fervent commitment to attend daily prayer services throughout the period of mourning. The primacy of Kaddish illustrates how customs can evolve organically, and testifies to the desire of those left behind to stay connected, and if possible to assist their departed loved ones.

How did the custom arise? A strange tale appears in sources as early as the twelfth century, in which the tormented soul of a deceased man appears to Rabbi Akiva, and is ultimately released from eternal punishment only when his son is taught to lead the congregation in prayer, specifically eliciting the response "*Yehei shmei rabba mevorach*, May God's Great Name be blessed." On this basis, a custom later arose for men who had recently lost a parent to act as prayer leader, in an effort to benefit the soul of their deceased. Since only men above the age of bar mitzvah could play that role, a custom then arose for young children to recite an "Orphan's Kaddish" (*Kaddish Yatom*). This brief responsive prayer, more commonly known today as the "Mourner's Kaddish," echoes the Kaddish prayers recited elsewhere and elicits the same communal praise of God. Over the centuries, saying Kaddish became a cherished and widely practiced custom for adult mourners, as well as children. Those who are ineligible to lead public prayer can nonetheless lead a congregation in the recitation of *Kaddish Yatom*. Affording them the opportunity is this Kaddish's *raison d'etre*.

Many people assume that the phenomenon of women saying Kaddish is a recent innovation, perhaps an outgrowth of secular feminism. In fact, women have been reciting *Kaddish Yatom* for hundreds of years in communities across the world.

Nonetheless, the practice never became normative, and women who stand to say Kaddish in Orthodox synagogues today frequently find their motivation to be suspect, or encounter outright opposition. As more women opt to do so, synagogues are challenged to make room, literally and metaphorically, for women and their voices. Rabbinic policies vary regarding how loudly a woman may recite Kaddish, or whether she may do so unaccompanied by a male voice. This book presents essays by three Orthodox rabbis, who share their own perspectives and discuss the laws of *aveilut*.

The Torah tells us that in the desert generation, there was a man named Zelofchad who had five daughters and no sons (Numbers 27). At that time, Mosaic Law stated that land in Israel was to be inherited only by sons. After their father's death, the daughters of Zelofchad approach Moses and the other leaders and advocate for their right to inherit their father's land. God tells Moses that they speak correctly, and the law is changed.

Both Moses and later authorities recognized the purity of the intentions of Zelofchad's daughters. The rabbis of the Talmud deem them "wise, learned, and righteous" (*Bava Batra* 119b). The biblical episode is introduced with an important phrase: "*vatikravna banot Zelofchad*, and the daughters of Zelofchad approached" (literally, came closer).

Like the daughters of Zelofchad, the women you will encounter in these pages were not looking to challenge authority or to sow discord, but only to claim their rightful inheritance and in so doing, to come closer to God and the Jewish community.

Saying Kaddish may not be the right choice for everyone. Women with young children, for instance, frequently can't participate in a regimented schedule of prayer services. This book voices the viewpoint of one woman who chose not to say Kaddish, as well as others who did not succeed as they'd planned.

When we do something worthwhile in memory of a loved one, our deeds reflect and extend their impact on the world. It is said that any positive action can bring merit to the deceased. Other traditional venues for honoring loved ones include learning and/or teaching Torah, increasing one's observance of *mitzvot*, performing acts of *chesed* and giving *tzedakah*. These continue to be available to us after the last "Amen."

Death steals those closest to us and takes them to another realm, seemingly beyond reach. Through Kaddish, we extend our arms into that void, seeking to stay connected and to aid the departed on their journey. Knowingly or unknowingly, in so doing, the mourner embarks upon a journey of her own.

This book is a record of the journey that is Kaddish, its dark corners and unexpected vistas, told with clarity, candor, and depth. It is a precious record of women searching for their place within Jewish tradition, and exploring the connections that make human life worthwhile. I hope you will feel as I do, that it is a privilege to accompany them, and we resume our own journeys enriched.

Acknowledgments

BARBARA ASHKENAS

M Y ABUNDANT AND MOST HEARTFELT gratitude to Michal Smart, editor extraordinaire, without whom *Kaddish, Women's Voices* would *never* have been completed. Her long, dedicated solo hours, patience, wisdom, expert writing and editing skills along with her Jewish philosophical sensibilities created a volume that is both thoughtful and compelling. Our special friendship that has grown while working together will be warmly cherished for years to come.

To Tzvi Mauer and Urim Publications for giving us this opportunity to publish *Kaddish, Women's Voices*.

To our incredible writers, I am so grateful to all of you for reaching into your emotionally packed Kaddish experiences in order to share and inspire us all.

With love, appreciation and thankfulness to my caring family whose patience and support has enabled me to pursue this project. To my husband, Ron, you consistently inspire me. You are my rock. Thank you for your ever-present love, help and encouragement. To my adult children Eli, Shira and Ari and their spouses, Elie and Rebecca, your love through loss, grief and Kaddish gave me strength to continue on. Hashem has truly blessed me and I am so proud of you. Finally to my precious grandchildren, to be your Bubbe is the best gift of all.

With loving appreciation to Dr. Vera Schwarcz, my *machatanista*, who introduced me to Michal and saw the benefit of our working as a team; who shares the joys of grandparenting with me, and played a constant role in making this book cross the finish line. To my *machatonim*, Jason Wolfe, David and Eve Thaler, for your loving support during this project.

With gratitude to my sister Suzie, sister-in law Lynne and my "sister" Adele, for your loving support through our journey through grief, loss and renewal.

With loving thanks to Nilda, your caring devotion dedication and friendship to our family is invaluable to me.

Many thanks to Rabbi Mark Dratch, for his warm support during a most difficult period of family illness and loss. His consistent advice and wisdom will always be fondly remembered. Additional thanks for his encouragement in selecting Urim Publications.

With gratitude to Rabbi David Walk, for being a friendly nudge. It was with his constant encouragement that I began this project.

With appreciation to Rabbi Daniel Cohen, for his warm welcoming support for women mourners who undertook the Kaddish commitment at Congregation Agudath Sholom.

With warm appreciation to my Kaddish companions, for standing beside me and giving me daily doses of strength, courage and love throughout my year of saying Kaddish.

With loving appreciation to Penny Cohen whose supportive counsel helped me through the most difficult days of loss and mourning. She lit a fire underneath me and fanned the flames in order to ignite the dream of this book into a reality.

Many thanks to Ari Goldman for his early and continuous encouragement to go forward with this book in the early stages of its conception.

With abundant gratitude to Hashem for blessing me in countless ways and for giving me the vision and courage to pursue and complete this project.

Acknowledgments

MICHAL SMART

I T HAS BEEN a privilege to work on this project, and I thank all the amazing women who generously shared their experiences. I am grateful for the assistance of Tzvi Mauer and the staff of Urim Publications in bringing *Kaddish, Women's Voices* to print.

Barbara Ashkenas not only conceived the idea for this book, she originated the collection of essays, arranged for publication with Urim, and supported my work and the project in myriad ways. Working with Barbara has been a gift. Her humor, kindness and extraordinary sensitivity have been enriching and often sustaining. This would all have been worthwhile just for the friendship we gained.

My family has been wonderfully patient and encouraging as I have worked on this book, even on nights when there was a pile of revisions on my desk but no dinner on the table. Thank you James, my *bashert* and best friend, and my children Zachariah, Jonah, Sarah, David and Tani. You are my joy and I thank God for every day that we all have together. Loving thanks to my wonderful and ever-helpful parents-in-law, Robert and Martha Smart, my sisters, Heather, Erica and Amy, and my cousins, the Schneiders and Minkoves for all your support.

I am grateful to Vera Schwarcz for reminding me years ago that I was a writer, and making the introductions. I will always think of you and our dear friend Levana Polate, *z"l*, as our guiding angels. Thank you also to Michael Feldstein for helping us to connect with potential authors and with rabbis supportive of this endeavor.

Several people reviewed parts of this manuscript in draft form and offered valuable feedback: Martha, James, and younger Smarts, Rachel

Mesch, Leah Levy, Vera Schwarcz, Erica Fox, Ronnie Sichel, Jackie Schiff, Maria Reicin, Naomi Messer, and Elizabeth Paddon. I especially thank Rabbi Mark Dratch for his insight and guidance. Rahel Berkovits generously shared her halachic expertise with us, as we awaited publication of her invaluable sourcebook, *A Daughter's Recitation of Mourner's Kaddish.*

In the span of seven years, I birthed five children and buried both my parents. I was supported throughout by the friendship of Rabbi Daniel Cohen and the West Hartford Jewish community. Those friendships continue and I am so pleased that he has participated in this book.

I would also like to express my appreciation and respect for the men and women who attend *minyan* each day in *shuls* around the world. This simple yet remarkably committed act keeps our community functioning, and makes it possible for mourners to find support while saying Kaddish.

Most of all, I thank Hashem for the gift of life, for sustaining me and enabling me to bring this project to fruition.

יִתְגַּדַּל
וְיִתְקַדַּשׁ
שְׁמֵהּ
רַבָּא

This Is the Way the World Ends
you go downstairs
in the morning
sip your coffee
browse the news while you
finish your toast
go about errands
that keep you
clothed and fed

miles away
a tiny ball of matter
smaller than a pea
lodges in the pathway
to the brain

phone rings
levee breaks
slowly
midst the roaring
it begins
to seep in

this is the way the world ends
with an ordinary breakfast

My Final Gift

HODIE KAHN

M
Y FATHER, LEON KAHN, *z"l*, was larger than life. He was born Leibke Kaganowicz in 1925, in Eisiskes, Poland (a small town near Vilna) where he lived a classically traditional *shtetl* life until the *Einsatzgruppen* arrived there in September 1941. Over two days, they rounded up and massacred nearly all of Eisiskes's 3,500 Jews. My father's family managed individually to survive the liquidation. He and his older brother hid on the rooftop of a home close to the killing field, a perch that offered them the perfect vantage to witness the horrors of genocide, and to feed their hunger not just to live to tell the tale, but also to fight back.

The family regrouped and together they embarked on an odyssey for survival that took them to farms, haylofts, ghettos, and ultimately the forest, where my father spent nearly three years as a partisan fighter. Sadly, he was the only member of his family to survive. His exploits and recollections are chronicled in his powerful memoir, *No Time to Mourn*, and immortalized in the films, *Genocide* and *Unlikely Heroes: Stories of Jewish Resistance*.

After the war, my father applied the same skills that served him as a partisan to building a new life. He arrived in Vancouver, Canada in 1948 in the guise of a tailor, having paid a fellow survivor in his displaced persons camp to sew a pocket for him, so that he could qualify for a Jewish refugee resettlement program for garment factory workers. The program's sponsors quickly recognized that their "tailor" was a fraud, and reassigned him to a toy manufacturer, where he began his rise from penniless refugee to successful business entrepreneur. He married (my mother is also a survivor), and became a husband, father, zeide, community leader, philanthropist, and loving and generous patriarch to new generations.

Family came first and last to my father. We were his world and he was ours.

His passing in 2003 was sudden and shocking. As I stood by his grave on a cloudy day in June, watching his coffin disappear under a mound of earth, I could not conceive – or accept – that my superhero Dad was gone. In the haze of my distress, I latched on to the words of the Mourner's Kaddish, not as a final goodbye but as the beginning of an extended farewell. I understood the prayer to be a vehicle for exalting God on behalf of my father, its purpose to facilitate the journey of his soul to eternal rest. I also understood it to be a tool for mourners, compelling us to pray with a community so we would not be isolated in our grief.

From the minute I first uttered the Aramaic words so familiar from years of listening to them in *shul*, there was never any question for me that I would utter them again and again for my entire year of *aveilut*. My father never had a chance to say Kaddish for his own parents, something I knew pained him greatly. I and my two brothers would make sure this piece of family history would not be repeated.

Saying Kaddish for my father was not a point of law for me. It was a point of love. Aryeh Leib ben Shaul HaKohen, *z"l*, was as much my Dad as my brothers' and I felt equally duty bound to make sure his soul got "home" safely. Saying Kaddish was the last opportunity I had to honor him. It was my final gift.

My father never distinguished between my brothers and me on the basis of gender during his lifetime, and I was sure that he would not have distinguished between us now. I was equally sure that Hashem wouldn't either. It never occurred to me that God would not acknowledge my Kaddish, even if some mortal men did not. The God I believe in hears without prejudice the prayers of males and females, regardless of obligation.

My year of saying Kaddish was nothing like what I'd expected. Then again, I didn't really know what to expect. *Shacharit* and *Mincha/Maariv*. Every day. For eleven months. Looking back on that year, I often marvel at the forces I marshaled to make it happen – and the blind ignorance I had of the emotional and logistical challenges I would deal with along the way. On more than one morning, I found my husband anxiously, but quietly, pacing in the driveway when I pulled in later than usual. My children and I often drove straight from their after-school lessons to synagogue and my daughters did their homework in the *shul* vestibule while I davened. Lucky for me, I was blessed with a patient husband, two loving and obliging young children, and devoted friends – all of whom accommodated my need to honor and mourn my Dad my way.

I remember one particular Shabbat morning at my then-*shul*, Hebrew Institute of Riverdale. I arrived a bit late and missed the first Kaddish of the morning. Rabbi Avi Weiss happened to be coming out of the sanctuary just as I was arriving into the lobby. Without a second's hesitation, he told me to stay where I was and to say the introductory blessings. He turned and re-entered the sanctuary, returning to the lobby in about two minutes – together with nine other men who made for me a *minyan* to listen and respond to my Kaddish.

What started as a gift for my father became in the end also a gift for me. By the time I uttered my last Kaddish, I understood the brilliance behind this prayer that compelled me to be a part of, and not apart from, a social group. It provided me with a tool to engage others to help me heal, and facilitated for me the creation of new and lasting bonds of friendship in my community. Each man and woman who added his or her voice to mine strengthened the power of my Kaddish. Each one who listened to me say the words acted as a buffer against the overwhelming pain of the loss of my father, at the same time gently moving me toward the dawn of a new world without him. Each Kaddish for me was a chance to keep my father "alive" a little longer. It was our special time together. And it was a way for me to help him reach the end of his journey.

I really don't know what to believe about after death or afterlife. But I like to think that the soul of Leon Kahn, *z"l*, my beloved father, now rests peacefully for eternity in the place where it was created.

My brothers and I often joked, even while my Dad was alive, that when he passed he would definitely merit "front row seats" in the World to Come. I'm hoping that when the time comes for my soul and my father's to be reunited, my daughters will say Kaddish for me – so that I can get close enough for him to see me wave.

HODIE KAHN is a native of Vancouver, Canada. After receiving her BA from University of British Columbia, she embraced the concept that "life is a journey" by spending a quarter century traveling, studying and working in a host of fabulous cities around the globe. Along the way she completed an MSJ (Medill School of Journalism, Northwestern University) and MBA (Columbia University) before navigating her way from Jerusalem back to Vancouver, where she resides with her two witty and wonderful daughters. She splits her time helping to manage the family investment business and communal work – but her most favorite job is motherhood.

A Mother's Kaddish

SHELLEY RICHMAN COHEN

I T IS HARD TO BELIEVE that it is four years since Nathaniel's passing. I still feel his presence throughout the day and miss his warm, smiling face and upbeat outlook. The name Nathaniel means "gift of God," and that is what he was. He woke up almost every day with a smile, eager to greet the world. An optimist by nature, the words "no" or "can't" were not a part of his vocabulary. He viewed life as a series of opportunities to explore and experience. Although never seeking the limelight, he always desired to be where the action was. He loved people and places, and was always ready to try something new. Although Duchenne Muscular Dystrophy, a progressive deteriorative disease, reversed the normal course of his life, he managed to enjoy all that he could participate in.

From the time of Nathaniel's diagnosis at age 6 he began to decline. He lost his ability to walk at age 8½ and by his early teens was fast becoming a quadriplegic. Instead of being a mother who slowly let her child grow towards independence, I was forced by necessity to be a mother who had to involve herself in every aspect of my child's life. From showering, to toileting, to dressing and feeding, as Nathaniel deteriorated his every function became the responsibility of those who loved him most, his family.

With his death at age 21, on that cold day in April, my constant physical orchestrations ended, but my emotional desire to care for my son did not. The desire to do for one's child does not die with that child.

When Nathaniel passed away, we in his immediate family were obligated to say Kaddish for the *shloshim*, the thirty-day period of mourning. My husband, Ruvan, my other children, Jonathan and Jackie, and I were steadfast in taking on this *chiyuv* (halachic obligation). After all, didn't

Nathaniel deserve this last act of devotion? As the days of that first month dwindled, Ruvan told me that he wanted to take on the obligation of saying Kaddish for the full eleven months. The minute he said that, I too knew that I wanted to take on this longer obligation, as well. Had Nathaniel had the *zechut*, the privilege of living a full healthy life, chances are he would have had children to say Kaddish for him. Since that was not to be his fate, who would be more appropriate to say Kaddish for him than his mother? I carried him in my womb, I birthed him, and I orchestrated the life he led. For his 21 years our lives – his and mine – were inextricably bound together. It was out of a profound sense of loss that I took on the commitment to say Kaddish.

At that moment, I don't think I fully grasped what saying Kaddish would really mean. Yes, I knew it was said at three different prayer times every single day. Yes, I knew I would have to say it for close to a year. But no, I don't really think I thought about how difficult it would be for a person like me who is, despite the best of intentions, perpetually tardy. All I knew was that I was grieving for almost every aspect of my son's short life and I wanted desperately to be able to connect to him. Kaddish was a means for me to continue doing for Nathaniel.

Since I was a little girl, I was told that there are many levels in heaven and that when a Kaddish is recited for a loved one, that *neshama* gets to move to the next level. Although I'm not quite sure what I presently believe, I do know that hearing "his *neshama* should have an *aliyah*" was quite comforting to me. It helped to make that nebulous void of death feel like a slightly more tangible, cause and effect relationship. If people heard my Kaddish they would say "Amen" and help to make Nathaniel's ascension in heaven happen.

I most often said Kaddish at my Modern Orthodox synagogue on the Upper West Side of Manhattan. I was not the first woman in my congregation who chose to say Kaddish and I am certainly not the last. At one point, we had as many as six women saying Kaddish, some out loud, some in a low voice, according to the way they are comfortable, not dissimilar from the ways different men say Kaddish. For the most part I felt comfortable saying it there and felt that the men as well as other women answered "Amen."

Nonetheless, certain customs of the daily service began to grate on me. For example, in *Shacharit*, our congregation has the *shaliach tzibbur* recite the *Birchot HaShachar* (morning blessings) out loud, to which the congregation answers "Amen." At the point where he recites the blessing for "God having not created me a woman," the women on the other side of the *mechitza* (divider) are supposed to say silently to themselves the blessing for "God creating me according to His will." I have learned and fully understand why that blessing is there, that it refers to the fact that according to tradition men are obligated to do more *mitzvot* than women are and for that they are thankful. But the truth is, despite understanding where the blessing comes from, it is insulting to hear a hearty refrain of "amen" to the line praising God for not making one a woman, day in and day out. In a religion where it is customary to cover the challah bread at a Friday night Shabbat meal during *Kiddush* so as not to embarrass or make the challah feel jealous while the wine is being blessed first, I couldn't help but wonder how a community could not devise a method where the man leading the service would take note before he starts if there is a woman present, and if so, he could say this blessing silently to himself. If we demonstrate compassion for an inanimate object like a loaf of bread, why can't we show more sensitivity towards women choosing to pray with a daily *minyan*?

I occasionally encountered problems saying Kaddish when I traveled to a different *minyan*. One time in Florida, I davened at a *minyan* set up for Yeshiva boys, and I was the only mourner. Midway through my first Kaddish, I realized no one was saying "amen" to my Kaddish. By the time I finished my second Kaddish, I turned to the men on the other side of the *mechitza* and said out loud, "Great, not one of you is going to say amen to my Kaddish?" They would not. Although I felt grateful that they didn't try to drown me out (as happened to me once in a Haredi synagogue in upstate New York), I felt shocked and angry that high school age yeshiva boys couldn't display enough *kavod ha-briyot*, basic human respect, to muster an "amen" to my Kaddish. After all, what could be so wrong about uttering the word "amen" when a fellow Jew praises God? The friend I was visiting contacted the principal of the Yeshiva, who promised to give them a talk the following day on the laws of answering a person's Kaddish. I hope they learned a life lesson!

The controversy I sometimes encountered prompted me to research the halachic discourse regarding women saying Kaddish. I was grateful that JOFA (Jewish Orthodox Feminist Alliance) had collected sources on the subject and made them readily available on its website. I was bolstered by the long history of rabbinic responsa that permit women to say Kaddish.

Interestingly, Rabbi Moshe Leib Blair said that saying Kaddish is an integral part of mourning, for which a woman is obligated, rather than an integral part of *tefillah b'tzibbur*, public prayer, from which she is exempt.

Despite the upsets, as the year passed, my inner dialogue with God grew through prayer. I realized that throughout Nathaniel's illness I had been so angry with God that essentially I had stopped praying. My yearning for a miracle that would stop his slow steady deterioration was so strong that it rendered me speechless for prayer. But as the year of saying Kaddish wore on, I felt a level of comfort from the steadiness of the repetition of prayer. Eventually, I was able to reconcile myself to the concept of a "merciful God," a formulation that I had a great deal of difficulty with from the time of Nathaniel's diagnosis. Despite being aware of the abundant blessings that I had in my life, throughout his illness I kept feeling that if our omnipotent God were truly merciful, He would create a miracle and cure Nathaniel's disease. Over the course of my year saying Kaddish, I finally internalized that which I always knew to be true. We are all here on this Earth for only a moment, and although Nathaniel's moment was especially brief, at least he was given the two most wonderful caring siblings and fabulous father that any person could ever want, and the love and devotion of his entire family. I finally understood that the quality of his life made it a merciful one.

Through *tefillah b'tzibbur*, and participating in it by saying Kaddish out loud and having it responded to, I was able to reconnect to a relationship with Hashem that I wasn't sure that I would ever regain. I think that in a fundamental way that is the very purpose of *tefillah*, whether one is a man or a woman. I urge all of you to consider that regardless of which side of the *mechitza* one is on, people who come to daven are striving to find their connection to and peace with Hashem, equal in intent, equal in merit and equal in importance.

There was one prayer in particular that I would sit and say very contemplatively. I began to think of it as Nathaniel's prayer, and it somehow enabled me to gain acceptance of his passing. It is found in the part of davening that is supposed to be said after one rises in the morning. It reads:

My God,
The soul You placed within me is pure.
You created it, You formed it, You breathed it into me,
And You guard it while it is within me.
One day You will take it from me,
And restore it to me in the time to come.

These words spoke to me. They seemed to convey a simple truth. Nathaniel had the purest of souls. God created him, bestowed him upon me and my family and ultimately God decided to take him back. Of course the last line that I quote gives me hope that I will one day be reunited with my beloved son.

Nathaniel was my first. He made me a mother and an adorer; he was an object on whom to bestow a love I never even knew I had within me. He altered my entire being as no one ever had before him or since. His diagnosis altered my world and his death destroyed an inner piece of me that will never recover. But even with that knowledge, another part of me needs to live and grow for my other two children, for my husband, and even for myself. In some small way, the year of saying Kaddish helped me to want to continue to grow despite the devastating loss of my firstborn son.

May Nathaniel's *neshama* have an *aliyah* to the highest level where it so richly deserves to be.

SHELLEY RICHMAN COHEN became an advocate for inclusion of Jewish Children with Special Needs starting with the diagnosis of Duchene Muscular Dystrophy of her eldest son, Nathaniel. A graduate of Barnard College, Shelley dedicated herself to raising her children after beginning a career in politics working as a political consultant and later as a congressional liaison for a number of Jewish communal organizations. She continues to be active in the field of disabilities advocacy as a public speaker and as a board member of day schools and Jewish organizations. She lives in Manhattan with her husband, Ruvan, and her two children, Jonathan and Jackie.

Loss for Words

RACHEL MESCH

M Y MOTHER DIED ON PURIM, a holiday she relished. It was less than two weeks after her sixty-fifth birthday, and two days after her sixth grandchild was born in the same Boston hospital, two floors and several hallways away.

Baby Noah was born at the wrong time (he was due a week later) and the wrong place (he was supposed to be delivered in New York, where my sister Elana lived). He met his Baubie twice in the hospital. Seeing my sister with her baby in her arms, my mother met my father's gaze: "She's glowing," she murmured. Elana decided it would be better to leave the hospital first. So she and her husband, Lou, shepherded their new son to my parents' empty house in the chilly March night. Three hours later, my mother was gone.

As death and birth coincided, we all found ourselves in awe before a powerful life truth: that it was possible to feel at once joy and sorrow; that a *bris* can indeed take place inside a *shiva* house. We lived those days in raw intensity, stunned, bewildered, amazed, our tears buffeted by the primal presence of this infant, so new, so alive. We were reservoirs of feeling, aching, flowing. During that time, Noah provided the comfort to which his Hebrew name attests. He and his cousin, my seven-month old Sam, were passed around like enchanted touchstones, their magical baby energy providing welcome escapes from a death that was too much to bear, too much to comprehend, too *fast*. My daughters and nieces were also a source of comfort, to be sure, but they knew too much already; at ages 3, 7, 10, their faces could mirror our pain.

In those first days, I struggled to reconcile the Jewish clock, cycling relentlessly towards the next ritual obligation, with a much less reliable children's timetable of diapers, meals, bedtime. I finally understood why the rabbis exempted women from what they referred to as "positive time bound commandments," *mitzvot* to be performed at fixed times. How could anyone be expected to be at *shul* every morning when they have children to nurse, clothe, send off to school, I wondered? But my mother would have wanted me to say Kaddish, this much I knew. A *frum* egalitarian Conservative Jew and a principled feminist, she said it daily, and with pride, for both of her parents. And so I did too, during the first month. I sneaked out of bed in the dark of early spring and found my way to *shul* for *Shacharit*, or bolted from the house between dinner and tuck-in, to catch *Mincha*. Once the *shloshim* were over, Kaddish became compulsory for me on the weekends, and a lofty, mostly unachieved goal during the week.

From the beginning, I felt most connected to my mother as I sat in *shul*; she loved davening, she loved Hebrew. For her the words in the *siddur* were thrilling characters in an epic story, and she was eternally dazzled by the alternate roles they played in the *Tanach*, in the *tefillot*, in Modern Hebrew poetry.

Davening for me suddenly meant speaking my mother's language, and inhabiting a space I had never quite adopted as my own. It meant being at once unbearably close to her and excruciatingly far. Those Hebrew words, many of which I had chanted my whole life, felt newly alien; they were awkward instruments tumbling clumsily from my mouth, their meanings opaque, locked away in a distant world.

Sitting in *shul*, I felt something foreign to any notion of grief I had ever contemplated, a whole that was much more, much different, than the sum of its parts. In some sense it was as if I had returned to what the psychoanalyst Julia Kristeva describes as the pre-linguistic phase, that period of infancy when one is boundlessly attached to one's mother in a chaotic amalgam of emotions – a kind of pure connection to reality that will eventually be broken by the sundering effect of language. In *shul*, I was internal chaos, at once buoyed by the comfort of that seamless connection and shaken by the recognition of permanent loss.

And then I needed to stand up and fit this feeling into a set of ancient Hebraic words, and to say them loud enough to be heard.

One morning, I brought Sam with me, now eight months old, and as I stood up to say Kaddish, he began to talk, a long melodic ahhh. I couldn't speak. I opened my mouth, but nothing came out. Hearing Sam's cheerful coo, rising and falling as he navigated the contours of his newly discovered voice, I was confronted with that juxtaposition of life and death that had defined my mother's passing. What I wanted to say was not *Yitgadal v'yitkadash*, not the somber, tuneless rhythm of the Kaddish verses, but something closer to my baby's wordless release of sound. I wanted a sound that would somehow capture the intensity of my feelings that would loop across time and generations, between my mother and my son and me, between Hebrew and English, between language and emotion.

Kaddish, I think, is meant to do this; it is meant to offer words for those who are wordless. And yet for me, sometimes, the words simply would not come out. A song, I have sometimes thought, might have been easier. A melody through which to thread emotions that don't wrap easily around words. I was there to remember my mother, but the force of memory and emotion always threatened to sabotage the mitzvah itself. Is Kaddish meant to express my loss or to contain it, I wondered? You can't cry and say Kaddish at the same time, I discovered, again and again and again.

In the rabbinic tradition, the words of the Torah are famously described as black fire upon white fire. The black fire is to be interpreted, both the words and their form: their various inky strokes and curls. But the white fire, too, is laden with meaning. Some say it is even holier for its opacity, its esoteric fullness. Black fire is language and thus contraction; white fire is reflection, emotion, expansiveness. In *shul*, I was white fire fighting with black fire, reaching for the words to enclose my feelings, but then spilling back again into the margins, refusing interpretation, meaning, and the solace of tradition and structure.

Despite the challenges, I was appreciative of the public space that was carved out for me as a mourner in *shul*, a space in which to recognize my loss. Kaddish was the ritual that was handed to me; that I would continue to say it went unquestioned. Even as I hit up against its limits, I clung to its dependable rhythms, to its ancient roots, to its potential as an outlet for the grief running through me.

At home, on the other hand, I had to find my own words, and they did not come easily. From the beginning, I was daunted by the difficulty of expressing my grief with my own children, particularly my daughters. I valued honest communication, but I did not want to frighten them. I wanted to be present; but I did not want to deny my own needs. I was repeatedly stunned to find that I lacked the vocabulary with which to make my way through this foreign emotional terrain, baffled by my own loss for words.

Days after the *shiva* had ended, I was tucking my three-and-a-half year old, Eliza, into bed. "Let's play a game," she whispered. "I'll be the mommy and you be the baby. I'll take care of you." It was, somehow, just what we both needed.

Sometimes when I left for *shul* my seven-year old, Abby, pleaded for me to stay. She was, like me, experiencing a loss that was both profoundly Jewish and profoundly maternal: that of a grandmother whom she associated with Pesach and Chanukah, chicken soup with matzah balls, Shabbat candles, *tefillot*, the Hebrew language. One evening, she began screaming angrily as her sister flipped through a book about making challah, with, naturally, a Baubie protagonist. Alone with her, I proceeded with trepidation. "It's okay to still feel sad about Baubie," I whispered. "Even if it hurts, you have to let it out."

"But Mommy," she pleaded. "You don't know what it's like to be *afraid* that you're going to cry."

And there, staring me in the face, was a mirror image of my own confused grief – relaying frantically between words, tears, and the fear of losing control. Stunned by my daughter's belief in a strength of mind I knew I did not have, I fumbled for a reassuring response. Within seconds, we were clinging to each other in a heap of convulsing sobs.

There is no right time, no perfectly comfortable place for the unleashing of emotion so raw and forceful that you don't recognize it as your own. But lying in my daughter's narrow bed, her tear-soaked blond hair pressed against my own damp cheek, I felt a small measure of comfort. We were exhausted, the two of us, but lighter.

As my mother's first *yahrzeit* approached, my family wondered how we were going to mourn on Purim, a holiday defined chiefly by merriment. But, by the end of that first year, Purim seemed only to capture and magnify what I had experienced in the preceding months as a grieving mother of young children, what we had all learned by witnessing my nephew's uncanny arrival. You find yourself laughing, even as you feel your sadness pressing, sometimes lightly, sometimes fiercely, against your chest. You become used to the perpetual disjunction of feeling joy as you inhale and sorrow as you exhale.

At the last minute I decided to dress as a cowgirl, to match Abby. I stood in *shul* with my father and sister, flanked by my kitty cat toddler and four-year old princess, and recited the Kaddish. On Purim, of all days, pleasure conjugates easily with pain. One moment the king wants to kill all the Jews; the next moment they are glorified. "*V'nahafoch hu*" is the line of *Megillat Esther* most often cited to describe this phenomenon. "And all was turned upside down."

That was me, flipping my way through the holiday, as I had flipped my way through the year, through my various emotional costume changes. I am a mother delighting in my kids; I am a child mourning the most difficult loss. I am happy; I am having fun; I am sorrowful; I am lonely. Most of all I am connected: to my mother, my family, and my tradition.

"How are you?" well-meaning people want to know. I have no words in which to answer them. There is no box to put me in, no formula to express it all, no conclusion to be drawn.

But there is Kaddish.

In the space between the Hebrew words, I am the presence of all feeling. I am pure connection and boundless emotion, the highest high and the lowest low. I am white fire on black fire. I am alive.

RACHEL MESCH grew up in Gainesville, Florida. She holds a BA from Yale College, an MA in French and Romance Philology from Columbia University and a PhD in French literature from the University of Pennsylvania. She currently teaches French language and literature at Yeshiva College, where she chairs the Department of Languages, Literatures & Cultures. She is the author of *The Hysteric's Revenge: French Women Writers at the Fin de Siècle* (Vanderbilt Univ. Press, 2006) and numerous articles on French women writers from the 18th, 19th and 20th centuries. She is currently at work on a book entitled *Having it All in the Belle Epoque: Women's Magazines and the Invention of the Modern French Woman*, which examines efforts to reconcile feminism and femininity in France in the early 1900s. She lives in Riverdale with her husband, Eric Fisher, and their three children, Abigail, Eliza and Sam.

Leaving Cochin

FIONA HALLEGUA

THE JEWISH COMMUNITY IN COCHIN is the oldest in India going back centuries. When my ancestor Abraham Hallegua came to India three hundred years ago from Aleppo, Syria, he did not envision that his family would join and later lead the Paradesi community in Cochin. For eight generations, Halleguas were owners of farmland property earning their sustenance from the sale of the products of the land including coconuts, rice and spices. Meanwhile, wealthier families built the synagogue in Cochin in 1568, later adding a clock tower and importing the famous hand painted Chinese tiles for the synagogue floor. About a hundred years ago, a learned man by the name of Isaac Hallegua took on the role of the *Hacham* (literally, wise one). Since then, Hallegua family members have been prominent in the affairs of the synagogue and community.

Samuel Haim Hallegua, my father, became the Warden (similar to the synagogue President), *Chazzan* and the leader of the Paradesi community. Being the daughter of the leader made it easier to get the respect and co-operation of the non-Jewish business and government stake holders in the City of Cochin and the State of Kerala. My younger brother, David, and I were encouraged to say our daily prayers at home in Cochin. Our father insisted on both of us learning Shabbat songs as well as basic written and colloquial Hebrew. Our father was also particular that we were present at the synagogue early in the morning at 7 a.m. before service started for Rosh Hashanah and Yom Kippur. I had a very good relationship with my father; he was always there for me when I needed him, and I give him credit for who I am today.

In Cochin, the roles played by men and women follow the Sephardic Orthodox rites and customs. Baby naming, *brit milah*, prayer and Torah services and burial rituals were performed by the male members of the community. Even though women did not take an active role in the synagogue, they knew the prayers and their voices were heard along with the men during regular prayer and Torah services. They maintained a Jewish home and carried on all the traditions for *Chagim* in the home. Cochin Jewish women composed biblical songs about various events such as the story of Joseph's captivity by the Egyptians and his final redemption and reunification with his father Jacob. Their songs were composed in the local Malayalam language and were sung by the women during festivals and weddings. One of the customs of the Cochin community was making Passover matzah as a communal event, and this was largely done by the women. Jewish women in Cochin were educated as well as their male counterparts and were respected by their male peers and by the non-Jewish Indians as well.

As one of the younger members of the community, I witnessed the changes that took place in Cochin since the creation of the State of Israel. Despite the fact that we never faced any anti-Semitism, community members migrated to Israel for religious reasons. It was a constant struggle for my father to get a *minyan* for the Sabbath and once his health failed in early 2009, Sabbath prayers were infrequent.

My parents wanted me to leave India because there was no future for me, professionally and religiously, in a community that was so small. I was very apprehensive about leaving my home, family and friends, but twenty years ago, I immigrated to the United States. After leading a privileged life in India, I was alone in a new country and I realized that I had to adapt to the Western culture in order to fit in. I gradually shed my inhibitions and became an independent woman. For example, in India, women who were not married often needed a male chaperone to go to a public event such as a movie or a concert. I realized that women in the West would not be denigrating themselves by going to similar events on their own or with other female companions. My Jewish life and observance also grew since I moved to New York, with the empowerment I felt in being independent and outside the restrictions set for women in Cochin.

I am proud that I have been able to say Kaddish for my father from the very first day after he passed away on the 28th of Elul, 5769 (September 2009). The advent of Rosh Hashanah one day later and Yom Kippur ten days from his burial resulted in his *shiva* being cut short to one day instead of seven days, and his *shloshim* to about ten days. I felt that I was unable to mourn his death and experience closure because of the shortened mourning period and the fact that I could not be present by his side when he passed away.

I was hesitant initially because I did not know if it was possible to say Kaddish, as women did not say Kaddish in the Cochin community. However my fears were put to rest by Rabbi Hayyim Angel from the Spanish and Portuguese Synagogue in Manhattan. The *minhag* here is to recite Kaddish with the congregation every day except on Shabbat and *Chagim*. I was pleasantly surprised that I was not the only woman saying Kaddish.

It has been empowering and fulfilling for me to say the Kaddish every day, easing my pain by sharing the prayers with other mourners and realizing that my prayers would actually help my departed father in his time of need, while his earthly deeds are being judged by the Almighty during his first year in the World to Come. I have had very vivid encounters with my father's spirit at nighttime, and I believe he is happy and content where he is, and with my attempt to elevate his soul through prayer and praise for Hashem.

It is also a communal feeling for me to say Kaddish with the other mourners and congregants, whom I got to know very well in these months. The earnest request for healing, comfort and atonement towards the end of the Kaddish brings inner peace to me, since I feel that I am praying with my female companions for the ultimate salvation for my father and their loved ones.

I intend to continue to go to synagogue after my year of mourning, and to follow my father's and my Cochin Jewish community's traditions of daily prayer and self-improvement. Praying has given me a different perspective on life. Several of the Psalms provide me with comfort and guidance through daily trials and tribulations, and have been a positive influence in my personal and work life.

I have often wondered why the Kaddish, which has no mention of death or mourning, was chosen by the rabbis to be recited during the time of bereavement. As I delved deeper into its message of praise for omnipotence over all creation, I realized that the souls that touch our lives on earth are only given to us on loan by our Creator. When the time is appropriate for the soul to return to its Creator, we have to acquiesce to that request. The verses in the Kaddish that extol and glorify God's greatness make me feel both humble and special at the same time. Humble when I realize that my life and the life of my loved ones are not entirely under my control, yet special because of the unique connection that each soul, including my own, has to Hashem.

———————

FIONA HALLEGUA is originally from Cochin, India, once the city of a thriving Jewish community. She attained a Master's degree in Sociology from The University of Kerala where she completed a thesis on "The Jews of Cochin." Currently, Hallegua lives with her husband in the New York City area.

בְּעָלְמָא
דִי בְרָא
כִרְעוּתֵה
וְיַמְלִיך
מַלְכוּתֵה

If I Had that Sunday Back Again
I would yell
   I don't want you to die
I would confess
   I'm scared to live without you
I would cry with you
but the doctors said there was hope

If I had that Sunday back again
I would ask
   Are you scared to die?
I would try to share my God with you
but my job was to encourage

If I had that Sunday back again
I would thank you
I'd say
   You did a great job being my Dad
I would confide
   It's a boy, and we'll name him after you
but we watched the ballgame instead

If I had that Sunday back again
I would offer to disconnect
those damned machines
I would tell you
   I'll always love you
   I'll look for you when I die

If I had that one day
back again
I would crawl
onto that bed
and let you hold me
just awhile

I Will Not Fail You Now

PEARL TENDLER MATTENSON

I am living in pain, and I know it is a scary thing to hear me say but I want to be out of my suffering. I want to die. I was born at 9:12 am on June 8th. I was hoping I would die today so there would be some symmetry to my life. I understand those people who say they are not afraid of death. I understand 1000%. There is not an ounce of fear in me. I love you. Okay, honey.

MY YOUNGER SISTER left these words in a phone message to me on her 46th birthday. She died on June 13, 2010 – five days later. It is hard to remember Karen at a time when she was not broken. She had struggled for over thirty years with an eating disorder and the many mental health issues that inevitably go along with anorexia: OCD, depression, anxiety and personality disorder. The last decade of her life was complicated by a series of surgeries that further weakened and debilitated her. In the end, her heart stopped; she was trying to prepare a meal for herself.

I think my sister was close to God. It was not a calm relationship. The only time she really prayed from a *siddur* was each year during *Ne'ilah* on Yom Kippur, standing next to my mother in my parents' living room. She railed at God, *Why me? Could I be that bad that I deserve this suffering?* Sometimes when she had banished God, she would turn to me as her intermediary. *Why?*

Our relationship was rocky too. Often, she resented me for the normalcy of my life. And her death – the finality of it coming to me in waves as I stayed with her frail, emaciated body all day in her New York apartment waiting for the medical examiner – meant there would never be a path to true connection. There would be no moments in our old age when we could come together, peacefully assessing the contours of our troubled life, and accept each other for who we had been and who we had become.

I would say Kaddish for my sister for the required thirty days. Of course I would. I am an educated and committed Jewish woman. I never even considered the alternative. Still, reeling from the shock of my sister's death, I probably did not give much thought as to what to expect from the experience. I thought of this as an obligation. I only knew that I must do this for my sister. (*Karen, there are so many ways that I failed you in life, I will not fail you now.*)

The *shiva minyan* sparked deep gratitude in me as I welcomed completely strange men into my parents' home each morning and evening. They had come simply to make it possible for me (and my parents) to say Kaddish. I never once wished that I could help make the *minyan* or lead services. I have loved being part of women's *tefillah* groups; love the intimacy of women's voices creating a community of prayer. I believe women have a crucial place as teachers and leaders of our religious communities. I believe there is an aspect of the Divine that will only come to light through women. And yet, in my grief, I found myself grateful for the opportunity to be alone in my prayer, silently holding up my mother, and buoyed by a group of men who would enable me to speak the words that would honor God and my sister at one and the same time.

Somewhere I had read a rationale for Kaddish that sustained me. This is what I remember: God has lost a unique living being whose very existence served to praise Him. (*Yes, Karen, you added to that which was good in God's world. Your life had meaning. To God, to the people who knew you. To me.*) By saying Kaddish, we try to fill, in some small way, the gaping hole left in God's bereft world. This idea informed my overwhelming sense that I was honoring all that my sister was and could have been in her life by speaking the words of the Kaddish out loud, in a *minyan*, each day. (*Karen, I declare our relationship each day. Is this enough to show you that I am proud of being your sister?*)

I had not prayed regularly in a daily *minyan* since high school, and I came to welcome the forced pause in my mornings and my evenings. The process of preparing to come to *shul* during the week was new, and pulled me into a new state of consciousness. I often needed to go home and change clothes before entering *shul*; it was summer and I wanted to wear longer sleeves, a skirt. My car now held a *siddur* and head covering in the passenger seat. I knew the daily *minyan* schedule by heart. Somehow, this more than anything marked me as a mourner. Some days I would almost forget that my sister wouldn't be calling me. Not in need. Not in anger. Not in love. (*Karen, I miss you.*) I could go through days in a foggy haze of memories and tears. And then *Shacharit* and *Maariv* would ground me. At least twice a day, I knew what to do. I knew what to say. I knew when to stand and when to sit.

> *May they and you have abundant peace, grace, kindness and mercy, long life, ample nourishment and salvation from before their Father who is in Heaven (and on earth) . . .*

The biggest surprise for me was the attachment I developed to certain prayers. For instance, the *Kaddish D'Rabbanan*. I rushed to get to services for the beginning so that I would not miss the first reciting of this version of the Kaddish. I found great comfort in this expanded prayer for peace and compassion (and nourishment!) for all living beings. (*Karen, I didn't always have the capacity for compassion and kindness that you needed from me. I can't make amends to you any more. I have to suffice with being kind to others and I know that it is forever a* tikkun *on my part.*)

Those early mornings also brought me into conversation with the story of the *Akeidah* (the sacrifice of Isaac). My parents lost a child. They never could have sacrificed her. They sacrificed so much else for her. Abraham only came to the brink of a loss. My father had to see my sister, lifeless, in her bed. (*Karen, we filled the room with pictures of you in your teens. Beautiful. Smiling. Full of life. You would have been so proud.*) I preferred the reciting of Temple sacrifices, which came next. For me, they brought to mind Aaron's own loss of his two sons. He understood.

As a young student I remember feeling impatient with the *Tachanun* prayers. Really? And we have to say all that and put our head down too? As a mourner, however, my heart was already broken open. I didn't have to conjure up tears or emotion.

> *I am exceedingly distressed. Let us fall into Hashem's hand for His mercies are abundant but let me not fall into human hands. Oh Compassionate Gracious One, I have sinned before You . . .*

I felt that hiding my eyes was an apt stance as I wrestled with my inner demons. I found in this prayer an outlet for my guilt. For beating myself up over all that I didn't do for my sister. All the ways I sinned against her. I desperately wanted to believe that God and my sister could find compassion for me. (*Karen, sometimes I hear your voice – so angry with me. So raw from a sense of betrayal that you could not even count on your own sister. And then sometimes, too, I hear your sweetest little voice call me Pearly. In my heart I hold you and hug you.*)

> *Hashem, do not rebuke me in Your anger nor chastise me in Your rage. Favor me, Hashem, for I am feeble; heal me, Hashem, for my bones shudder. My soul is utterly confounded . . . Amid rage remember to be merciful.*

The thirty days ended. I no longer stood alone (or one of only two or three women) on my side of the *mechitza*. I went back to my old routines – exercise, coffee, e-mail. I was still raw. And yet I found wisdom in a rationale I read for the 30-day limit. Sometimes the grief can be so intense, that unless we cut it off quickly, we will never stop mourning. Did I deepen my relationship to God through this process? Actually I deepened my relationship to qualities of God, to kindness and compassion and appreciation. (*Karen, I deepened my relationship to you. Is that possible? It's true though isn't it?*) And with Kaddish behind me for now, I connect to God through my living relationships – through the divine in each of us.

PEARL cares deeply about learning, doing and creating with integrity. She believes in making a contribution. She believes that success comes from a deep consonance between who you are and what you do. Pearl became a certified leadership and relationship coach after a 25-year career in Education and non-profit leadership. She has been a teacher, family educator, and Principal and has consulted to private schools on governance, teacher development, and school change initiatives. She also grew up in Japan, and is conversant in Japanese and fluent in Hebrew. Together with her husband and two teenaged boys she makes her home today in New Jersey.

You Can Do It, Mom

KAREN MARKOWITZ MICHAELS

MY PARENTS OWNED A DRUGSTORE called Noble Drugs in Crown Heights. Today, the neighborhood is known as the headquarters for Chabad, but when my three sisters and I grew up there, it was a mixed Jewish neighborhood. Reform, Conservative and Orthodox Jews all lived and went to synagogue there. My family was Modern Orthodox, but we had very strong ties to the Old Country through my European grandparents. They would regale us with stories about their hometown of Bircza (now in southeastern Poland).

When I was 8 years old, I overheard my mother speaking with my father about a funeral that she had attended. The family had no sons, but four daughters had recited the Kaddish for their mother. My Mom said it was beautiful and meaningful. At that moment I knew that when the time came ("after 120 years"), I would say Kaddish for my parents. This was not a decision that I could talk about with my friends in Yeshiva, or even with my family. I feared I would get my grandfather's typical response – *Men darf nit*! It literally meant "it's not necessary," but it carried the implication that it was at best silly and probably a violation of some law. My friends and my teachers would have simply thought I was play-acting and when the time finally came I would come to my senses.

My mother died in 1983. Following a very old European custom, the funeral took place in my parents' house. The street outside was filled with people. Her casket was carried from the house to the hearse. We then walked behind it as she was driven slowly past the synagogue where my parents had davened. From there we all rode to the cemetery.

Of the four daughters, my youngest sister and I chose to say Kaddish for my mother. My father also took upon himself the obligation to say Kaddish for the eleven months (not just the obligatory thirty days for spouses), but he encouraged my sister and me to say it, too. I suspect he felt that his prayers would reach the heavenly throne, and ours used his to get there.

Saying Kaddish every day was truly a team effort. Although my husband, Jim, a Conservative rabbi, had normally gone to *shul* early in the morning, I was now the one to go. Jim could only manage cold cereal for breakfast, but he got the kids off to school. In the evening, he would stay with them as they did their homework and went to bed, while I went to the evening *minyan*. Despite their young years (the oldest was only ten), nobody complained. My children would write notes and draw pictures of flowers with the words, "Mom, a little longer," or "You can do it, Mom." I have saved these notes of love because they got me through the year. Later on, my daughters decided to join me at services on Friday evenings; it became our special private time.

Each morning, I went to *shul* and cried through most of the service. At the end, I pulled myself together to say the Kaddish. Our synagogue wasn't egalitarian, so we needed ten men for the *minyan*. It annoyed me when nine men were present and the *gabbai* would make phone calls to get one more man. Some of them slept while I prayed, but I persevered in my mission. I had been taught that the words of the Kaddish helped push the soul of a loved one into Gan Eden (heaven), and I was determined to make it happen. As time went on, the outward crying became less common, although the inner pain was still intense.

When I was growing up, *Yizkor* was a very powerful experience. All the young children were sent out and the prayers seemed to last for an hour. Many Holocaust survivors were in our *shul*, and we could hear the sounds of men and women wailing. When it was time to re-enter, all the women had red eyes and when they saw us, we all were hugged and kissed and revered.

It's a strong custom for mourners not to recite *Yizkor* during the first year. On Yom Kippur, however, my grandmother was with us and I didn't want to leave her alone, so she initiated me into the group of those who stay. For the past twenty-eight years I have stayed, but if they're with me, I still send out my children, and now my grandchildren.

Each day after my Mom passed away we had direction – *shul*; we had a purpose – to help my Mom's soul reach its final destination. The day of the last Kaddish, I decided to daven with my father at his *shul* in Crown Heights. The day was full of reminiscing: Where did the time go; could Mom possibly be gone so long? The *minyan* was at 4 p.m., and we had dreaded it for the entire day. At 3:55, the doors of the drugstore closed as my father, my youngest sister and I went to *daven*. Before the last Kaddish I turned to my sister and said, "This is it. Kiss Mommy goodbye for the last time." With that, we began the words, "*Yitgadal v'yitkadash*..." As I said the last words, I felt my mother ascend to the place near the heavenly throne where she deserved to be. We all felt a breeze and her final kiss as she ascended. The men each took a glass of schnapps, said *l'chaim*, and we walked to the drugstore in silence.

The next morning, my children asked for pancakes for breakfast.

Blessed Be

REBECCA E. STARR

"To everything there is a season," Ecclesiastes reminds us, ". . . and a time to every purpose under the heaven. A time to be born, and a time to die."

I was raised in a Jewish home in the Upper Peninsula of Michigan. Our Jewish community was small, for sure: a synagogue of about twenty-five families located fifty miles from our family farm. But we managed, and my parents made sure that I understood the fundamental concepts of our tradition. My mother always invited many guests to our Passover Seder, although very few of them were Jewish. She always said, "It is important to invite people to our Seder, so that is what we will do!" Our family farm produced sheep as its main animal crop, and when Passover came in the spring, it was also lambing season. There was often a lamb or two that had been rejected by its mother, and my mother always took great pride in nursing those little orphans back to health. So there was often a cardboard box sitting by our wood stove, and throughout the Seder one could hear the little sounds of the lamb coming from the box. Looking back, I wonder how those animals felt as we read about the sacrificial lamb in the Haggadah! Each year, my mother came to my classroom to teach about Chanukah, serve latkes, and make sure that the entire class knew that not everyone celebrated Christmas. This was a difficult message to relay in a small town with little diversity, but she was committed. I know her lessons and belief in education impacted my life then, as they do now.

After making my way to college, I met my future husband, Aaron, who was planning to become a rabbi. We were married and he received his rabbinic ordination at Hebrew Union College in Cincinnati. He was then hired as the rabbi at his home congregation in Detroit.

We were thrilled to be living in Detroit, relatively close to my family and around the block from his. My husband enjoyed his work and I enjoyed mine, as a social worker and community educator at the Jewish Federation. We were overjoyed when I became pregnant, but then disaster struck – my mother suffered a stroke.

She fought for six weeks, but in the end, she was unable to beat it. I remember visiting her one day in the hospital, and although she couldn't talk, she looked at my stomach and one shaky hand reached down to touch it. It was one of the only times while she was in the hospital that I truly felt like she was actually "in there" and understood what was happening around her. I still believe that after I told her that the baby and I were both fine, she said to herself, "This is ridiculous. This child needs to go and have her baby and not be spending time worrying about me." A few days after that moment of clarity, she passed away. I held her hand as her soul ascended. It was the seventh day of Passover.

Our congregation and extended community were a huge support to us. They visited us, and prayed with us, and of course, they fed us! I always knew that the Jewish mourning practice of *shiva* made a lot of sense, but until I went through it, I did not really comprehend its brilliance. Slowly we made our way out of the fog of loss and back into some semblance of life. I will never forget taking that first walk around the block when *shiva* was over. It was spring and the flowers were blooming, the sun was shining, and the air was beautifully fresh. The baby growing inside me was kicking and moving around. The signs of life were all around me. I remember thinking that my mother was looking down and telling us to get on with life and appreciate the beautiful things that awaited us. But I was still not sure how to comprehend that the baby inside me was going to come into a world without her.

I made the commitment to say Kaddish at least once a day until the baby came. I did this for my mother; I wanted to do everything in my power to help her find her way to God's presence. My husband's congregation did not offer daily prayer services, though, so I turned to a local Conservative synagogue.

I experienced great comfort in the community around me. They surrounded me in my prayer, and the 90-year old Holocaust survivor who led the prayer service reached me with his voice. Perhaps I was more open to the prayers themselves at this particular time, especially those that addressed God's greatness and power over life. Whatever the reason, I found myself being drawn closer and closer to our tradition and to our rituals. The day after I completed the *shloshim*, I became a mother myself.

The prayers had reminded me of all that God wants of us in this life, and that includes observance of the *mitzvot*. Our home had always been a kosher one, we were regular service attendees, and certainly our home was filled with ritual. But now we found ourselves wanting to take on more of the commandments.

Our Reform community was certainly open to our desires, but ultimately we decided that we wanted to be part of a more observant community, and not the only observant Jews within one. This meant my husband would need to leave the Reform movement, and to find another job. Our home was not walking distance to any synagogue, yet we couldn't sell it in those difficult economic times, so we worried about the financial impact of our decision. Moreover, we'd have to leave my husband's family, perhaps to a community far away. Then, coincidence of all coincidences, the very congregation where I'd been saying Kaddish needed a rabbi! My husband got the job and we moved across town. Now, we are able to be *shomer Shabbat*, we are close to a day school for our children, the food within the synagogue is always kosher, and we have been able to take on many other *mitzvot*, as well. We find joy and meaning in our new existence, and every day we are grateful that we were able to make the change.

This growth in our family life came about because of my experience as a mourner. The comfort that I found in those observances led me to wonder what other rituals might add meaning to my family's life. The profound sense of loss that my husband and I felt was eased by our tradition, and we wanted to cling closer to it. This desire was intensified when our son was born. We wanted him to feel the same love of tradition that we did, and to surround him with it. I stood to recite Kaddish just before his *brit milah*.

As I recite the Kaddish on my mother's *yahrzeit* each year, I pray that she is walking with God now, and is able to experience God's goodness first hand. As it says so powerfully in the Book of Job (1:21): "Naked came I out of my mother's womb, and naked shall I return thither; the Lord gave, and the Lord hath taken away; Blessed be the name of the Lord."

REBECCA STARR lives in Southfield, Michigan with her husband, Rabbi Aaron Starr, and two sons, Caleb and Ayal. She is a Jewish educator and trainer, as well as a social worker by profession. Rebecca was born and raised in Michigan's beautiful Upper Peninsula, also known as God's country. She and her family visit the great white north as often as possible.

Learning to Live Without

DEBBIE YATZKAN JONAS

THE PHONE RANG at 5:00 a.m., waking me from a deep sleep. My mother's voice was jarring. She didn't apologize for waking me, or ask about the kids. She sounded like she was under water. "Debbie," she said, "Daddy just . . ."

The human mind is an incredible thing. In that synapse, the space between "just" and what came next, the possibilities were still infinite and hopeful. I ran them through my mind . . . "just got a raise," "just wanted to say hello," "just . . ."

"Died," she said. "Daddy just died."

My father, a marathon runner who had just celebrated his 59th birthday, had gone to Central Park to run a 10K race, and now he was dead.

My screams of "no, no, no" woke my husband and my children. It was Friday morning, and we were at the tail end of a six-week, idyllic vacation in Israel. All I wanted to do was get home. We didn't pack or think. We grabbed our passports and our kids and fled to the airport, where the only flight to New York was over-booked. We tried every permutation of travel to get me home – perhaps I could go through London, Greece or Canada. The manager of El Al finally sat me down, kindly, and told me there was no way to get home before Shabbat. My father was dead, I was trapped half way around the world, and there wasn't a darned thing I could do about either.

Shabbat, I was promised, would be a comfort. It was, after all, *Shabbat Nachamu*, which since that day has seemed like a cruel joke. As the rest of the Jewish world breathes a sigh of relief that the dreaded Three Weeks are over, my heart gears up to be broken once again.

On Saturday night we returned to the airport. I couldn't sleep, couldn't think, could barely take care of my children. We got off the plane and went straight to the *shul* where the sight of my father's coffin sitting in the back of a hearse brought a new wave of horror. Somehow we got to the cemetery, where my father's body was put in a jagged grave. The first shovelful of dirt had a huge rock in it, and it crashed onto the coffin with a sickening thud. There was my father, dead in the ground in a cracked box with a rock over his heart. And then the rabbi handed me a *siddur* and said, "It's time to say Kaddish." My sister and I stumbled over the unfamiliar words, just one more element of the ordeal.

When my father's parents died, he paid someone to say Kaddish for them. He was not one to go to *shul*, and certainly not every day, morning and evening. So that was Kaddish as I knew it, something you paid someone else to do while you grieved privately and got on with your life.

Yet when people gathered back at my mother's house after the funeral, and it was time for *Mincha* and *Maariv*, I moved to join them and say Kaddish. It was not a decision so much as an impulse. There was no intellectual foundation, no Torah learning about Kaddish, or the role of women, or the mysteries of Aramaic in my choice to say Kaddish. It was primitive, primal and necessary to my survival. It was the last and only thing I could do for my father. If someone had told me I had to crawl across sub-Saharan Africa licking the ground with my tongue to give comfort to my father's soul, or to heal my own open sore of a heart, I would have done it gladly. And since it was the only thing I could do, the thought of not doing it was unthinkable.

And so the next morning I said it again, and then that evening again. It gave shape to the *shiva*, something beside the endless rounds of repeating the story of my father's death, which threatened to replace the much more compelling story of his life. When *shiva* ended, we went home. It was Friday morning once again. The world felt fragile and tentative; I felt fragile and tentative. I wanted to crawl into a cave and stay there, but I had three little boys, ages six, three and one, and I couldn't allow myself the luxury of total despair. I had no choice but to function, and so I did. But as Shabbat fell, I was drawn to *shul*, back to the room that had last held my father's body, to say Kaddish once again.

It is hard to remember how this impulse, at once so casual and intense, became the scaffolding on which the rest of my life hung. Strangely, I never made peace with the words. I dreaded the staccato, rapid-fire intricacies of the *Kaddish D'Rabbanan* every single time. The Aramaic always felt like shards of glass in my mouth, sharp and a little dangerous. Yet my life revolved around it. I rarely left my neighborhood, tethered as I was to my home *shul*, a place where no one looked at me funny or showed anything but respect for my daily presence. Even on days when I could barely put one foot in front of the other, even in the dead of winter when I couldn't get the image of my father, frozen and unprotected in the ground, out of my head, I dragged myself out of bed and into the community of worshippers at 6:30 a.m., and then back for *Mincha* and *Maariv* a heartbeat later. Even when all I wanted was solitude, the meager warmth of my aloneness, I had to venture out. And on some level, this saved me.

It also made me appreciate the brilliance of *Halachah* in a way I never had before. This framework was so in tune with what makes us human that it could only have been Divine. The progression of *aveilut* from *shiva* through *shloshim*, the thrice-daily recitations of Kaddish, and the forced abstention from communal celebrations, coupled with the forced attendance in *shul*, gave dignity and structure to my life in that first year of learning to live without. At first, I didn't want to go to weddings and bar mitzvahs and smile hollowly at joy that I could not be a part of, and *Halachah* gave me the dignity to stay away without insulting anyone. But towards the end of the year, I wanted to jump back in, to dance a little, to kick up my heels. For me, a year was just long enough to be champing at the bit of returning to the world.

When I said Kaddish for my father way back in 1987, I was the only woman in my *shul* to do so consistently. In a way that is hard to explain, saying Kaddish was a holy time, and a memory that I savor. Often, I remember how I brought my sons, who played or bickered on my side of the *mechitza*, at my feet. They have since grown into men, married with children of their own, where they dwell on the other side of that divide.

I am used to being needed. I am, after all, a mother. When my father died I had three children, and in the years that followed we had six more. Feeling needed is how I know I'm alive. And yet, for the eleven months that I said Kaddish, I depended on the men to create the necessary community. I wanted nothing more than to be extraneous to the process of creating a *minyan*. I wanted to be the beneficiary; for once, the one receiving rather than giving.

One cold winter morning after a snowstorm, there were only nine men. Phone calls were made. The clock ticked. Still only nine. One of the older gentlemen wanted to count me as the tenth. There was much discussion as to the propriety of the suggestion. In an Orthodox *shul*, you might be able to count a *Sefer Torah* or a 12-year old boy, but not a woman. But I did not want to be counted; I did not want it to depend on me. When the tenth man showed up and ended the discussion, I was grateful beyond measure.

My father had one great dream, which was to live forever. He loved being alive, and didn't take it for granted. I am now approaching the age that my father was when he died, and I share that dream. I am still young, as he was, but I know the day will come when I will be the one in the grave, and those little boys who sat at my feet will stand at the head of my grave with their brothers and say those ancient words. Perhaps my daughters will say Kaddish as well; it will be their choice.

When I think about my father's death, I am always amazed by how my father, inadvertently and much against his will, was the source of the deepest pain I have ever known. This great and gentle man, who wanted nothing more than to protect his family from harm, threw us all for a loop that twenty-three years later we're still reeling from. You fight day and night, tooth and nail, to protect the people you love, and then you land up being the cause of their deepest anguish. So I always tell my children that they should not ask *mechilla*, forgiveness, of me when I die, but that they should know that I ask it of them. I would never want to hurt them, but if God is good, and the natural order of the universe prevails, I will shake them to their cores. I hope Kaddish will be a balm on their wound, as it was on mine.

DEBBIE is the mother of nine children, and the grandmother (so far!) of ten. When her youngest child was in kindergarten, she fulfilled a lifelong dream, and returned to law school. She graduated Cardozo in 2010, clerked for a Federal Judge, and now works in a legal clinic for poor and homeless people in the Bronx. She likes to think that this would have made her father proud.

בְּחַיֵּיכוֹן
וּבְיוֹמֵיכוֹן
וּבְחַיֵּי
דְכָל
בֵּית
יִשְׂרָאֵל

Wracked Again
this body
this time in grief

graveside, childbirth
surrender is
the same

souls come into this world
beloved, depart

the pain is not theirs, but
ours, who bear them

Into the Void

JENNIE ROSENFELD

I DON'T WANT TO FOCUS on the negative. I don't want to use Kaddish as a feminist battle cry, at least not now. Four months into my *aveilut* for Abba, I don't want to write about being kicked out of my childhood *shul* – my father's *shul* – for saying Kaddish. I don't want to write about the times when I come to a *shul* as a guest and there is "no one" [read "no man"] saying Kaddish, and so I am left with no voice, destined to wander the streets in search of another *minyan*. And I don't want to write about the number of times that I've spent the entire davening just worrying about whether a man would be saying Kaddish at the end so that I can mumble along to his tempo and perhaps get the congregation to answer "Amen" to my Kaddish, too. There are a lot of negative things that I could write about being a woman saying Kaddish within the Orthodox world. But I don't want to focus on the negative – not in this piece.

And I don't want to paint a picture of negativity. There are the men who see me in *shul* and offer to say Kaddish with me or to ensure that someone else says it. There are the places where I can say Kaddish alone; and there are the people (both men and women) who make sure to answer loudly, joining me in the praise of God that is Kaddish. One man was so inspired by my Kaddish that he brought his teenage daughter over to meet me. To these friends and strangers I am truly grateful. But I don't want to write about them either.

So what do I want to write? What does saying Kaddish mean to me?

When people ask me why I choose to say Kaddish, my answer is immediate: It is because my father would have expected it; he would have taken it for granted that of course I would say Kaddish when he died. I'll admit that I haven't studied the sources, even though I study and teach Torah. I know this was my father's expectation and so I go to *shul* and do the one act that I see myself as being able to do these days, in the great void of his absence, on his behalf. And ironically, often at the most painful times, I feel his presence or, more correctly, his absence. I miss him.

Growing up, I was a *shul*-goer. I was a girl who went to a right-wing/ black-hat New York *shul* amidst throngs of men. It wasn't a place for a woman alone. But I wasn't alone, my father protected me. My father had a presence and he was an imposing – even intimidating – figure, especially to those who didn't know him well. If ever a man, or boy, were to be in the women's section of our *shul*, my father would come and kick him out. If this happened when my father wasn't in *shul*, he would follow up – calling the rabbi who dared to daven in the women's section to explain to him that this was not his territory, or speaking with the fathers of young sons telling them to better educate their children. In this way, he protected me, and stood up for my right to pray as a woman in *shul*. Today, years later, there is a sign that hangs by the woman's section, asking men to refrain from entering: "By order of the rabbi." Every time I have a negative Kaddish experience I think of my Abba and I miss him. I think what he would have done. I think how he would have stood up for me – not in a feminist way, because feminism wasn't his thing, but simply in a basic human way. And now he is gone. I should stand up for myself.

When my grandparents died, my mother said Kaddish. I was fifteen when my grandmother died, and I was attending the daily *minyan* at that time anyway. And my grandfather died just under three years ago – then, too, I stood by my mother's side as she said Kaddish. Answering "Amen," helping her signal to the rabbi across the ironclad *mechitza* when there was no man saying Kaddish. Kaddish was something that brought my mother and me closer; it gave us the excuse to meet every morning and walk to *shul* together. And it gave me the chance to feel that even as she did some-thing for her parents' memories I could do something in her honor. When my father died, davening next to my mother throughout the *shloshim* gave me the strength to say the Kaddish myself without breaking down. I was used to her saying it and now I simply added my voice to hers. Coming back to Israel after the *shloshim*, saying Kaddish alone, was different.

But I think the deepest feeling that the Kaddish brings out for me is a sense of this being the wrong time, and of my father having died too young, too soon. I see myself through the eyes of the people around me. I see a young woman in a colorful scarf and I see the question echoed back to me of why someone so young is saying Kaddish. Of course, I know that there are many younger than me whose parents have died; but still, I am not yet thirty. My friends stay outside the *shul* playing with their kids, while I am inside davening, trying to juggle my daughter back and forth with my husband who needs to be inside to say Kaddish along with me. It is hard to find meaning in the recitation of Kaddish as my two-year old runs away; I can barely hear the final "Amen" as I run out to catch her. And during the week, each time I leave she knows I'm going to *shul*, and each time I feel again that my father died too soon. Too soon to hear Shami sweetly saying "Mimi *shul*" (Mommy go to *shul*). Too soon.

It is a late *Maariv minyan*. The service ends and there is silence. The people wait a few moments to see whether anyone is saying Kaddish and in those moments my heart leaps to my throat; what if no man is saying Kaddish? This is not the type of *shul* where I could hope to evoke a response by saying Kaddish alone. Tonight was one of those nights. One of those nights when no male mourner's voice broke the silence, and I walked out unfulfilled and angry. I ask myself who I am angry at. I was a stranger in a strange *shul* and behind the ceiling high *mechitza*; I was anonymous. Even those who saw me walk in had no clue why I was there. Who am I angry at? Is it at myself – at my inability to shatter the silence with my voice and let those on the other side pick up the pieces? Perhaps I am too timid, or perhaps I don't want to offend, or perhaps I am scared of what lies on the other side. The last thing I want to do is to bring shame to my father's memory and I dread speaking out into the void and receiving no answer. I kick my way home, debating the merits of screaming the Kaddish alone into the Jerusalem night, daring God or my father to answer from the heavenly realms. But I walk in silence.

JENNIE ROSENFELD holds a PhD in English from the CUNY Graduate Center. Her doctorate, "Talmudic Re-readings: Toward a Modern Orthodox Sexual Ethic" was a fixture on her parents coffee table and entertained many a guest visiting her father in his illness. She co-founded and directed the Tzelem Project at Yeshiva University which aimed to increase sexual education within the Orthodox community. During her three years working on YU's Wilf Campus she often enjoyed lunching with her father, Former Dean of Yeshiva College and then Professor of Mathematics, in the Skycaf in Belfer Hall. Jennie made *aliyah* in 2008 and teaches Talmud and *Hasidut* at Havruta: The Beit Medrash for Hebrew University Students. She lives in Jerusalem with her husband, Pinchas Roth, and her daughters, Neshama Malka, who has fond memories of her zeida, and Neta Shira, who is named after her zeida and answered many an Amen in utero.

Choose Life: Kaddish after a Suicide

LAILA GOODMAN

UNTIL THE MOMENT I heard that my 79-year old father had committed suicide, I had never understood the compulsion to rend one's clothes. The deep shock, the intense soul pain upon registering the words of my brother on the phone, tore a hole in me. The rip of cloth more accurately represented my feelings at that moment than any words I could utter.

My father wasn't sick though he was having some slight discomforts that come with an aging body. But he was still working full time in his law firm and kept a busy social calendar, as well. My father always called himself a professional magician who practiced law for a hobby. Just ten days before his death, he performed a magic show for family and friends at his birthday party. None of us had any inkling that he was thinking about killing himself. He called all of his children in the morning and left us messages saying he loved us. I called him back and we chatted for ten minutes or so. He paused for a long time which I thought strange, but I didn't guess the truth.

The funeral and sitting *shiva* and the whole whirlwind of activities that happen in the first week was more automatic than thoughtful. The presence of my siblings, my cousins, aunts and uncles, good friends and hundreds of people who came by or wrote in that first week made the grieving deep and even fulfilling, in the way that entering fully into a process can be.

After that week, I felt like a buoy bobbing up and down in an ocean of grief and intense abandonment. Long before his suicide, I had come to terms with my father's imperfect ways. We had said everything that needed to be said and I know he loved and appreciated me in a way that no other person on Earth could. His pride in me and love for me was something I counted on when I was feeling down or insecure. And yet he had chosen to end our relationship. I had to explore the depth of my anger and confusion about his action and the grief of losing my father.

I resented his narcissism and his unwillingness to give us the opportunity to nurse him to a natural death. I felt sad that he didn't want to live to hear the news about where my eldest child was going to college or to be part of any of the details of his kids and grandkids' lives. I uttered curses at him, which sometimes shocked my friends, and I often used the starkness of his death as a weapon. I would blurt out in a casual conversation, "my Dad shot himself in the head."

I never doubted for a moment that I grieved differently because my father had committed suicide. One of my brothers worried about our father's wandering soul. I was comforted to follow ancient traditions rather than having to figure out for myself. On the way to the airport, a good friend who happens to be an Orthodox Rabbi guided me on the traditional *Halachah*. Abstaining from alcohol was not something I knew about and skipping the glass or two of wine helped me not to suppress the hard feelings.

I believe that suicide is wrong, that it is our obligation to choose life, *and* my responsibility is to choose my life, not to judge others. I chose to say Kaddish as a response to my father's death, not particularly to help his soul reach heaven. The fact that he committed suicide only added to my sense of obligation to pray, to make meaning of the life I live, to let go of the shame, to keep my heart open in a time of deep sorrow and despair.

Before my father died, I didn't understand why our tradition calls for us to say Kaddish for a year for one's parents but only thirty days for a spouse, sibling or child. To me, the loss of one of my children would be the worst possible thing that could happen. During my year of *aveilut*, I saw it differently. I came to understand that my parents were my first "God." They created me; they brought me into the world and raised me. My father ended his life but I wanted to show my respect, to honor his memory, to honor how much he meant to me.

Saying Kaddish for my father through the year was surprisingly healing. The daily davening was comforting. Feeling obligated to say Kaddish gave me *kavana*, purpose and intention. The words of Kaddish weren't particularly meaningful for me. I loved the rhythm and the familiarity of the sounds. The other prayers helped me to center, to keep my heart open, to ask for forgiveness for my harshness, cynicism, and loss of hope. I loved the English translation from *Tachanun* in the *Mincha* service: "We look to You, for alone we are helpless . . . Have pity, for we are sated with contempt." At the end of the *Amidah*, I felt *Modim anachnu Lach* was written for me: "May You continue to grant us life and sustenance." While mourning my father and hating the fact that he committed suicide, I was boosted up each day as I prayed for sustained life, as I chose life each day. Every morning or every afternoon or both, I would say Kaddish and at the end, after taking steps forward I would say, "I love you, Dad."

My last week of saying Kaddish, I was in Israel. On the last day I visited the Pardes Institute in Jerusalem for *Mincha*. When it came time for Kaddish, the *shaliach tzibbur's* deep, full voice enveloped me across the *mechitza*, and I was lifted up. He chanted the words and still made room for my voice. I felt heard and part of something bigger than me. After davening, I went over to convey how "fathered" I felt at that moment and I burst into tears.

Eleven months and thousands of miles from my father's last breath, I felt accepting and accepted, whole and empty, scarred and healed, spent and recharged. I felt my soul yelling, "Praise God, Praise God" and I walked out into the Jerusalem sun.

LAILA GOODMAN is a Biology teacher and Dean of Students at Gann Academy, The New Jewish High School of Greater Boston. She grew up in Hollywood, Florida but made a sharp turn north and married a Gloucester, Mass. native. She and her husband, Barry Moir, live in the house his grandfather bought in 1934 where they raised their two children and now happily attend to the chickens, dog and cat. When needed, she performs a bit of magic for a class or a Shabbaton to keep the students alert, but mostly she relies on the beauty of photosynthesis to do the trick.

Kaddish for My Sweet Son, Steven

ABBY ELLISON KANAREK

Losing a child is like no other loss. Sadly, by the time I was twenty-six I had lost both parents. My husband, Arnold – my lover, my best friend, my champion – succumbed to lung cancer in his mid-fifties. But none of this prepared me for what I felt when my 43-year old son died suddenly. Everything turned black; I couldn't catch my breath, I wanted to disappear.

Steven died on the 6th of Tishrei, in the midst of the Ten Days of Teshuvah between Rosh Hashanah and Yom Kippur. The abbreviated *shiva* was over a few hours before *Kol Nidrei*. As I took off my torn mourning blouse, I could not believe that very shortly I would dress in Yom Tov (holiday) clothes, go to *shul*, exchange the "*G'mar chatima tova*, May you be inscribed for a good year" greeting. Most of all, I could not fathom the idea of praying to the God who had just taken my child from me, the God who had decided that Steven would no longer be inscribed in the "good year" book.

It was during the first Kaddish during *Mincha Gedola* that something incredible occurred. I was in the upstairs women's section, and when I stood to say Kaddish, I was all alone. As I started to say the words "*Yitgadal v'yitkadash shmei rabba*, May Hashem's name grow greater, may Hashem's name become holier" – my body felt warmer and for the first time in many days I was able to take a deep breath. As I got further into the Kaddish – "*Yehei shlama rabba min shmaya*, May Hashem in Heaven send us much peace" – my enunciation became even stronger – even clearer. When I took the final three steps forward after completing all the words, I knew. Something truly extraordinary had occurred.

I knew, with absolute and perfect faith that Hashem was listening very carefully to all my words. I knew Hashem truly appreciated that I was making the effort to praise Him and affirm His existence despite my profound sadness and my anger toward Him because He took my son away from me. He in turn showed His appreciation by hugging me to warm my body, to free my breath, to begin to re-open my heart and soul.

During the eleven months of Kaddish, I grew to think of Hashem as a truly close personal friend. He invited me three times a day to have a talk. Whenever I entered His Home I knew He was waiting to hear what was on my mind, as willing to listen to my *tzoros* as He was to hear my praise.

The bond that began to form because of my need to mourn my sweet Steven via the Kaddish grew stronger and stronger. Once I completed my Kaddish I was unwilling to let this go. After all, how often does one discover a truly close friend at a relatively late stage of one's life? I therefore continue to go to *shul* regularly. Now, when I do miss a *minyan*, on my next visit, I particularly focus on *tefillot* that express thanks and appreciation. I want Hashem to know that even though I occasionally turn down His invitation, He nevertheless remains my closest friend and confidant.

The notion of "time healing wounds" is, for me, a terrible lie. The hole in my heart remains cavernous. Multiple times a day I think of Steven. I think about all he has missed and will continue to miss since he left this world. I think of how much mankind will miss because Steven still had so much left to give. I think about how I will never again hear "Hi Maw. It's your favorite youngest son."

However, when my thoughts and feelings get especially dark, I think back to the "Kaddish chasing" days and remember that a wonderful new relationship began. As it states in Psalm 130: "*MiMa'amakim karaticha Hashem*, I called to you, Hashem, out of the depths of despair."

Acknowledgment

MARLYN BLOCH JAFFE

I cannot ask you to say Kaddish after my mother. The Kaddish means to me that the survivor publicly and markedly manifests his wish and intention to assume the relation to the Jewish community which his parent had, and that so the chain of tradition remains unbroken from generation to generation each adding its own link. You can do that for the generations of your family. I must do that for the generations of my family . . . I believe that the elimination of women from such duties was never intended by our law and custom — women were freed from positive duties when they could not perform them, but not when they could. It was never intended that, if they could perform them, their performance of them should not be considered as valuable and valid as when one of the male sex performed them. And of the Kaddish I feel sure this is particularly true.

IN MY RESEARCH ABOUT WOMEN saying Kaddish, I came upon this 1916 letter from Henrietta Szold to Hayim Peretz, explaining why she was refusing his generous offer to say Kaddish for her mother. When my mother died, my husband offered to ask his parents' permission to say it on my behalf. (Some people consider it bad luck for their children to say Kaddish while they themselves are still alive.) Like Szold, however, I knew recitation of Kaddish for my mother was something I must do myself.

As her daughter, I had in some way stepped into a place my Mom had occupied in the community. In fact, the first day I went to morning *minyan* to say Kaddish for my mother, something remarkable happened.

· Acknowledgment ·

When I arrived home in time to see my children off to school, my husband told me our oldest daughter had just had her first period. I felt in a very literal sense that day my mother's survivors had moved up a generation. Our oldest child was entering womanhood, while I was rising a generation, too.

On the phone with my sister one night, she asked, "Do you ever just forget that Mom died? I mean, you go about your life, and then it hits you that she's dead?" "When that happens," my sister continued, "I get so sad . . . not just because she's not here, but because I feel like I am betraying her by having *forgotten* for the moment that she's not here." It was different for me. Kaddish defined my day. Every day, I established a time and place to remember.

During my year of *aveilut*, I kept a list of twenty-three different congregations where I said Kaddish in seven cities. Even now when I look at my list, I can remember the places in which I felt alienated and those in which I felt welcomed. The brilliance of the laws of Kaddish is that a *minyan* is required; yet sitting alone on the other side of the *mechitza* sometimes led me to wonder whether my presence as a mourner was truly being acknowledged.

For most of the year I attended the high school *minyan* in my children's school. The principal welcomed me warmly, and discreetly asked another rabbi to say Kaddish so I could accompany him. The girls were kind, albeit somewhat bewildered by my presence. Over time, I not only deepened my understanding of the weekday *Shacharit*, but also gained insights into the spiritual challenges of adolescence (their *kavana* was noticeably higher during exams), and even noted some high school fashion trends (various ways to push the boundaries of the dress code). And I noticed something else. After a while, one student who regularly sat next to me started to respond "Amen" to my Kaddish. Interestingly, she was the daughter of a Conservative rabbi. I started to feel a kinship toward her, because she was acknowledging me.

At its basic level, the act of saying Kaddish is to acknowledge . . . the loved one who has died, one's own role as a mourner, and ultimately, God. Moreover, the mourner is herself acknowledged by the congregation. Acknowledgment of this kind composes part of our humanity; we can recognize others, and their reciprocal recognition helps us to define ourselves. Martin Buber referred to it as an "I-Thou" relationship. I-Thou, between man and fellow man; I-Thou, ultimately between man and God.

73

Much of the year of mourning is about absence, not presence. Not just the fundamental absence of the loved one in your life, but also the mourner's own absence from public celebrations. My year of mourning could be catalogued by the events from which I was absent: bar and bat mitzvah celebrations, weddings, concerts, my niece's debut with a professional theater. But saying Kaddish within a *minyan* was, in some ways, an antidote – whenever my presence was recognized by the response "Amen."

Over the past five years, I have embraced the lessons of my year of Kaddish and tried to "pay them forward." Several times after a service, a woman has come to me to say how consoling it was that I responded to the words specifically of her Kaddish, at her tempo. I smile, recognizing that underlying our exchange lies the truest expression of our human connection: acknowledging that we are all created in the image of God.

During my *aveilut*, my daughters and I started to join my husband and son at our synagogue for *Kabbalat Shabbat* on Friday nights. Gradually, my daughters' friends heard we were there, and they started to come, too. To this day, dozens of girls and young women arrive at our *shul*, singing with joy to welcome Shabbat. When I see the women's section filling up, I think of it as one of my Mom's legacies, and it fills me with gratitude.

Annually on my mother's *yahrzeit*, I sponsor a breakfast for the high school *minyan*. It is my way to offer *hakarat hatov* (appreciation) to the school, and is the most uplifting part of an otherwise emotionally difficult day. (There is no more cheerful feeling than serving food to 120 hungry, chatty teens!) Every year, I feel that the girls are less bewildered by my presence, and I hear a few more mutters of "Amen" to my Kaddish. This year, one of the rabbis thanked me for setting such an important example for the students – male and female – in demonstrating that a daughter saying Kaddish for her parent is the "right thing" to do.

This was the ultimate acknowledgment of my actions – at once recognizing my relationship with my mother, the integration of Jewish law into my life, and my desire to model my behavior for the next generation.

· *Acknowledgment* ·

MARLYN BLOCH JAFFE is director of planning and evaluation at the Jewish Education Center of Cleveland (JECC). She graduated from Yale University with a BA in English, and the Mandel Center for Nonprofit Organizations of Case Western Reserve University with a Master of Nonprofit Organizations. She continues her graduate work in the department of Educational Studies at the University of Cincinnati. A lifelong Clevelander and married to the boy next door, Marlyn and her husband are the parents of three teenagers.

Praise Him All His Angels

DEBORAH FINEBLUM

TWELVE YEARS HAVE STOOD between my two months of *shloshim*, those twelve years that separated the passing of my two sisters.

Losing my little sister, Tobi, a month before her 46th birthday, I was nothing short of terrified. That illness could daily rob my little sister of more of her strength, that death could steal someone so young, so close. I would wake in tears from dreams that she was whole and healthy again, but in the light of day, she felt to me so wholly gone.

I said Kaddish for Tobi in our big Conservative *shul* in Upstate New York, surrounded by twenty old men and the occasional wife. Walking in from the cold, it was warm in the basement chapel with its tiny stained glass windows. I remember loving the men's voices, their old-country accents, plaid flannel shirts and shuffling feet, their masculine warm beard smell.

Now twelve years have gone by. During those years, I left Upstate New York, changed careers, and became an empty nester, a mother-in-law, and a grandmother. In the midst of those twelve years I also became religious.

I was in my fifties when it happened to me. *Frumkeit* (religiosity) came to me, not the other way around. It snuck up on me slowly and now that I think back on it, stealthily. One day I heard myself tell an editor I couldn't review a Friday night concert, a year later I'd begun postponing grocery shopping till Sundays and ignoring the TV and computer from Friday evening till Saturday night. By early 2005, whatever was happening in me was gaining serious momentum. I insisted our new house be near a *shul* – I who'd always happily driven on Shabbat suddenly needed to walk. I signed on for a Torah class with women from the nearby Orthodox *shul*, women who patiently took turns learning in English with me. I began reading the daily Psalms on the commuter train. And I found myself buying up hats of all styles and colors and stashing them in a big white garbage bag in the hall closet.

It took months for the first hat (a pink velvet model) to wiggle free of that bag and plop itself on my head, followed by another and then another. By hat three, a colleague asked me, "Is this a fashion statement or does it mean something?" "I guess it means something," I answered somewhat sheepishly. I'm glad he didn't press, because, back then, I couldn't have told him exactly *what* it meant. I just knew that hatless my head felt naked. Within the month, I was wearing only skirts and had shoved my jeans onto the top shelf of the closet. It took another six months for me to give them away.

Now that I look back on those lifestyle changes, as seismic as they felt at the time, I can see them for what they were: surface signs of my shifting subterranean spiritual plates. Underneath it all, I was struck with the overwhelming evidence that God has His fingerprints on every piece of my life. He has plans for us, big plans, I was beginning to realize, plans we need to pay attention to. And the clues to those plans are hidden deep in the Torah and other ancient books I'd never heard of.

My husband, poor man, looked on with equal parts amazement, confusion and horror. He simply could not fathom what was happening to his wife, the Woodstock veteran. Or to our kitchen, for that matter. New dishes! New pots! Dipping laundry baskets of glasses into 40-degree lake water while saying a Hebrew prayer! With his (albeit weak) assent, pretty soon there was a new *shul*, new friends and an infinitude of new rules in our lives.

This was pretty much the place I occupied when my sister, Susan, left her body in December. Although I could see her getting progressively weaker, when she died, I was stricken bone-deep at the thought of never hearing my sister laugh again, or watching her eyebrows shoot up at the birth of one of her fiendishly clever ideas.

But the truth is that Susan, not unlike Tobi before her, had a clear sense that the body's passing isn't the end of the story at all. Though she wasn't religious in any traditional way, Susan's own certainty that her soul was just getting warmed up for another one of her great adventures met my newfound awareness of God's presence halfway. And so it was that I entered *shloshim* again.

At first waiting for the tenth man to arrive ruffled my still-prickly feminist feathers. But to my surprise, once I got out of my own way, the arrangement provided me large doses of comfort and unexpected gratitude. I began to see those men who came to *shul*, wrapping themselves in phylacteries at daybreak, as a *holy team*. Whether they're college kids home on break, retirees (more flannel shirts) or family men with minutes to spare before their commuter train, beginning with their first "Amen," *minyan*-makers are no longer ordinary guys, but divine agents charged with illuminating a nearly-visible path of light to escort our prayers straight up to *Shamayim*.

Roughly half the time, another woman in mourning was there too, wrapping us in that comforting cocoon of sisterly intimacy. "It's the club no one wants to join," sighed one, finishing up her year of Kaddish for her Mom. "But when you do, it sure is nice to have company."

Still, in moments of solitary prayer I was anything but lonely, free to immerse myself unselfconsciously in the powerful waters, the silent readings that make up the bulk of the daily services. "Praise Him all His angels," King David prays in Psalm 148, never failing to bring tears to my eyes. "Praise Him, sun and moon . . . praise Him all bright stars . . . Young men and also maidens, old men together with youths." I looked forward to Monday and Thursday mornings, when the Torah is read in the lovely quiet of a non-Shabbat service. This may be Kaddish's most ironic blessing of all: when those who were less-than-devout, by passing on, bring us close – literally and figuratively – to the Torah.

Yesterday it all ended. So now I am like everyone else, free to attend parties, get a haircut, take an Alaskan cruise. When *shloshim* ends, some people light a candle; others plant a tree, learn Torah, give charity, or host a *siyum*. But it seems the most important thing we can do is will ourselves back to the business of life.

For me that life brings with it new life: a grandson, our son's first child, born during *shloshim* and named after Susan. A blizzard shook the trees outside that day, but there was light and warmth in little Asher Sivan's dwelling as the *mohel* welcomed this new soul into the Covenant. It was at that moment, feeling God blessing both the comings and the goings, that the words of the *Amidah* came fully alive for me: "You give life to the dead and have great power to save."

DEBORAH FINEBLUM is a Sharon, MA-based writer, editor and memoir coach. A former reporter with the *Democrat and Chronicle* in Rochester, NY, Deborah spent 8.33 years as Public Relations Manager for Combined Jewish Philanthropies in Boston. She now writes and edits for such clients as Gateways: Access to Jewish Education and the Ruderman Family Foundation and is a regular contributor to *Hadassah Magazine*. Best of all, Deborah is Bentzion Yair, Ayelet Rina, Nachum Tuvya Kalev, Amiel Adin and Asher Sivan's Bubbe.

בְּעָגָלָא
וּבִזְמַן
קָרִיב
וְאִמְרוּ
אָמֵן

The Mourner Sits Low
knocked down, dizzy
unable to stand

the mourner sits low
humbled, assumes her place
amongst ants, beetles, dust

the mourner sits low
gristle faced, clothing rent
naked hearted

the mourner sits low
looking up to meet your gaze
childlike in her not understanding

the mourner sits low
begging crumbs of comfort
from those kind enough to stop

the mourner sits low
chair encircled by others
in a mirthless whirl
cruel perversion of the nuptial dance

the mourner sits low
lingering in the doorway
not ready to rejoin the living
not ready, just yet
to take her leave
from those she's left below

A Sacrifice of Time

BELDA KAUFMAN LINDENBAUM

IT HAS BEEN ELEVEN YEARS since my mother's death and over thirty years since my father suffered a fatal stroke. After so many years, it is hard to recall my exact feelings and thoughts at the time, so I can only surmise why I did not say the Mourner's Kaddish for my father, as I did for my mother. What stands out in my memory is that my children were young at the time of my father's death, and it was not accepted or expected practice at that time. Although I had already self-identified as an Orthodox feminist, I was not ready to flout tradition.

When my mother died suddenly, there was no question in my mind that I wanted to – and would – say Kaddish for her on a regular basis. My children were no longer living at home; my time was my own; and, more profoundly, I felt ready and able to challenge and withstand a "system" that could be unwelcoming. With age had come greater self-assurance, strength, and determination to pursue what I felt was my right within my religion.

My sister, with whom I shared the Kaddish recitation, opined to me on one occasion that saying Kaddish was like catching a plane three times a day. During the week, if I was in New York, I crossed Central Park each morning and evening to pray in the synagogue where I had grown up, and where my parents had been members. It was a welcoming *minyan* with a friendly rabbi and a friendly *mechitza*. On Friday nights, I attended a Sephardic synagogue near our home, where the Kaddish was slightly different, and mine was recited in a booming voice from the balcony. I wanted to be heard and acknowledged. On Shabbat I was back in what was then my "home" *minyan*, which was fine on Shabbat because of the rabbi's welcoming and open attitude, but less so during the week when the group prayed in a different venue – one that had a very high *mechitza* which made me feel absent. On the one occasion when I attended, I had to remind them that I was there and to send over the *tzedakah* box. Although I recognize that for many women this is not a problem, and they prefer their anonymity, for me it has always seemed a denial of me as a functioning member of the community.

My husband and I spend a part of the year in Israel, and it was trial and error until I found my comfort zone in the synagogue. Israel then was more conservative than New York, and fewer women were to be found in daily *minyan*. I finally settled on one *shul* for morning *minyan*, where a friend would come over to the *mechitza* and answer "amen" after I recited each Kaddish. I arose early on those mornings, and took a taxi to another neighborhood, rather than go to one closer to my home where I was not welcome and no place was made to accommodate me. For *Mincha* and *Maariv*, I was in yet another venue, where the rabbi was not happy with my attendance, but the male congregants seemed nonplussed. On one occasion, there seemed to be no one other than myself reciting the Kaddish, and I feared they might skip it entirely. I called down from the balcony, "No Kaddish?" and the president of the congregation shouted back, "So say it." And I did, alone. For me it was a significant moment. I ran home to my husband, excited as a child, to tell him the news.

The rabbi of this synagogue happened to be saying Kaddish at this time for his mother. He would have no cadence to his delivery, and it was difficult for me to recite it with him. When I asked him once to say it slower, he responded, "I never know when you are there." My response to him was twofold. "Rabbi," I told him, "I am always there." Each evening as I stepped into my row, I would bang down the seat of the chair to announce my presence. Each time he would look up, but he never slowed or changed the pace of his Kaddish.

This same rabbi offered me another glimpse into how he viewed women in his community. On the eve of the Passover holiday, my husband remarked that since I was attending daily *minyan* and he was not, perhaps I should sell our *chametz*. I approached the rabbi after services and told him that I would like to sell my *chametz*. He asked me in turn if I had my husband's permission to do so. It was a pointed reminder to me that the synagogue is truly a male preserve and that they wish to keep it that way. It seems to me, and it has been echoed in conversations with others, both men and women, that there is a fear of "feminizing" Orthodoxy, much in the way that people feel has happened to Conservative Judaism. As women assume more roles and take more responsibility for themselves, the men are marginalized and begin to drift away.

I still remember reading a quotation from a distinguished rabbi, Rabbi David Tendler, in which he described women as "guests" in the synagogue. I called him to make sure that he had not been misquoted and he stood by this statement.

The liturgy of prayer, which was written by men, in male language for men, only serves to reinforce this view. I continue to be struck by phrases such as "God, our Father, or our Father our King." In my own prayers, I have begun to make substitutions such as God our Creator, and regularly add "our foremothers," the *imahot*, in my prayers. It helps me to feel that as a woman within Orthodox Judaism, I am not living in two parallel worlds – one world that acknowledges my creativity and potential, and another that circumscribes my role to mother, wife, and enabler of men. Language is important, as it helps to define us. The language of prayer, its poetry, is no exception. It can inspire or deflate me, draw me close or make me feel like "the other." While many today speak of the rabbis' stamp on prayer that cannot and should not change, I do believe that in times past creative change was employed to make a more just environment. In those days not every change was labeled "Reform."

During the summer months, I was at yet another synagogue where the rabbi, a gregarious person, hugged and greeted everyone, except me. After a few days of being ignored, one man approached me, introduced himself as an officer, and inquired for whom I was saying Kaddish. The ice was broken. After a few weeks, one of the "regulars" invited me to join him at the rabbi's Friday class. I demurred saying that it was a busy day. He responded by telling me, "I've already poured your coffee," and with that gesture I was hooked. I began to attend class every week and to contribute on a regular basis. I became part of the "men's club" – and a friend of the rabbi. At the end of the summer, he sent me off with a farewell lauding me as "heroic." What I really attained, though, was that I was no longer invisible.

One thing that you notice about a *minyan* with people who attend on a regular basis is that it tends to move quickly. Everyone has to go to work during the week, and Sundays are for play. I once complained to my nephew about how fast the morning blessings were recited. They are so beautiful, and yet they are said in a rote-like, unremarkable way. He responded by asking me what form prayer used to take. We all know that the prayer service came to replace sacrifices when the Temple was destroyed. "What do we sacrifice today?" my nephew asked me. Of course, the answer is our time. Time, which has become so precious in our busy, multi-tasking lives, is what we bring as we pray each day. That was a profound lesson for me. If I ask myself why I said Kaddish for my mother, it was because of my love and respect for her. I wanted to give back a gift, in this case, the gift of my time and effort each day, three times a day, to devote to her and to God.

My mother, during her lifetime, gave me many gifts and insights that have made my life more meaningful. Even with her death these gifts continued. Saying Kaddish for her taught me about the cycle of the Jewish year. I thought that I knew it from the perspective of preparing for the Sabbath and the ritual of the holidays. That was only one aspect, however. There is also a rhythm to the year – the parts of the liturgy that we add or omit, the fast days, the New Month, and the whole panoply of Jewish life – that one experiences each day only within the *minyan*.

One custom that I began was to bring a breakfast of muffins and juice on Rosh Chodesh, which is, after all, a women's holiday. In this way my male co-daveners were able to celebrate with me.

The most difficult part of saying Kaddish turned out to be stopping at the end of eleven months. Dealing with the finality of my mother's death, and even the camaraderie and support of the *minyan* was not what I had expected. Who could predict that this could be so painful? My eleven months ended while I was in Israel for Sukkot. That last morning I went to *shul* as usual, and a friend, as a loving gesture, brought a group of women to daven with me for this last *Shacharit* service. For me, who was used to being, for the most part, the lone woman, it was a moving experience to pray with women, their voices added to my own, and to hear their Amens to my Kaddish.

I ended my year with a *Mincha minyan* of family members at my home. As we were short one male for a while, we solicited a passerby off the street to be our tenth man . . . this after all was Jerusalem. After hearing me recite the Kaddish he fled rather than stay for *Maariv*, a reminder to me that we were still dealing with an imperfect world.

My very perceptive nephew, the one who taught me about time, also taught me to create mnemonics in my prayer, so that with certain prayers I think of particular people. When I say in the morning, "From the rising of the sun to its setting, God's name is praised," I think of my mother. Some one remarked to me upon her death that it reminded them of a line from the Sabbath song "the sun from the top of the trees has disappeared." The two verses juxtaposed in my mind. For my father, for whom I will always regret not giving this gift of time and respect by saying Kaddish for him, I have a phrase from *Ashrei*: "From generation to generation we will tell of Your greatness." He was a quiet and modest man, who achieved so much despite difficult circumstances and left a great legacy for his children and grandchildren.

I learned great respect for those men who continue to come on a daily basis to make *minyan* for those of us who come sporadically or for the year. And yet, I wonder if we were counted, would it make a difference in our priorities and commitments, and our willingness to attend. There is a beauty and solidity to starting one's day in prayer in the company of a familiar group. While the group gives much, they are also greatly rewarded.

Since my year of Kaddish I have noticed change when I attend the daily *minyan*. There are more women coming to *shul*, and they are being accommodated. For some women it is no longer a lonely experience. Still, the road to understanding women's spiritual needs and making room for them, both figuratively and physically, is a long one, and we have barely begun the journey.

Most of the liturgy is wonderfully poetic. A phrase that is dear to me appears in the morning prayers:

> *You have changed my mourning into dancing*
> *You have removed my sackcloth and girded me with joy*
> *So that I might praise You, and not remain silent*
> *God, my God, forever will I thank You.*

Is this not a paradigm for loss and acceptance? For me, it also speaks to women's need to be seen and heard within Judaism. If God sees us and hears us, and acknowledges us as part of God's community, then where is man?

BELDA is the wife of Marcel Lindenbaum and the mother of five children, three boys and two girls. She has been interested in the role that women play in Orthodox Judaism for over twenty years and has tried to expand the learning opportunities for women and girls by opening new opportunities for them in professional Jewish life and education. To that end, with her husband, she founded Midreshet Lindenbaum, a school in Israel, and was a founding member of Drisha Institute in New York. Belda has served as President of the Board of the American Friends of Bar Ilan University, and Drisha. She is a founder and vice-president of JOFA, the Jewish Orthodox Feminist Alliance.

Whispers in the Dark

ELLEN COPELAND BUCHINE

BETSY WAS MY YOUNGEST SIBLING. Her diagnosis of Type B Lymphoma and death a mere nineteen days later shocked us all. She had struggled her whole life, academically, socially and emotionally. Now, her suffering was over.

I stood at her bedside, stroking her arm, whispering to her, removing hair from her eyes and giving her teary kisses. Betsy's twin, Kathy, kept vigil with me, neither of us willing to leave her alone. Betsy had felt alone through so much of her life, we dared not leave her now. Fortunately, I have many memories of playing with and helping Betsy during our younger years and into our adulthood, despite the geographic distance between us. She often opened up her troubles to me, looking for validation or advice. While I felt complimented by her trust, it was a helpless feeling to have only this to offer during some of her darkest times. Now, I reflected on our relationship, and in some way attempted to soothe the many sad memories. We were out of time . . . or were we?

In a certain sense, my participation in Kaddish was a private and spiritual way of "tucking her in," forever. The whole image of comforting Betsy and giving her *neshama* an *aliyah* seemed to me a final *chesed* and fitting tribute. Saying Kaddish took slow and deliberate concentration the first few times around. How I wish I could have given her more of this same deliberate attention during her lifetime. Over the next several weeks, Kaddish presented me with several lessons, some overt, others more subtle. From my vantage point, our conversations were not over.

During her *shloshim*, I joined the *minyan* at my sons' nearby day school. With my vulnerability at the surface, I felt every set of teenage eyes boring through me as I stumbled through the davening with which they were so familiar and cavalier. I couldn't help but be reminded of Betsy's challenges with school and making friends, both of which had been so hard for her. Now she was giving *me* a turn at that feeling. It was as if, in her death God channeled her exquisite sensitivities into me, forcing *me* to feel them instead of her. I had always felt so protective of Betsy. Suddenly, I had the job of comforting us both, simultaneously. Even if it could have brought her back, I don't think I could have apologized enough during those last days of her life and *shloshim*. Kaddish was all I had, so I grabbed on and stumbled through the words and emotions in my darkness.

The darkness only deepened when my father passed away, only eight months after Betsy. Dad, generally the master of his business, tennis, and family worlds, had always been overwhelmed by Betsy's differences. The fact that she alone of his six children remained nearby during adulthood had kept her difficulties in his field of vision. The other five of us used to speak constantly of the negative dynamic between the two of them, always hoping to fix the unfixable.

So it wasn't only that I had lost them both that was so tragic. It was that the two of them had run out of time. Her years of vulnerability, his inability to connect with her, and my own need to be some sort of peacekeeper all came rushing to the surface after both of their deaths. My involvement in Kaddish proved to be the beginning of a healing balm, not only for my loss of each of them, but for the damaged and profoundly sad parent-child relationship that I had been privy to all these years.

Jewish men in mourning are expected to lead the prayer services. I'm no wallflower, but, in this case, the part of the morning blessings where women thank Hashem for "having made me according to His will" made perfect sense to me. I was in no way interested in leading others in any public forum. Rather, I counted on time to pause and reflect in that cocoon-like time and space. Sort of a spiritual insurance plan. I sensed the envy of some of the men, were it "permissible" for *them* to weep openly for their departed! Many of those in attendance shared a unique bond, as a large percentage of us were mourners. In many ways, however, we were each alone, wrestling with memories amidst one another's softly melding voices.

Over time, words and ideas sprang off the pages, forcing me to re-evaluate myself, my relationships, and all aspects of life. Strands of truth that might have resonated, perhaps, with either Dad or Betsy also wove their way through my thoughts. Themes of compassion, humility, righteousness and forgiveness are all mentioned during davening. They wended their way from the *siddur* to my tear-blurred recitations. Was I just imagining Dad and Betsy's quiet misgivings as to what each of them might have done better? Were they, at last, at peace with one another? Did these thoughts come to mind to encourage me to ratchet up certain *middos* of my own, to guide me, perhaps, to put more effort into all my relationships, lest they go sour? I felt, through Kaddish, that they wanted me and our entire family to heal, not to let spiritual opportunities such as these pass us by. The verses we recite during davening speak in praise of God, yes, but also, of each of *our* potentials, since we are made in His likeness.

Certainly, I missed some sleep during my two rounds of saying Kaddish, but I gained a mindfulness I could not have developed any other way. Nineteen days between Betsy's diagnosis and her departure. Nineteen months, until the mourning for Dad was completed. Like the nineteen blessings of the *Amidah*, participation in Kaddish brought me spiritual shelter and peace within the tenderness of my community. Darkness became light.

ELLEN COPELAND BUCHINE became a *baalat teshuvah* within UOS, Houston, in step with her all-boy household toddling off to her community's fine Jewish day schools. Now, with three young adult sons ready to segue into adulthood, and a married stepson, to boot, she takes great comfort in her faith and insists she is still thirty-ish while concocting clever promotional copy for businesses and non-profits.

A Child of Old Age

SARA WISE PRAGER

EACH YEAR ON MY FATHER'S *yahrzeit*, I am transported back in time, and tonight, I do not need to look in the *siddur* as *Aleinu* ends. The words flow back to me and roll out of my mouth, as I stand there and proclaim the greatness of God and His wisdom, which is beyond our understanding. I find myself carried by the rest of the Kaddish-saying *tzibbur*. I feel lucky to be among them instead of saying it by myself. Whatever stage of mourning we are in, we are united by an understanding of each other's loss.

I was sort of a *bat zekunim* (child of old age) to my father; he was fifty-two when I was born. My father, Rabbi Joseph H. Wise, was the rabbi of a *shul* in Yonkers, NY, which was his final pulpit in a lifetime of service to the Jewish community. In those years, my father was often on the phone to ensure there would be a *minyan* for a congregant who had a *yahrzeit*. He always said Kaddish with the congregation, and his clear resonant voice was a fixture in the *shul*. My father was especially dedicated to teaching boys for their bar mitzvahs, regardless of their background. As a child, I would sit and listen to their lessons, and learned the sing-song of the Torah *trup* by osmosis.

But by the time of my own bat mitzvah, my father was showing early signs of an Alzheimer's-type illness. When I was sixteen, he moved into a nursing home for around-the-clock care.

During the seven years he lived in a nursing home, my father's decline was gradual, like going down a staircase and suddenly realizing you are at the bottom. Sometimes he was aware of my presence, more often he was not. Sometimes he smiled when he saw me; sometimes he just slept the whole time I was there. He lived in the nursing home but not in my life. I graduated high school; I went to Israel for the year; I started college; I had my first serious relationship and my father was alive but not present as I navigated these milestones. In that age before cell phones, I worried about where I would be when he died and how my mother would reach me. I had no idea when to expect it, so I half-expected it any time.

As a college student at Barnard, I became a regular *minyan* goer. Students davened together, ate at the kosher meal plan, and we learned Torah together in the *beit midrash*. Davening in a *minyan* helped me focus, and I liked that my prayer carried with it the added weight of everyone else's. When I said *Refa'einu* ("God heal us") I thought, "My father is not healable, please just do what is meant to be." I did not know how long he would live, but I saw myself saying Kaddish whenever that time came.

My father died when I was twenty-three, at the start of my life as a working adult. It was still a shock to get the phone call that *Asarah B'Tevet* morning, the morning he did not wake up. In all the years he had lived in America, and even served America as a reservist chaplain in the U.S. Army, my father yearned for the land of his parents and grandparents: Israel. He had told us in no uncertain terms that he had to be buried there when the time came.

The night we buried my father, not far from his mother's grave, was a clear Jerusalem night with a bright, nearly full moon. For me, walking through the Har Hamenuchot cemetery in Israel is like walking among the branches of a family tree. Family graves are scattered throughout the first section of the first cemetery to have been opened after the state was established in 1948. The tears came, however, when I looked around and saw that I had been embraced by a community of people who cared about our loss, and wanted to do a *chesed* for my father.

During my year of mourning, I davened with a *minyan* at least once a day. Saying Kaddish was the last thing I could do for my father, and in some ways, it filled a hole. When I had visited my father during the last years of his illness, I no longer felt like I was doing something for him; I was going for me, just to see him alive and present. In contrast, saying Kaddish was for him. There was relief in having reached the end, and there was satisfaction in doing something that I believe would have been meaningful to him, and in carrying on his legacy. While my father's long illness was something I had experienced privately, saying Kaddish was a public act that allowed people around me to understand the depth of my sorrow.

Tonight, as I said Kaddish on the eve of my father's *yahrzeit*, I relived the experience of having a community of people carry me along on a clear, moony night in Jerusalem fourteen years ago. My rabbi came over to me and said the customary "Your father's *neshama* should have an *aliyah*." I am not exactly sure what that means, but I find it comforting and hope that saying Kaddish is something that helps my father's *neshama*. On some level, it helps my *neshama* as well, as I connect with a community of mourners who understand how it feels to lose a loved one.

SARA WISE PRAGER serves as a consultant to a New York law firm and does volunteer work for her children's day school and her synagogue. Sara is a self-described beginner writer, avid reader, enthusiastic cook and homework helper to her children. She lives in New Jersey with her husband and four children.

The Prayers of Other Hearts

LAURA SHEINKOPF

I N A HOSPITAL SETTING, the chaplain is the tree that holds its ground in the chaos that is illness. As a rabbi and chaplain, I have always imagined my role as that of a guide; more akin to a shepherd than a savior, prophet or preacher. I momentarily step into someone's life when they are confronting death and that means being still and present without impeding the story that is unfolding. Having to confront one's mortality is a universally challenging thing, and it's like looking at the sun. You cannot stare into it endlessly without going blind. So we look and turn away and look again. The shepherd stays with a person, never insisting that s/he see something in a particular way but instead remaining present throughout. Taking a piece of another person's story, lifting it up and dignifying it by placing it in the context of the Jewish experience is what differentiates a rabbi from a counselor. But you cannot be that guide, you cannot assume that position without being nominated by those in need.

I am a female Reform rabbi, and therefore automatically off the list of potential shepherds for a certain group of people. It's not personal and I have never felt offended by it. Death and illness are profoundly disorganizing experiences and people look for familiar words uttered by a familiar voice when they find themselves in the chaos of tragedy. I have no trouble stepping aside if I am not the right person to counsel or assist for any reason, gender or otherwise. But in these instances I have felt useless and feeling useless in a time of extraordinary need is very uncomfortable for me.

I first learned these lessons years ago as I drove to the hospital in response to a call, just as dawn was breaking on a Shabbos morning. The father of a Jewish family had just died. At that time, I was immersed in my rabbinic studies, a new baby, and my job. I did not stop to wonder why this Jewish family's own rabbi was not able to get to the hospital that day, I just responded to the call.

I went to the designated floor and made my way to the nurses' station.

"Hey, I am the chaplain on call and . . . ."

A blond bobbed nurse popped up. "Oh great, but you are a rabbi, right?" she asked, a bit too perky for 5 a.m.

"Well, yes and no . . . I am still in school but close enough for most people."

"These folks were really relieved when I told them we had an actual rabbi on call . . . ," she replied. But that relief would soon turn to horror. The well-meaning nurse led me to the room and just as she opened her mouth to announce I had arrived, I saw the long skirts and the bearded men and realized too late that I was not the kind of "rabbi" they were expecting. So when the nurse blurted out, "Your rabbi is here!" they all looked up. There was a round of sniffles, a second of silence and then a collective wail. And I am not talking about a little bit of crying here. This was a heart-wrenching, throw yourself on a coffin sort of wail uttered in unison, and all because I walked into the room.

I summoned my most compassionate voice and simply said, "I am not your rabbi. I am just your chaplain." They were still too shocked to even respond so I stepped out and considered leaving but then thought better. After a bit, I returned to ask if I could do anything helpful like call a funeral home or arrange for a *shomer* (guardian of the body). They were genuinely grateful for the offer and I stayed for a bit just trying to be a presence. I learned that the deceased had been a very devout man and the patriarch of a large family. At some point one of the sons said he wanted to sit by his father and recite Psalms, but he did not have a *siddur* and could not do all of it by heart. I offered my book of Psalms, but he politely declined. I took my leave soon after.

The daughter followed me out the door and down the hall. She was sobbing and asked, "Could I please borrow your book of *Tehillim*? I know my brothers would not want me to but I need to say them. I need a *siddur* to hold in my hands. I can't explain it. I was holding his hand in the ambulance and it was cold and now I just want to hold a *siddur* in my hands . . ."

I gave her my book but it felt like I was giving something back to its rightful owner. I understood her need completely, not as a rabbi or a chaplain (neither of which I was completely sure of at that moment), but as a woman, the way you know to start swaying back and forth when the baby you are holding begins to fuss. The gender that limited me in one context became the bridge in another. Looking back, this seems right to me now. While I can pray with the men in my tradition and I do, it still lacks the import and the power of the cooking and soothing that I came to know in the presence of women. Even as a rabbi, I have often felt more connected to the life of the community in the kitchen or the social hour among other women, and this feeling deepened when I had children and sometimes had to leave events in order to care for my child. I did not feel frustrated at those times. I did not feel demoted or excluded as a woman, or that taking time to rock or feed or soothe was antithetical to my role as a rabbi. Quite the opposite; I felt ennobled. I felt the comfort of clarity. Though being a rabbi demands words, the most sincere and powerful connection to Judaism I have experienced is all about the hands.

She asked me to come with her to where her father's body lay so that she could recite the *Tehillim*, and I stood at the door as she whispered the Psalms through tears. She said that her Dad would probably have objected, wanting only her brothers to do this but, "I just have to. . . ." This was a Jewishly knowledgable woman who was extremely close to the father who had just died. Though they did not sit side by side in the synagogue, they uttered the same words and I imagined holding that prayer book was akin to hearing the beating heart of the father who could no longer utter its words. Before I left, she grasped my hands and looked into my eyes and said "Please promise you will say Kaddish for my father after he is buried. I may not be able to do it, I don't know . . . Will you promise me that you will say it wherever you are?"

That was the last time I would ever see or hear of that family, but I did say Kaddish for their father and have on the day of his death in all the years since. From our different perspectives, this woman and I share a deep appreciation of the power of Kaddish. Her prayer would be from the heart and I would be the privileged voice that spoke its truth.

LAURA SHEINKOPF grew up on Cape Cod and attended Northfield Mt Hermon School in Western Massachussets. She received a BA in Religious studies from Columbia University. She was awarded a Master of Hebrew Letters and rabbinic ordination by Hebrew Union College in 2002. She resides in Houston, Texas with her two children, Max and Isabel.

El Malei Rachamim

DEB KRAM

ON THE OCCASION of my mother's, *z"l*, first *yahrzeit*, I prepared myself to recite Kaddish with a local *minyan*, and invited an intimate group of friends to join me at my home to be present when I kindled a *yahrzeit* candle and taught a text in her memory. Kaddish fulfilled a public expression of loss ending the year of *aveilut*, chanted however in haste to keep up with other mourners, while the learning among friends illumed by the light of a *ner neshama* fulfilled a personal expression with the luxury of time for reflection. Upon moving to a new community, I found another ritual expression connected to my loss that holds much meaning.

The prayer of supplication, *El Malei Rachamim* (God full of compassion), is recited at funerals, when visiting the gravesite, and is included in the *Yizkor* liturgy. Historically, it was recited for the martyrs of the Crusades and the Chelminski massacres. The Ashkenazic custom is also to include it after Torah reading, some time during the week of a *yahrzeit*. Unlike the proclamation of God's majesty echoing in Kaddish, *El Malei Rachamim* is an intensely direct and personal prayer on behalf of the soul of the deceased, who is specifically named. It articulates a plea that the *neshama* of the deceased should come to rest *upon* the wings of the *Shechina* (Divine Presence), "*al kanfei ha-Shechina*," signifying a spiritual elevation. This is opposed to the more familiar imagery of being sheltered protectively *under* these wings. We further articulate our desire for the *neshama* to find peaceful repose in Gan Eden.

Shortly after joining Congregation Shaarei Tefillah, in Newton, Massachusetts, I requested that the *gabbaim* include my mother's, *z"l*, name among the deceased when reciting *El Malei Rachamim* at the Shabbat *Mincha* service. To my surprise, the *gabbai* informed me that I had the option of reciting *El Malei Rachamim* myself. While the *Sefer Torah* was held by the *shaliach tzibbur*, I could approach the *mechitza* and say the prayer aloud. I had never contemplated this possibility before. I had never heard of or seen it recited publicly by women, and was unaware of any historical or contemporary source text on this practice. The rabbi of the congregation, Rabbi Benjamin Samuels, reassured me of its halachic validity. He explained that *El Malei* was a personal prayer that did not require a *minyan*, though its recitation at both *Yizkor* and on occasion of a *yahrzeit* customarily took place amidst community.

I wrestled with my decision. Why the hesitation? I value *tefillah b'tzibbur* highly, and continually invest intellectual time and spiritual energy towards understanding prayers, so that my davening not be a rote practice. I am not reticent about public speaking, and have taught Torah to mixed audiences. Yet the closest prior experiences I could summon were my *bentching Gomel* at a Shabbat morning Kiddush after the birth of my daughter, and *l'havdil*, tearing *kriyah* and reciting the blessing of *Dayan ha-Emet* (the True Judge) at the funeral of my father, *z"l*, five years ago. Neither of these took place in a *shul's makom tefillah* or within the context of communal prayer. This opportunity would truly be unprecedented for me, and certainly different than blending my voice in with others when reciting Kaddish. This was giving my singular voice resonance within a communal prayer setting. Was I prepared to do so?

I was undecided all week as to what I would do, up until the actual moment arrived. I did recite *El Malei Rachamim* that Shabbat on behalf of my mother's *neshama*, trembling with intentionality and deep-felt emotion. Recited at my own pace and cadence, undistracted by all else, focused on the words in a way that *tefillah* is surely designed. I found it comforting, juxtaposed to straining with frustration to catch the fleeting mention of her name recited by unrelated others on this occasion in previous years. I am so grateful for having the ability to participate in this practice, and for feeling supported by my fellow congregants while doing so. It was a vastly meaningful prayer experience for me, beyond my recitation of Kaddish on the occasion of their *yahrzeits*, or davening *Yizkor*.

When the calendar date approached some months later close to the *yahrzeit* of my father, *z"l*, there was no question of where I would be on that Shabbat afternoon. The communal prayer experience has been transformed for me in ways I had not imagined, as I now memorialize my parents annually in this public expression.

DEB KRAM is a consultant and senior scholar who lectures widely. An alumna of the Mandel Jerusalem Fellows, she has served in Greater Boston as Director of Adult Learning for the Combined Jewish Philanthropies, Family Education Consultant for the Bureau of Jewish Education, and Co-Founder and Director of Ma'ayan, an award-winning program for life-long learning.

יְהֵא

שְׁמֵהּ

רַבָּא

מְבָרַךְ

לְעָלַם

וּלְעָלְמֵי

עָלְמַיָּא

The Shoes
still sit there
two days after shiva has ended
caked with mud
from my mother's grave
I don't want to clean them
I want to throw them away
once was enough to
immerse myself in the
dirt of her death

I was terrified of the burial
It was not so horrible, actually
my mother whose emptiness
had been infinite
had only one need remaining and
I who never succeeded
in loving her, really
was fully able to give

It must be on account of these
mud-caked shoes
Halachah prohibits wearing new clothes
the laws of mourning
the laws of Mo'ed
coexist
within one tractate

So I sit
again
shake the dust from my skirt
step outside

Fulsome Grieving

VERA SCHWARCZ

*Sometimes it is the artist's task to find out how much music you can
still make with what is left*   —*Yitzhak Perlman*

IN NOVEMBER 1995, Yitzhak Perlman broke a violin string at the
very beginning of his performance at Lincoln Center. To the marvel
of the audience, he continued to play with only three strings. In his
moving book, *Consolation*, Rabbi Maurice Lamm recounts this event as a
metaphor for life after loss: We can, and indeed must go on, making the
music of our lives with what is left after the wrenching separation of death.

When my father died in 1984, I experienced only raw cacophony. Only
three days before his death, our first child was born, and needed immediate medical care. We held one Kaddish *minyan* in my hospital room, and
then I hurried back to my baby in the incubator.

My mother was the active mourner, and she bore her long widowhood
with grace. After all, she had long ago mastered the art of composing
a life out of broken chords. A survivor of the Shoah (like my father),
she had gone on long after her holy parents were consumed in the fires
of Auschwitz. She lost a baby daughter in the ghetto of Budapest, she
mourned quietly a grandson who had died of hemophilia. She treasured
life's pleasures – especially opera music – but eventually, a series of strokes
and a growing cancer spelled an end she was fully prepared for. Often she
would say that she was ready to meet my father, to see her own parents.

The last month of Mother's life began with an inchoate phone call:
an eerie chortle followed by a rapid stutter. This could not be one of the

many languages my mother knew, and which we had learned to speak together. It was the beginning of the end.

I returned to Florida, where she lived. Early one morning, I saw Mother's face in my own tired wrinkles. Dying inscribed her into my flesh more deeply. Mother's closed eyes, sunken cheeks, and labored breathing during her last days of life are all part of a mournful symphony that still echoes in my heart. There was no choice but to witness the breaking of yet another violin string. My sister and I stood at her bedside on that last Erev Shabbat, *Parshat Lech Lecha*. We knew we were being sent forth, like Abraham, into a new land.

On Motzei Shabbat (Saturday night), the *yahrzeit* of Rachel Imeinu, my mother returned her soul to Hashem. Yitta bat Tzivia v'Tzvi Hersh, who had not been able to mourn her own mother or father or child, was now finally at rest. She left us an opportunity for fulsome grieving that she had never known.

Back home in Connecticut for *shiva*, I was truly free to sink into the loss of my mother. I had a small album of photographs I'd prepared to share with my comforters: a visual testament to my mother's irreplaceable life. I did not want to talk about politics, weather, and the kids. I was determined to mourn, to live out the grief that I had no time for when my father died. This time, I knew the string had broken. If I were going to go on, it would have to be with a different tonality. I was looking for Torah, something enduring to stitch up my broken heart, even as I let the tear in my shirt show.

One rabbi drew my attention to the last line of the Mishna that one customarily studies in a house of mourning, drawn from the section on *mikva'ot* (ritual baths): "If a needle was placed on the steps of a cave, and one moved water to and fro, as soon as a wave passes over it, the needle is cleansed." Who cares about how you kasher a needle, was my first, impatient thought. Then, I listened more closely: To what can a needle be likened? The soul, which is a slim connector between the disparate realms of the physical and the spiritual. Just as a needle pulls together what is severed, so too, the mourner's soul weaves together the rent fabric of life and death. What is water? Always, Torah. By the time the rabbi left, I saw how my own tears had become a *mikvah* of a certain kind, and my mother's *neshama* became more present to me. Loss was being bathed and cleansed in the very act of mourning, and of Torah study. Learning this one Mishna made me thirst for more. A daily dose of Torah study – one paragraph of Mishna each morning – has become mother's enduring gift to me, even now.

In the days after *shiva*, however, I needed more. My friend Judith, a pioneer in Kaddish, had warned me that it would be hard to take that first walk around the block. And it was! She suggested that I might find solace in coming to *shul* to continue saying Kaddish, and offered to pick me up the next morning.

At first I felt lost, but Judith's simple wisdom prevailed: don't try to say all the prayers; listen for the key words that lead into each Kaddish; don't be shy about asking the men to slow down. In a couple of weeks, with my mother's large print *siddur* marked with a dozen yellow stickers, I stood as any mourner in the morning's *minyan*.

As the words of the Kaddish became smoother on my tongue, I could listen more attentively to the subtle music of soul going on around me and within me. I began to distinguish – and to wait for – the sweet melodies of specific men I knew in our community. One Kohen from Safed, with roots in North Africa, brought his unique tunes to the *Psukei D'Zimra*. The principal of our day school would sing out certain words in the *brachot* before the *Shema*. He helped me hear afresh Hashem's will to renew the world each day.

All along, Judith's quiet presence near me was reassuring. When another woman lost her mother, we arrived early to the *shiva* house, holding cups of coffee, lingering to talk, and giving the new mourner strength to say the words that were now part of the fabric of my daily life.

As I entered the last months of saying Kaddish, I found myself deeply connected to both my parents. Having had time to articulate grief in the midst of community, I am now able to hear new music seasoned by loss.

Two survivors came together immediately after the war; two broken souls made room in the midst of fear for hope. Daily, I beg God to help me become a living Kaddish for my parents; to grant me strength and wisdom to make my actions worthy of them in this world, and in the world of truth they now inhabit together.

BORN IN ROMANIA, Vera Schwarcz is a China historian and poet. She is the author of eight books on Chinese and Jewish history, including the prize-winning *Bridge Across Broken Time: Chinese and Jewish Cultural Memory* (1999) and most recently, *Place and Memory in Singing Crane Garden* (2008). She has also written four books of poetry, including *Brief Rest in the Garden of Flourishing Grace* (2009) and *Chisel of Remembrance* (2009). Schwarcz holds the Freeman Chair in East Asian Studies at Wesleyan. Her work won a Guggenheim Fellowship and is featured on the web at: between2walls.com.

Leaving a Stone

LEAH BRAUNSTEIN LEVY

Y MOTHER. MY SISTER. My aunt. Myself.

We were all with my father when he died. We had been with him for days, since my mother called to tell us that he was leaving the hospital. He wanted to go home.

My father had no brothers and no sons, but he had a wife, a sister, daughters. We surrounded his bed for three days, dabbing his lips with a moist sponge, stroking his hair, holding his hands. We told stories. We asked, "Do you remember, Tatti?" "Paul, do you remember?" We laughed, and cried; he blinked and tried to smile.

My father was the bravest person I have ever known. In 2006, he was diagnosed with a rare and aggressive cancer – the six to nine months kind – but he refused to give in to despair or self-pity. He remained hopeful and determined through seven rounds of chemotherapy, through so much radiation that his skin crackled and broke like old leather. The damage to his leg resulted in a complete amputation in spring 2010.

Loss of a leg didn't even slow him down, and he was determined to walk again. He worked for hours with a physical therapist, hopping around the patio in a safety harness. When new tumor growth made a prosthetic leg impossible, he bought himself a wheelchair with handles that folded away, because he refused to allow anyone to push him. He went to appointments himself, pulling on fingerless gloves to make the pushing easier, tucking a book into his wheelchair pouch, rolling himself onto the senior wheelchair transport, tipping the driver. He wrote on his blog and followed the news and talked to his friends. He lived his life. But the tumors that consumed him could not be stopped.

My father, among his many other talents, was an in-demand *chazzan* for the Yamim Noraim (High Holidays). Throughout my childhood, it was my father's voice I heard singing *Kol Nidrei*, lifting his voice from a whisper to a shout; it was my father I heard pleading for forgiveness for us all. *Accept my prayer like the prayers of an experienced elder, whose life has been well spent, whose beard is fully grown, whose voice is sweet, and who is genial with other people* . . . This past Rosh Hashanah was the last time he davened from the *amud* as the *baal tefillah*. My father – an amputee fiery with tumor fever – sat in his wheelchair and sang *U'Netaneh Tokef* before the *aron kodesh*, ten weeks before he died.

❧

My father had no sons, so when he died, my rabbi asked me if I planned to say Kaddish. I had not realized that this was even a possibility. I found the idea of preset, daily times to think about my father – and something concrete to do for him – very appealing. It seemed like somewhere firm to walk in a world where very many things had become uncertain, out of balance. But life with four children of varied ages has long since convinced me of the wisdom of exempting mothers from time-bound *mitzvot*. It's complicated; I spend every weekday *Shacharit*, *Mincha*, and *Maariv* driving my children to and from their yeshiva, an hour round-trip. How, then, could I be in *shul* at the same time? My husband told me that he would be happy to say Kaddish on my behalf, and he had loved my father too. That seemed easiest and best.

One afternoon towards the end of my *shloshim*, my husband fell victim to a particularly nasty flu. I called the rabbi and asked him if he could arrange for someone to say Kaddish for my father that evening.

"Wish I could," he told me, "but I'm in a traffic jam and can't promise I'll be there on time myself." He suggested that I pick up the children early, go to a *shul* near the school and say it myself.

There was nothing else to be done, so that's what I did.

Because I was reading the words from the *siddur*, I didn't look across the *mechitza* to see if I was shocking anyone when I raised my voice and chanted along with the men. Women have been saying Kaddish for centuries. Not every halachic authority agrees that they may, but mine is hardly a fringe position. I didn't need to consult Moshe, like the daughters of Zelophchad (another man with no sons). They had to ask for a change in the law to receive their inheritance. In this time and place, Kaddish was freely offered to me by my rabbinic authorities. And in any case, my father himself was never swayed by worries about what other people thought.

I was surprised at how comfortable I was, for the first time in memory, making myself heard in *shul*.

As we waited for *Maariv*, the rabbi gave a *Dvar Torah* "in honor of those we are remembering with Kaddish." He asked all of us in attendance to call out the names of our loved ones, and we did, one at a time. I said his name, Pinchas ben Tzvi Reuven. It was strangely exhilarating just to say his name out loud. My presence at the *minyan* seemed significant, somehow; it reminded me how much it meant to my father to daven with a *minyan* on Rosh Hashanah, for what we had refused to admit was the last time.

At *Maariv*, I recited the Kaddish once more. It felt like a gift to him, that day, like the wobbly handmade ones I gave him as a little girl. It was a gift to myself, too.

Now, I am happy to make time to honor my father this way, when I can – on weekends, at the early *minyan*, on snow days. And of course, my husband continues to say Kaddish for my father, steady and true, to free me from my time-bound constraints when I am pulled by love in too many directions at once.

෨

My father's grave is not far from where I live, and I visit as often as I can. In accordance with Jewish custom, I have left a stone every time. Leaving that stone feels very much like saying Kaddish. It is the same sort of gift for my father: a thought made manifest, a marker of my love.

And remembering how my father loved the beach, sometimes I leave a seashell, too.

LEAH BRAUNSTEIN LEVY is the author of *The Waiting Wall*, a Sydney Taylor Notable Book for 2010, and a contributor to *Highlights for Children*. She is also a freelance editor who specializes in scholarly works of Jewish philosophy, history, and Bible Studies. Leah lives with her husband and four children in Atlanta, Georgia.

Good Thing I'm Not Claustrophobic

JONI NATHANSON

WE WERE GOING TO Atlantic City. I knew there was an Ortho-dox community near our hotel, and I called the rabbi to ask where I could find a *minyan* the next morning. He told me, "There is none." I asked about the yeshiva high school and he said, "No." I asked if he knew where I could go to say Kaddish, and he answered: "Why don't you call the Conservative rabbi?" I'm sure if my husband had called him to find a *minyan*, he would have had no problem. I did call the Conservative rabbi, and he was so nice! He told me he would make a *mechitza* for me and have a *minyan*. I went the next morning and was relieved and honored that he went out of his way for me.

On Thanksgiving, we were at the Homowack, and I went down early Thursday morning to the *minyan* to daven. It was held in a large gym, and there was no *mechitza* set up yet. I went over to the rabbi and asked if I could daven in the back – where there was a little partition and I would stand behind it. He said, "Fine." As I was in the middle of saying Kaddish, a man comes over to me and is very angry and says, "Please leave now. Go daven out in the hall." I continued my Kaddish, as the tears were streaming from my eyes. He yelled, "Because of you, I can't daven. Are you going to leave or not?" By now I'm just crying outright and I couldn't think of an answer so I just looked at him and said, "Not." He spent the rest of the time finding a *mechitza* and moving it around me.

Another time, we were in Las Vegas mid-week and there was barely a *minyan*. During the middle of the service, the rabbi and the *gabbai* got into a loud argument and one of the men started to walk out. And then there were only nine – I went into a panic. Suddenly a 16-year old boy said, "What's wrong with you? Don't you see someone has to say Kaddish? If you leave there won't be a *minyan*." The man who had left walked back in. Later, the *gabbai* made an appeal to raise money to expand the building. At the same time, I overheard that same boy asking for donations for him to be able to attend Yeshiva University. Needless to say, we gave a donation to the 16-year old, who acted with more sensitivity than any other member of the *shul*.

Even at home, there were challenges. Each Sunday morning, the door to the ladies' section was locked and I had to search for someone to find a key to open the door for me. Each week, as I entered the building, I noticed a beggar standing in the lobby, who would approach me and ask for money. I decided one week that I would make it worth his while. I asked him what time he arrives for "work" every Sunday. He told me he comes at 7 a.m. I told him I would make a deal with him. I said that since I come each week at 9 a.m., if he has the door unlocked for me, I would pay him for his diligence. The following week and all the subsequent weeks of the year, the door to the women's section was unlocked and ready for me to enter. He even went so far as to hold it open for me! It cost me $5 a week, but it was well worth it!

Another time, we were in Miami and I went to a *shul* for *Mincha* on Shabbos. As the men's section began filling up, I knew there would be trouble. When they ran out of seats, men started to walk into the women's section, and then did an about face as they noticed me. One very bold man came over and started yelling at me that I was taking up the whole section and what was I doing there anyway?! I told him I was davening and saying Kaddish. He got angry and told me to move to the back, and proceeded to "build" a *mechitza* around my one little chair.

Some people just forget how to be nice.

JONI NATHANSON grew up in Crown Heights, Brooklyn, NY, went to Public School and Talmud Torah, but always felt connected to davening and a closeness to Hashem. She was a teacher and director of the early childhood department at her local yeshiva and then continued to expand her pursuit in the field of Early Childhood Special Education. Joni has a supportive husband, four children and numerous grandchildren.

Building Character

RACHEL COHEN

M Y OLDER BROTHER was killed in a car accident in 1997, at the age of 36. My parents were devastated by his death. During the *shiva*, I remember my Dad sadly remarking that he no longer had a "Kaddish." It never occurred to me to promise him that he would indeed have a Kaddish; that he still had three living daughters. My siblings and I were raised in a dynamic and traditionally observant home in an environment that encouraged higher education for all in both the secular and religious realms. I felt relatively informed about the halachic issues surrounding hot topics such as women's *aliyot* and reading *Megillah* (Book of Esther). How could it not have occurred to me that I could say Kaddish for my parents?

My father, George Kaplan, was born to staunchly secular parents and raised in the Bronx. A lawyer by training, my Dad enjoyed philosophical debate and was supremely interested in people. After moving to Atlanta and marrying my mother, herself the daughter of secular parents (of the "Driving Miss Daisy" set), they began a lifelong journey towards religious observance and *aliyah* to Israel.

Three years after my brother died, my Dad had an aneurism and died suddenly. During *shiva*, a friend of my Mom's shared that she had recently finished saying Kaddish for her parents. When I looked surprised, she promised to provide me with the halachic sources. True to her word, the following day she presented me with a pile of xeroxed sheets with all sorts of traditional and modern halachic sources supporting the saying of Kaddish by women. Reading through these texts, I couldn't understand how saying Kaddish evolved into solely the son's responsibility. My father left behind a wife and three daughters, many friends and even more good deeds. Why shouldn't I proclaim these accomplishments through sanctifying God's name in public?

Rabbi Shlomo Riskin, the rabbi of our community of Efrat, was unequivocally supportive (not surprising at all). Rabbi Riskin ruled that even when there were no men accompanying me in the prayer, I should say it aloud on my own. I was the first woman in our *shul* to say the Kaddish in such an open and public manner.

It was so odd to hear my own voice ringing out in the *shul*. I believe this is at the root of my blind spot in not considering the possibility of a daughter saying Kaddish. In the *shul* I grew up in, women didn't even say the *Birchat HaGomel* after giving birth (a prayer said in gratitude for surviving a dangerous experience), rather the husband made the blessing aloud and the community responded to him. After giving birth to our first *sabra*, I had been both very surprised and gratified, and admittedly a bit terrified, to be able to make for myself this thanksgiving blessing aloud in synagogue. I knew that the Mishna discusses women getting *aliyot* on Shabbat. Nonetheless, I had an irrational yet visceral reaction to hearing a feminine voice in *shul*, especially my own.

We are fortunate to live in a warm and supportive neighborhood. The comments I received from my neighbors on the other side of the *mechitza* were mostly along the lines of "Speak up! We can't hear you!" Rabbi Riskin's *psak* (ruling) was my shield against the very few who may have found this practice objectionable.

Our youngest child was ten months old when my Dad died, so getting to *minyan* every day was a challenge. Our oldest daughters were twelve and ten at the time. I've always tried to avoid giving my children too many responsibilities around the house, believing that they deserved to enjoy their childhood. However, here I had no choice and they rose to the occasion.

Overcoming my inhibition about praying aloud in *shul* indicated my devotion to my Dad, and thereby increased the mitzvah in my mind. I believed I was truly becoming someone he would be proud of by stepping out of the box and doing something difficult; "building character" as he loved to say. I felt his approval and embrace with each recital of the prayer.

On Shabbat and holidays, some women would make sure to move closer and respond specifically to my recitation of Kaddish. Being encircled by these women brought home to me how different the daily davening experience is for men and for women. The ritual affirmed both my personal love and respect for my father and the general loss his passing was to the community at large.

After losing my brother, the hardest period came after I came back home from sitting *shiva* in the States. I was irrevocably changed, yet there was no sign I could wear that informed people I was a walking open wound. Saying Kaddish for my Dad gently guided me through that difficult period. I felt I was both helping his *aliyat neshama* through my prayers, and working through my grief one "*Yehei shmei rabba mevorach l'olam ul'olmei olmaya*" at a time.

RACHEL was born and raised in Atlanta, Georgia. She earned a Master's in Mathematics and worked as a financial planner after marrying her husband Kenny. Eight years later, she moved with her husband and their four children to Israel. They had seven years with her father in Israel before he passed away. Rachel and Kenny have six children, thank God: two married daughters, two sons in the IDF and two children still living at home. Eight years ago Rachel went back to school to study Neuropsychology at the Hebrew University in Jerusalem, and is now in the process of completing her residency in that field.

Baby Cries
half-hearted, sleepy moan
refuses to settle
into silence
she persists
because she knows
what I've wanted
her to know in every
cell of her body

A mother comes

long after quiet
descends, I lie
awake, tears
turned cold
I know
she's dead but
it's been four weeks, why
hasn't she called?

Ascent to Praise

NESSA RAPOPORT

KADDISH: *HINENI*

AYIN MI-YESH: Death inverts creation. One second, God is renewing each day the divine invention of the world. The next, a freefall into primordial chaos, *tohu va-vohu*, darkness without a horizon, pure, ruthless black.

So it is on the morning when a phone call tells you that the beloved friend your age, with whom you were laughing a mere night ago, is gone. Or the friend you loved since you were teenagers. But so it is, surprisingly, when the father who has been leaving, second by second for ten years, is released with finality while you watch his beautiful last breath.

There is no good way, and either way you are unable to cohere. They die. You labor to reconstitute the ones who are never, not ever . . .

The taunting paradox of mid-life: When at last you don the wisdom of experience, death strips away the accrual, leaving you whimpering. Loss steals language; you have nothing to say.

A loving community buttresses you, feeding you, telling you when to stand and sit, thrusting into your slack hand the prayer book containing the chanted words that, until now, only other people knew by heart.

You are the other people now. You are the one sitting on the low chair, slayed by memory. You are the one entering a synagogue, eons of previous praying useless, fumbling through pages, unable to find your place.

In the beginning, your fluidity in your tradition, your adeptness: gone. I shall not forget J., who handed me his *siddur*, open at Kaddish, on the first morning after *shiva* as I entered the *ezrat nashim*, the women's side, of the Modern Orthodox synagogue that became my Kaddish *minyan*, shocked both by death and by my plummeting awareness that there was no egalitarian *Mincha-Maariv* near either my home or my job. Or E., who interrupted her ardent prayer to show me the place.

Eleven Hebrew months later, we women are a fierce sisterhood, waning and waxing like the lunar calendar. When one of us completes her Kaddish, we are diminished as a community and yet relieved for her – no more panting up the stairs to get to *shul* in time for the first Kaddish, no more solidarity in our delight at being acknowledged in subtle ways as contributors to the culture of the *shul*, even if not citizens; or, more rarely, slighted by those who race through Kaddish on the other side of the *mechitza* as if we are not there. Or who ask in a strident voice, "Is anyone a *chiyuv*?" Does anyone have the mourner's obligation to lead the *minyan*?, to the resounding "No *chiyuv*" as we stand there, mute.

If we lower our voices in humility when we claim in the Grace After Meals that from youth to old age we have never seen a righteous person forsaken and his descendants begging for bread, can you not lower your voice when asking such a question? Or when every morning, to start the praying day, you bless the Lord "who did not make me a woman," as if we, a hearing, listening community, were not standing in the same sacred space, only a barrier away.

Ger: Convert to mourning, stranger at first to the rhythm of public thrice-daily prayer, halting, not enfranchised, orphaned.

Through holy days and fasting days, through festive days and grieving days, and through many ordinary days, none of which has felt ordinary during this mourning year, I have walked – more often run – to *shul*. Through seasons of dazzling light or brutal cold, through the darkening days and the lengthening ones, I have sat and stood and recited, almost never alone in the women's section and occasionally, refreshingly, in a mixed *minyan*. I have said Kaddish in New York, Vermont, Atlanta, Toronto and Israel. I have been in *shul* for the early *minyan* on Sunday mornings and for the latest *Maariv* of spring evenings. On an Erev Shabbat near summer's peak, in different cities and continents, my sisters and I concluded eleven Hebrew months.

I count the saying of Kaddish as among the highest privileges of my life. I entered a world and emerged a different person. Time unfurled, and my father's glittering facets turned toward me and away, the clutch of turbulent perfectionism he bequeathed me relenting in compassion – for all he did and could not do, for my own unfinished self.

In the beginning, Kaddish was like the frame that descends to right the bowling pins that have been mowed into patternless anarchy. The frame lowers painstakingly, setting in place, but only for an instant, what can never be in order.

Throughout the year, my soul was shipwrecked, but my body, that automaton, walked and bent and intoned. And from the *na'aseh ve'nishma* of assumed obligation has come a restored delight in my father's essence and in the profligate gifts he gave us, which I can see and savor.

By year's end, and not deliberately, I have reassembled him from the ailing, reduced man of his long illness to a man in the flush of his powers, exceptional healer, burnished honestly by recollection.

He is gone and will not return. But he has been returned to me in this terrible year, in ways oblique but constant, dappled by the knowledge that now he is a sanctuary. The thought is sweet. I am a parent and I know that what brings my child solace is my consolation. Somewhere in the Gan Eden my father earned by saving so many lives, he wants to ease my suffering.

Once I heard a son cite a passage of Talmud in memory of his father. Before his father's students he spoke these words:

"As long as you're alive, you're a *holech* – one who walks – able to go higher and higher in *kedushah*, holiness. But the second you die, you go from being a *holech* to an *omed* – one who stands still. Unless," said his father's son, "your students, or your children, continue your work."

So much death this year. So many sorrows unredeemed. Friend of my middle years, friend of my youth, father: May you accompany me all the days of my life.

YAHRZEIT: ONE YEAR

Reappearing to mark the day, I assume my place in the *ezrat nashim*, at home and not at home as the shade and sun of invisibility, of belonging, pass over me. This *Mincha* liturgy, the last of my *yahrzeit* day, is a homecoming, the words embodied by eleven months of daily service, alongside, inevitably, the unabated anguish of my not being counted, not counting.

The men on the other side do not see me – literally, metaphorically – and thus cannot acknowledge aloud, as they do for male mourners, that I am present because of my father's remembered absence. But the resident scholar, a woman, knows why I am here. And when I cannot recall (it has been a year) whether the *Kaddish D'Rabbanan* that comes between *Mincha* and *Maariv* on this Friday is the conclusion of *Mincha* (and thus my responsibility to say aloud) or the prelude to the *Maariv* after the *yahrzeit*, she does not say, "I'll go ask the rabbi." She tells me, immediately, the answer.

Because she *knows* the answer. Which is a transformative change in the architectonics of communal prayer. Braced for the pain of exclusion, I am suffused with thanksgiving. Beyond the boundaries of this Jewish world are women rabbis. Now, new, on my side of the *mechitza* is a religious authority.

My assumption of this mitzvah gave me irreplaceable gifts, gifts that partake of eternity. But the saying of Kaddish each day, *Maariv, Shacharit, Mincha*, also confirmed irrefutably that separate can never be equal.

When you do not count, you cannot simply join the impromptu morning *minyan* in the El Al lounge at JFK after your midnight plane was delayed until dawn. You can run up Broadway to your cherished Shabbat *tefillah*, lungs sliced by brittle winter air, to find that there are nine women but only six men. You make ten – but not the right ten. And so, again, despite your being on time, despite your commitment to honor your father in this time-stringent way, there is no initial Kaddish for you.

Sisters in Kaddish: Here is a hard truth. There is an inescapable line between a woman who is not counted in a *minyan* and a woman who is an *aguna*, a line that no welcoming words from the *bima* and no woman scholar-in-residence can erase. When a man on the other side of the *mechitza* forgets to pass over the *tzedakah* dish during the repetition of the *Amidah*, the primordial shiver that afflicts me is not only about the deletion of the women who are saying Kaddish; it is the accurate perception of our elemental powerlessness in Jewish law.

YIZKOR: EVER

Last week, alone in the house on my way to work, I stopped in the kitchen to cut out a coupon from *The New York Times*. As I aligned the scissors, I was smiling in solitude at my flawless cutting, each unperforated dot bisected with the unique, *lishma* pleasure that has no greater utility. I am a sublime wielder of scissors!

Instantly, there was my father, not "with me" but genetically alive. Of four daughters, I am the one who inherited this quality: the inability to cut out anything unless it is meticulously on the line.

To my astonishment, my father returns, sometimes daily, with a power that is revelatory. In the immediacy of grief, the idea that he would be "only a thought away" or "always with me" seemed a not-believable comfort. Now, four years later, my sisters and I are amazed by his presence. We use his expressions. We laugh at his voice in our heads, for we can hear exactly what he would say.

My benevolent understanding of his being – at times a mystery while he lived – has deepened with such profundity that I can conclude only that Hashem has shared with me a tincture of *middat ha-rachamim*, the infinite mercy that is the chief attribute of *El Malei Rachamim*, the Merciful One.

Those we have lost, who are gone with the utter finality that death uniquely confers, can also return to inform our days. They, in partnership with us, can soothe regret, the raw edge of grief. We, in communion with them, can repair what was left undone, not by cheap forgiveness but with a trace of the discernment God continually offers us.

We say the words of *Yizkor*, praying in community that our dead know *menucha nechona*, perfect rest, and summon for each other, in our unredeemed world to which loss is intrinsic, *nechama nechona*, true consolation.

For they live.

NESSA RAPOPORT is the author of a novel, *Preparing for Sabbath*, and a collection of prose poems, *A Woman's Book of Grieving*. Her memoir of family and place, *House on the River: A Summer Journey*, was awarded a grant by the Canada Council for the Arts and nominated for the PEN/Martha Albrand Award for the Art of the Memoir. Her essays and stories have been widely published and anthologized. Her meditations are included in *Objects of the Spirit: Ritual and the Art of Tobi Kahn*; *Tobi Kahn: Sacred Spaces for the 21st Century*; and *Embodied Light: 9-11 in 2011*. With Ted Solotaroff, she edited *The Schocken Book of Contemporary Jewish Fiction*. She speaks frequently about Jewish culture and imagination. *Ascent to Praise* by Nessa Rapoport draws in part on an essay published in *The Jewish Week*.

Defying Death

NECHAMA GOLDMAN BARASH

Through the Kaddish we hurl defiance at death . . . . When the mourner recites "Glorified and sanctified be the great name," he declares more or less the following: No matter how powerful death is, notwithstanding the ugly end of man, however terrifying the grave is, however nonsensical and absurd everything appears, no matter how black one's despair is and how nauseating an affair life itself is, we declare and profess publicly and solemnly that we will carry on the work of our ancestors as if nothing had happened, that we will not be satisfied with less than the full realization of the ultimate goal of the establishment of God's kingdom . . .
Rabbi Joseph Soloveitchik, "Eulogy for the Talner Rebbe"

MY MOTHER DIED in Philadelphia and we brought her to Kfar Etzion, a settlement in Gush Etzion, where I live, for burial. It is hard to describe the pain, the emptiness, the longing. Often I am reminded of my ten-year old self, terribly homesick for my mother at sleepaway camp. Back then camp ended. Now I am left with the lump in my throat, the endless yearning to see, hear and hug the woman who was my mother, my friend, my conscience and my history. At the grave, I said Kaddish along with my father, brother and two sisters. It was a powerful moment, accepting the decree from above by sanctifying God's name.

I had thought about saying Kaddish for over twenty years, since I heard two sisters do so at Harvard University's Hillel. In subsequent years, I taught a course on Women and Judaism, and Sarah Reguer's article, "Kaddish from the 'Wrong' Side of the Mechitza," touched me. In my mother's last days I even thought of telling her – Mom, I will say Kaddish for you – but somehow, putting it into words seemed to acknowledge the terrible reality awaiting her and us, and I could not bring myself to do so.

Three other women were saying Kaddish on the *yishuv*, so I was not alone on the "other" side of the *mechitza*. The presence of my four daughters (ages 6–16) strengthened my resolve. My mother always told me to be a strong role model. And my brother upped the ante when he told me that since I have always wanted to be a man in Judaism rather than a woman, I finally have the opportunity and he will accept only three misses in the course of the year or I will have failed!

During the first few weeks, going to synagogue gave direction to my day. I had to get out of bed and say Kaddish. I had to pick myself out of my sadness and go say Kaddish. Three times a day, relentlessly, the prayer service was waiting. Interestingly, sometimes being the only female in a *shul* felt empowering and sometimes it made me feel vulnerable and exposed.

Embarrassed by the *gabbai*'s scurrying around to find someone to say Kaddish with me, I called the rabbi of the community and demanded that he take a stand. What does he suggest women do when no men are available to say Kaddish? His answer, published to the community, was that a woman could say Kaddish along with the *chazzan*. Thanks to Mordechai Telsner's book on Kaddish, I discovered that historically in Israel, this was the way Kaddish was practiced until less than a hundred years ago. At Machon Pardes, where I teach and usually daven *Mincha*, I say Kaddish loudly – alone or with other mourners. In the evening, my six-year old daughter accompanies me and we have turned it into a nightly outing.

Although I am a proud Orthodox-Jewish feminist, my Kaddish is not meant to be a platform for my feminism but is rather, an expression of my mourning and a sign of my respect to my mother. I did not want to cause tension in the community but in reality, I feel silenced, invisible, as if there is something wrong with my Kaddish that it has to be said with the *chazzan*. I don't really understand what is wrong with women saying Kaddish alone. After all, I am safely behind a *mechitza* and I am not singing. Male guests respond to my *zimmun* (invitation to pray) when eating in my home and eat challah after I say *Hamotzi*. They have come to hear me teach Torah on Shavuot night from the *bima* (podium), so why is Kaddish still taboo?

At the end of six months I still wonder why it is that when I enter a strange *shul*, I have a stomach ache over how loudly to say Kaddish or whether there will be male mourners to say it along with me or do I dare say it alone?

For years I have struggled with prayer, finding the words empty. Yet both my mother and my grandmother prayed twice daily, and it bothered both of them that I had lost this connection. They would love the irony that I am now in *shul* three times a day, sometimes connecting, sometimes disconnecting, and thinking of them constantly.

———————

NECHAMA GOLDMAN BARASH received her bachelor's degree from Yeshiva University in 1991 and made *aliyah* during the Gulf War. She is a graduate of the Matan Advanced Talmud Institute and received her Master's degree in Talmud from Bar Ilan University. She teaches at various seminaries including Emunah V'Omanut and Midreshet Devora, as well as at Pardes Institute and over the Internet to schools in the U.S. through Lookstein's distance learning program. She is currently a student in Nishmat's Keren Ariel *Yoetzet Halacha* program. Nechama lives in Gush Etzion with her husband and four daughters.

Don't You Have Any Brothers?

MERYL GREENWALD GORDON

M Y FATHER WAS SNATCHED from this world in August of 1990. He went to work on Friday, walked into the hospital emergency room with chest pains on Saturday morning, was gone from us by evening, and was buried Sunday morning.

After sitting *shiva* in my parents' house, I arrived home literally blinking in the sunlight, astounded that the world still did turn and the sun still did have the nerve to shine without my father. The next day, indeed the next few weeks, still deeply in shock, I would not have gotten out of bed to face the world, not even to take care of my two young children, except for this: I felt compelled to go to my synagogue to say Kaddish for my father at the morning *minyan*. I saw clearly the deep wisdom of our tradition in forcing me out into the community at a time when I would have much preferred to hide.

I had read Maurice Lamm's beautiful classic book, *The Jewish Way in Death and Mourning*. He writes: "The Mourner's Kaddish . . . blends in with the internal spirit of the mourner, imperceptibly healing his psychological wounds, and it teaches the mourner vital and profound lessons about life and death. . . . It is, therefore, no accident of spiritual history that the Kaddish has become so important to those stricken with grief . . ." I was comforted that, as a Jew, I could draw on such a rich tradition in my time of need.

I arrived at 7:30 a.m. and I took my place in the women's section, alone. I recited the Kaddish at the appropriate times, and I tried to keep up as the experienced worshipers raced through the service. I did expect questions and comments, but not the first one I received: "Don't you have any brothers?"

As if everyone does. As if my father, only son of an immigrant butcher, was woefully lacking in the two daughters he had been so proud of, sending one to Yale and the other to Princeton. As if I, as a woman, was not also entitled to be comforted by the ancient traditions of our people, or somehow had no need for a structured mourning ritual. As if, had I had a brother, there would have been no reason for me to say Kaddish. Was I not also a Jewish mourner "stricken with grief"?

I was surprised and hurt that an otherwise kind and gentle human being thought that it was perfectly acceptable to ask such an audacious question of a new mourner – "Don't you have any brothers?" From other women I have spoken with, it seems to be a common question for Orthodox men to ask.

I went faithfully to that *minyan*, morning and evening, through the thirty-day period of *shloshim*, then beyond. No longer surprised to see me, most of the men ignored me. The bank of light switches was on the men's side of the *mechitza*; if the rabbi or one particular gentleman was there, he would turn on the lights on the women's side for me. Otherwise I sat through the entire service in the semi-dark. The younger men made jokes about women in general, or their own wives in particular, women whom I personally knew. In front of me. As though I wasn't there. Not being counted in an Orthodox *minyan* is one thing; not being acknowledged as being in the room is quite another. Why was I completely invisible?

I had read all the lovely things about the wonders of the Jewish mourning rituals, and until then I just did not realize that they weren't talking to *me*. I had read that ". . . the recitation of the Kaddish and its cadences were so well patterned to the mood of the mourner that it became a cherished part of the whole Jewish people." Was I not a part of the whole Jewish people?

And "The recitation, nowadays made alongside other mourners, creates a fellowship of the bereaved in a time of profound loneliness and helplessness" – but not for women?

And "Kaddish is a spiritual handclasp between generations, one that connects two lifetimes" – but not for parents and daughters? Not for my father and me?

I have come to see a connection between the behavior of the men I encountered and the common use of universal language for circumstances in which the exclusion of women is a given. It comes from a mindset in which one can refer to the Jewish "people" and really mean only Jewish "men," or say "children" and mean only "sons." It is a mindset in which women are not merely not "counted," but are not taken into account at all.

As fall turned to winter, it became harder to find men available at, say, 4:00 in the afternoon for *minyan*. So one of the men would count, and count again, and eventually there would be nine men, my little daughter and me. Then someone would call someone's newly bar mitzvah'ed 13-year old son to come over and stand there to make a *minyan*, and I began to resent not being counted more and more.

One way women have traditionally answered death is with new life, and six months after my father's death, I became pregnant. Two months later, the day after the second Seder, I began to lose the baby, a process that a week of medical intervention could not stop.

There is no traditional Jewish ceremony or prayer to mark a miscarriage, an event in which a woman's body betrays both her and the next generation, and the promise of new life turns into the pain of blood and death. With the loss of that baby, who would have been named for my father, my father died again for me. I began to find it impossible to sit alone and invisible on my side of the *mechitza* as a woman in a man's world while I was so deeply in the throes of a woman-only experience, bleeding for what seemed an eternity, sobbing into baby blankets in the middle of the night.

Yet I still needed the anchor of Kaddish so badly. So one day, I tried the Conservative morning *minyan* in town. No one asked if I had any brothers. They asked instead whom I had lost, and expressed their condolences and their appreciation for my wanting to honor my father's memory. It was the supportive atmosphere and sense of community that I had imagined and craved. However, the Conservative *minyan* met only in the morning. Since I couldn't face going back to invisible status, my husband said Kaddish for my father in the afternoons and evenings for the rest of the eleven months, which was of some vicarious comfort to me.

In addition to attending *shul* each Shabbat, I return to our Orthodox weekday *minyan* to say Kaddish, every year on my father's *yahrzeit*. Over the past twenty years, I have become somewhat less of a curiosity. There is always at least one other woman besides me now, sometimes several, and that is comforting for me. But whoever is in charge that day will still always ask, "Are there any mourners? Anyone have *yahrzeit*?" looking to give the honor of leading the service to the one who is saying Kaddish, and I still bristle because I know he isn't talking to me or to the other women when he says, "Anyone?"

I am more at peace during *Yizkor*, the memorial prayers during the holidays, when there are so many other women in *shul* with me. I like to spend that special time with my memories of my father, though not a day goes by when I don't think of him. After all, I see him every day in the mirror, as well as in the face, expressions, and mannerisms of my youngest child. Born almost two years after my father's death, my youngest son carries his grandfather's good name and enough of his personality to make me almost believe in reincarnation.

MERYL received a BA degree in Mathematics and Philosophy from Yale University, and worked for a number of years as a computer programmer/analyst before receiving an MS degree in Computer Science from Iona College. While raising her three children, Meryl has been involved in many community activities, including starting a newsletter at her children's day school, co-founding (with her husband David) and co-running an after-school Hebrew High School, and serving on the executive board of the United Jewish Federation of Greater Stamford, where she has served on many committees and chaired numerous adult education events.

Lifeline

JERALYN GOLDMAN

ALONE FOR THE FIRST time in forty years, I set the alarm and went
to *shul* by 6:30 a.m. to say Kaddish. I'd go to work and be back
to *shul* to say Kaddish. In my house, I was surrounded by my
husband's things and our life together. I'd find a note in his handwriting
or a bill he paid. I would see his clothing in the closet and tears would
flow. I needed to spend extra time at *shul*; it was a safe haven away from
my loneliness.

My husband, Herb, and I were married for almost forty years. We were
both adventurous and Zionists, so we went to Israel in 1970 and helped
build Moshav Neve Ilan. We had three sons and lived in Israel for nine
years before returning to America. We lived in Albuquerque, New Mex-
ico, before moving to Las Vegas, Nevada, our final home together. Herb
had an amazing quality of always smiling and staying positive. He was an
easy going man and always helped me see the bright side of any situation.

When Herb died suddenly in 2006, I was in a state of shock. He caught
the flu, which turned into pneumonia. For eight weeks he was in intensive
care and then in a rehab hospital. I prayed constantly during that time,
asking Hashem to heal my husband and bring him home to me. In the
deepest recesses of my heart, I was sure that Hashem was listening to my
prayers. Then two days after being released from the rehab, my husband
died in his sleep. Why weren't my prayers answered? A huge frigid wall
grew before my eyes keeping me away from Hashem every time I tried to
daven.

I said Kaddish for the *shloshim* at Young Israel Aish of Las Vegas. There
was never a question in my mind that I would say Kaddish. The *minyan*

gave me a month of a steady schedule of davening. Who knows what I would have done without it? I was really angry with God. Would I not have davened on a regular basis? Would I have stopped talking to God altogether?

When the month was over, I continued going to *shul* to hear Kaddish said by my son. By regularly attending *shul* that year, my connection to Hashem was slowly restored. My Rabbi, Yitzchak Wyne, suggested that I study the six "constant *mitzvot*" as way to restore my *emunah* (faith). In the *Sefer Ha-Chinuch*, the author identifies six *mitzvot* that a Jew should constantly be aware of: know that there is God, know that He is one, love God, fear God, don't put any other gods before Him, and don't follow the desire of your heart or your eyes. When I wasn't at *shul* or at work, I'd listen to tapes on these *mitzvot* by Rabbi Noah Weinberg, *z"l*, who was the Rosh Yeshivah of Aish HaTorah. By internalizing these *mitzvot*, I realized that Hashem is there for me during bad times as well as good, and is always giving me exactly what I need. I cannot understand all His plans for me, but by keeping an awareness of Hashem in my heart, I slowly came to realize that I was never alone. By Rosh Hashanah, I was familiar enough with the material to give a class at the *shul* on *emunah*. To sum up my experience with Kaddish: it was a lifeline back to Hashem.

Many women have told me how they wished they said Kaddish for their parents or loved one. I know I am a stronger person because of the experience. Saying Kaddish gave me the time to reconnect with God after the tragedy of losing my husband and gave me the strength to continue my life without him.

JERALYN has been a *baalat teshuvah* for about twenty years. The biggest blessing in her life is that all her adult children are traditional Jews and all her grandchildren attend Jewish Day Schools. She is active in her *shul* community and has proudly been instrumental in the growing Modern Orthodox community in Las Vegas.

Afterthoughts

RACHEL GOLDSTEIN JUBAS

BEFORE MY FATHER DIED, Kaddish to me was the afterthought of the service. Like reading credits after the feature film, half an eye glancing at the words, a bit restless, the crowd standing up and reaching for coats, waiting for companions to file out. Once, my son, Ben, came home from a learning program at the local yeshiva amazed by the young boys in black hats who cried out in fervor when responding "*Yehei shmei rabba*," but where I sat an absent-minded mumble was the typical refrain.

For a time after my father passed from this world, the Kaddish was all I could see of the prayers. As though I had been staring at a hologram and with a tilt, the words of Kaddish came into view and everything else receded.

My father, Avraham Azriel ben Yitzhak v'Chasya, died the week before Passover while on a visit to my younger sisters and their families in Israel. The funeral began at twilight and my mother, sisters and I were led by the Chevra Kaddisha, in darkness to the grave. The text of Kaddish was thrust into my hands and a kind person beside us lit a flashlight to illuminate the words. Friday night, my husband and I went to *shul*, where the *gabbai* informed us that they did not greet female mourners. When asked about my saying Kaddish, he responded, "Okay, as long as she says it so quietly that no one can hear." I told myself a story then that I repeated throughout the year – that this was not a political act, and that I would endeavor not to take the cool reception personally. In an effort to keep my focus on the spiritual and personal nature of my Kaddish task, I then sought out *minyanim* where my Kaddish would be welcomed.

I had always assumed, particularly since my parents did not have sons, that I would try to say Kaddish when the time came. In my childhood community, women were given opportunities to study Jewish texts and participate in public Jewish life. Sitting in my kitchen as a child, I once overheard my father on the phone opining that there was no such thing as "separate but equal" when it came to Jewish education for women. Reciting Kaddish for my father did not seem like a break with tradition to me, but continuity.

At my home synagogue, there has been a tradition of women saying Kaddish. Still, there were days when I could not focus on the davening. The prayers would pass and I was on autopilot, waiting for "my lines" when I would assume the stance that I thought I should have, staring into the abyss and declaring God's greatness. On Shabbat, I was buoyed by the company of other women. I noticed that it was those women who had said Kaddish themselves who would respond "Amen" most deliberately, cutting through the restlessness around me. A touch on the shoulder, a quick comment of how important this was, helped steady me in the early days of mourning.

There were times when it was lonely on my side of the *mechitza*, times when I was keenly aware that we were waiting for a *minyan* and I was the tenth person in the room. I struggled to make sense of my place in the *minyan*, where I was praying as part of the group, yet extraneous to its functioning. From my side of the *mechitza* I observed changes over the year, like the seasons . . . new men leading the service as mourners rotated through the life cycle, variation in the melodiousness of the prayers, the improvement of skills as those who started out as novices gained confidence. Driving to work after *minyan*, it occurred to me that it was like enjoying flowers that had been planted by a road, or when the foliage turned. I wondered if from the men's vantage point, the women in the room changed the atmosphere, too.

Though my Kaddish "appointments" were not written down, each page of my daily planner was peppered with those words peeking out behind the scheduled events of everyday life. A reminder that life had not yet returned to normal and an anchor at those moments when it seemed that it never would. I gained respect for men who made it to *minyan* morning and night, and better appreciated why women are exempt from certain time-bound *mitzvot*. On those occasions when I might have been at *minyan* but was instead preparing pasta, or leaving work, or going through my daughter's backpack, I would hear the Kaddish playing in my head, the background rhythm of the year, its heartbeat.

My father was a psychiatrist, who would remark about the problems in families where people had stopped talking to one another. For me, Kaddish was a way to continue the conversation – with my father and with God. When the prayers for good health, or rain or a messianic era seemed distant, I could still utter Kaddish, and when my spirit faltered, I was carried by the response of the congregation. In the white fragments of space between the words and prayers were moments when I would contemplate and mourn. Within the ritual of Kaddish, I was able to unwind from the somewhat abrupt ending, to the unanswered questions that always arise, to the conversations of earlier times – advice, discussion of my own work in psychiatry, puns and silly songs, Candyland on the living room floor.

As the year wound down, my perspective normalized. My routine was no longer accompanied by the chant of Kaddish in my head. When the last Kaddish came, I felt ready.

When I go to *shul* today, Kaddish is not all I see. Yet once illuminated, its importance and meaning did not fade completely. So I recite "*Yehei shmei rabba*" with purpose, in response to those women in mourning beside me and to the men across the *mechitza*, as well.

RACHEL said Kaddish for her father along with her sister, son, nephew and brother-in-law. She is a psychiatrist and mother of four, who lives and works in the Tri-State area.

וִיתְהַדָּר
וְיִתְעַלֶּה
וְיִתְהַלָּל
שְׁמֵהּ
דְקֻדְשָׁא
בְּרִיךְ
הוּא

Grief Comes in Waves
knocks you over
scours, salty torrents
then releases
retreats

in time it is content to lap
at your feet, even tickling
toes as it tugs on
wet sands of
memory

grief comes in waves
you may trust it
yes, bless it
knowing the moon
which governs the tide
reflects the light of
the sun

Heartache

DEBRA SHAFFER SEEMAN

FTER MY MOM DIED, I found myself in inexplicable chest pain. It kept coming and going, getting worse with time. Doctors sent me for test after test. Thank God every test showed that I was healthy as could be. I called a medical friend and told him what was going on. He asked me whether my doctors had performed Test A and Test B and Test C. He checked to be sure that my X, Y, and Z levels were all appropriate. He covered all the bases. One day, he asked me to call him at home to review the results of one test. I gave him a call and his wife answered the phone. As she handed him the receiver, she said to him, "Would you please just explain to this poor girl that she is broken hearted and she simply misses her mother?"

She, of course, was completely right. My heart ached because it was broken. I missed my Mom more than words could say. When my first children were born, "Safta" came to take care of us. She stayed for weeks, and weeks became months. She did this out of deep love and commitment to her family. And when the time came for her to finish her life in this world, during a six-month fight with cancer, our small family did the same for her. We moved in with Saba to help. She taught us that everyone needs to be needed, and everyone accepts help when it is well offered and they are ready.

I had taken on saying Kaddish once before my Mom died, when my older brother passed away. My husband, Don, and I, were living in Jerusalem at the time. The most profound moment was when a friend also showed up to *minyan* in our apartment before 7 a.m., explaining that she didn't want me to feel alone as I began saying Kaddish. Though I was touched by her generosity, I don't think that I really understood what she meant until I said Kaddish for my mother nine years later. *I have never felt more alone than during the time that I said Kaddish for my mother.*

After my mother died, I spoke with a rabbi who suggested that I say Kaddish three times a day. I remember trying to keep a straight face and be polite as my head exploded with calculations. *Three* times a day?! At the time, we were parents of two children under the age of three. We were both supposed to attempt to be present at *minyan* during breakfast, bath, and dinnertime, while holding down two full-time careers? Driving home, I burst out laughing, which quickly turned to tears, which shifted into a rather ambivalent attempt to reimagine the hours when my children could be outsourced so that I could attend three daily *minyanim*. With a heavy heart, I came to terms with the reality that this was the wrong decision for my family, especially since we had just moved back to Atlanta after months at my parents' home. I decided to say Kaddish just once a day. The logistical calisthenics to make that happen were nothing short of a military campaign, replete with all the drama and tactical maneuvers that term implies. I can only imagine the cost that my young family and my marriage would have had to pay if I'd decided to say Kaddish three times daily.

I never considered not saying Kaddish for my mother. However, there was a piece of this open-minded Orthodox portrait of ritual fulfillment that I had painted completely wrong in my mind's eye. I had accompanied my mother to *shul* on occasion when she said Kaddish for her father. That was the image that I had painted for myself – a woman with grown children taking a relaxing hour out of her day to attend *minyan* and re-engage in her relationship with God on new terms. The picture that I saw was never a mother of two young children who was attempting to function as the head of a brand new Jewish day school while living in the Deep South of the USA. I did not imagine racing from a board meeting to sterilize sippy cups and then frantically careening into the *shul* driveway, praying that I had arrived in time for *Ashrei* (those parking lot prayers were some of my greatest davening moments that year!). And yet, this is the plan that Hashem and I made for that year. *I have never felt more frazzled by the competing pressures of life than during the time that I said Kaddish for my mother.*

Once, I had a rather toxic experience, ironically at the school that I was running. When it came time for Kaddish at a *Maariv minyan*, after an evening event for families, I joined in. I heard murmurs and whispers from the men's section and could feel eyes piercing through me. When I mustered up the courage, I looked up. Jaws were dropped. Some men left the room, asking whether this was a school for Reform Rabbis. *I have never felt more humiliated as a member of the Orthodox community than during the time that I said Kaddish for my mother.*

These challenges notwithstanding, each day, I stood and quietly reminded the Master of the Universe of my connection to the Jews of the past. The *siddur* regularly reminded me that I prayed to the God of Abraham, the God of Isaac, and the God of Jacob. Each had his own relationship with his Creator, and I was steadfastly adjusting mine to integrate my new life experiences and to find room for a woman's voice, a woman bereaved within this tradition of men.

I remembered how my mother used to complain bitterly about trying to keep up with the men when she was saying Kaddish for her father. Ironically, I found myself in the same situation, even though I had attended *minyan* regularly beforehand. It seemed like I was constantly deciding which *tefillot* to come back to later in order to make it to the *Barchu* or *Amidah* together with the *tzibbur*. Trying to support my parents through the last months of my mother's life took every ounce of strength I had. I used up my reserves in the battle against cancer. When I got to *minyan*, I had no strength left to race. Out of the depths of my exhaustion, the early morning *tefillah* took on new meaning:

> *Elokai neshama shenatata bi tehora hi. Ata Barata. Ata yetzarta. Ata*
> *nefachta bi . . . Baruch Ata Hashem ha-machazir neshamot*
> *lif'garim metim.*
> *My God, the soul You placed within me is pure. You created it, You*
> *fashioned it, You breathed it into me. . . . Blessed are You,*
> *Hashem, who restores souls to dead bodies.*

It was only when I permitted myself to daven at my own pace that I finally felt as though I was in conversation with God. So I learned to let the *minyan*-makers run up the hill ahead of me. I was not angry to be left behind, as those were the moments when I could walk together with Someone Else, "*v'halachta b'drachav*, You shall walk in God's ways" (Deuteronomy 28:9).

Those encounters with sweetness, those connections with the Divine, would shine through at the moments when I allowed myself to sit back and breathe. Surrounded by fifty empty chairs, the only woman in sight, I could just slow down and pray to the God with whom I so desperately needed to reconnect; to plead, to be angry, to thank, and to beg for help simply to get through the year. *I have never related to prayer in the same way as during my year of saying Kaddish for my mother.*

Saying Kaddish was physically exhausting; it was emotionally draining; it was logistically difficult; it was lonely; and it reminded me that there are parts of Orthodox Judaism that cause me deep pain. But I would do it all again. I went into my year of Kaddish searching for connection, for a way to fill the ache of loneliness that made my heart hurt. I came out of that year understanding that the empty space my mother's death left was not meant to be filled. It is the darkness which will one day become the starting point for a new light. The Jewish mystical tradition teaches: "*Leit nehora ela d'asi migo chashucha*, There is no light except that which comes out of darkness" (Zohar 2, 184a).

DEBRA SHAFFER SEEMAN recently returned to Atlanta, GA from Mandel Jerusalem Fellows where she focused her studies on the transmission of Moral Legacy within the organized Jewish community. Debra has been an avid teacher of classical Jewish texts for the past fifteen years and has served in a variety of educational settings in Israel and North America, including Rambam Atlanta Day School, Dror Elementary School, Tal Torah Center for Intergenerational Learning, Pardes Institute for Jewish Studies, Florence Melton Adult Mini School, and Yeshiva Atlanta High School. She holds a Masters in Education from Harvard University focused on Moral Development. Debra is a mother of three delightful little ones and is very lucky to be married to Rabbi Dr. Don Seeman.

Post-It Notes on My Siddur

ROCHELLE BAROUH SENKER

WHEN MY FATHER, ALBERT BAROUH, was twelve years old, his mother passed away. His father was unable to work and care for three small children, so he was placed in the Hebrew Orphans Asylum, in Manhattan. In spite of this hardship (or perhaps because of it), he grew up to be a kind, responsible, and loving individual – a true *mensch*.

During WWII, Dad served in the Merchant Marines and was stationed in Baltimore, where he met and married my mother. Mom and Dad had two children, me and my younger brother, Stan. They were happily married for over sixty-three years.

With his limited Jewish background, Dad managed to do so many mitzvahs. He spoke fluent Ladino, too. There is a custom among Sephardim to name a baby in honor of someone who is alive. In 2005, my son and his wife asked my Dad if they could give their new son his Hebrew name, Avraham. He was very touched and honored.

When Dad died later that year, my brother decided not to say Kaddish for him, so Mom suggested that we pay a yeshiva student to perform this mitzvah. My response was, "No way!" My husband, Eddie, had been saying Kaddish for his mother since July, and on several occasions I attended services with him. I noticed that at our *shul*, there was a group of women comfortable and accepted saying Kaddish on their side of the *mechitza*.

I unfortunately have little background in Hebrew. What I know is from begrudgingly attending after-school and Sunday Hebrew School. I was afraid and I was nervous. I didn't want to appear ignorant, but I was determined to do the right thing to honor and respect my father's *neshama*.

A friend of mine lost her father at the same time. Her sweet daughter, Lexi, probably fifteen at the time, often accompanied her to *shul*, and would always help to keep me on the correct page in the *siddur* and guide me when it was time for Kaddish. One day, Lexi asked to borrow my *siddur*. She returned it the next day neatly marked with colored Post-It notes, with instructions. Others have since used my *siddur* as a template for their own.

Our Kaddish group really went out of its way to extend warmth and compassion to others. Whenever I saw a new face in the women's section of the Chapel, I would reach out to welcome them. Our *shul*, with its wonderful clergy, was so welcoming and encouraging to the women. I never felt the least bit uncomfortable on the "other side" of the *mechitza*. My challenge was learning the Hebrew, and the order of the service.

That year, Eddie and I davened in thirty-six different synagogues during our travels. To this day, there are women who are friends of mine because we met at synagogue and they welcomed me. One time, we stopped in Savannah, Georgia and arrived at an Orthodox *shul* just minutes before *Mincha*. When we entered the sanctuary, there was no place for women to pray and men occupied every corner, so I stood in the doorway. I was soon approached by the most religious-looking man in the room, with a full white beard, long *peyot* (sidelocks) and Chassidic garb which included a large hat, black coat and *gartel*. I explained to him that I wanted to say Kaddish, but there was no place for me. He said, "come with me." In moments, he cleared the men out of that part of the room, and moved a small bookcase over to serve as a *mechitza*, so I could enter the room and daven. He commented, "That's what we call Southern hospitality." "No," I said, with tears in my eyes. "That's pure kindness."

This whole experience made me so much prouder to be a Jewish woman. It gave me a continued connection to my father, and a fuller connection to my family and community. I actually was sorry to see the eleven months end. I was proud of myself for assuming and completing this awesome responsibility.

ROCHELLE (SHELLEY) BAROUH SENKER is a non-practicing Registered Nurse, and is married to Eddie, her high school sweetheart, for 45 years. She is the mother of Ellen and Michael Muss, Joey and Bianca Senker, and Joshua and Limor Senker, and the grandmother of eight wonderful grandchildren – Jacob, Isabelle, Maxwell, Jonas, Liam, Nolan, Jude, and Noa. She volunteers for Bikur Cholim, and the Chevra Kaddisha of Stamford, and is an active member of Agudath Sholom of Stamford, CT and The Young Israel of Bar Harbour, FL. Rochelle is an avid gardener and crocheter, and enjoys traveling and reading biographies.

My Kaddish Journey

TOBA WEITZ GOLDBERG

A SMALL BLUE NOTEBOOK with a flower on the cover; given to me at the Jewish Day School where I am a principal, as a thank you gift. Little did I know it would chronicle my year of saying Kaddish for my mother.

MY FIRST KADDISH · Graveside, surrounded by family and friends. My husband and I had chosen this cemetery as my parents' final resting place, and ours, purposefully. The Chevra Kaddisha allows women to attend a funeral and will wait for children who need to come from abroad. Women are permitted to give a *hesped*, eulogy, and say Kaddish. Unseen hands wisely push us down onto low stools so the few minutes left before sunset will count as a day of *shiva*. From deep within me, I feel a howl rising up but I contain it. I cup my hand over my mouth and sob.

WEEK 1 · Although my parents' apartment is not a *makom kavua* for prayer, the man in charge of the *minyan* would not allow me to daven and say Kaddish in the same room as the men, even if I stood in the back. My brother, the least observant of the three of us, prayed with the boys' club. My sister relegated herself to the kitchen, but I stood in the doorway, needing to feel that I was part of the prayer group. My Kaddish then, as it would be thereafter, was recited out loud. For what point is a quiet Kaddish, a *minyan* required for *Kaddish*, if no one hears you and cannot answer "Amen"?

I am determined to say Kaddish through *shloshim*, the first thirty days. I am a believer in women's active participation in religious observance where permitted by *Halachah*; I attend a women's *Megillah* reading, and joyously take part in *hakafot* (dancing) on Simchat Torah when able. Our synagogue is an Orthodox one, certainly not black hat. A good friend was the first to say Kaddish daily for her mother two years ago, and now I will be the second.

WEEK 3 · Today I felt that my Kaddish didn't count. Our synagogue does not permit a woman to recite Kaddish alone. When I heard my husband's voice, I knew. It was his Kaddish the *minyan* was responding to, not mine. I made my voice louder. "Hear me," I was saying, "I am the one saying Kaddish." If I don't count why do I need this *minyan*? Won't Hashem hear my *tefillot* if I say them privately? Sitting behind the *mechitza* you are almost invisible. Not once, does the man who carries around the *tzedakah* box offer it to me.

WEEK 9 · I missed ten opportunities to say Kaddish this summer, in three separate instances of time. Not that I was shirking, not at all. Circumstances beyond my control.

WEEK 12 · I feel as if I am in a fog. When the doctors gave us the diagnosis back in February, I asked Hashem, while praying at the Kotel, to keep my mother alive for the bar mitzvah and for Pesach, when the family would be together. Having been granted both these requests, I thought I had come to terms with my mother dying when I left after Pesach, still three weeks before she died. But three months later, I realize that I have not.

WEEK 14 · One morning the *gabbai* tells me that there is a new *mechitza*, a folding screen, for me. I cannot see a thing through it. The next time I use a small straight edge razor and cut out little squares so I can see the men davening, see the *shaliach tzibbur*, see the Torah being read.

WEEK 19 · In the beginning, I continuously questioned why I was doing this, saying Kaddish at least once a day. Could it be because I believe my daughters expect it of me, or it is something I have started and can't stop because the men would surely comment, "That's why women don't say Kaddish?" No, it is just something I need to do, need to finish. I know that I would be very unhappy with myself if I didn't.

I have become enveloped by *tefillah*. The *mechitza* cocoons me. When I occasionally skip *Shacharit* on a Sunday and go to *Mincha* and *Maariv*, it's not the same. The prayer time is too short. When I return to *Shacharit* on Monday morning, the calm feeling returns.

WEEK 20 · At school, as in my synagogue, I am not permitted to say Kaddish alone. I hope someday that will change, but that is not my purpose here. I am grateful to Rabbi S. for saying the Kaddish with me. To Mr. L, who looks around each morning counting bar mitzvah boys, and goes out to look for latecomers so I won't miss the two Kaddishes at the beginning. Here, J. remembers to bring the *tzedakah* box over to me.

EREV YOM KIPPUR · *On Rosh Hashanah their destiny is inscribed, and on Yom Kippur it is sealed.* The tears flow, I can't control it. I always took it seriously but this year more so. It really happens; God decides. *Who shall live and who shall die.* How and when, so many different ways to die. Seeing a grey haired old lady in a wheelchair brings tears to my eyes.

WEEK 24 · Sometimes I feel like I'm cheating. I have an early meeting in the city so I go to *Mincha* that afternoon in lieu of *Shacharit*. Is it okay to go to *Maariv*, so I can sleep late the next morning? Going to *Mincha and Maariv* covers two days!

Some parents have mentioned that their sons have told them that I am praying with the *minyan* in the morning. I hope I am having an effect on these boys so they will view women's Kaddish and commitment to *tefillah* in a positive manner.

WEEK 25 · It's slump time. I find myself sitting in bed with my coffee far longer than I should, then rushing to get dressed. "I don't know how I am going to do this," I think, "it's getting on to winter, it will be so cold." In my mind, I am counting the months until Kaddish ends. Is it like this for everyone?

WEEK 26 · Tonight as I begin unfolding the *mechitza*, a man whom I do not recognize comes over to help me. At the same time, a friend tells me that I can catch an extra Kaddish, as the *gabbai* has finished his class after *Mincha*. Two men, both respectful of my place there and what I am doing.

WEEK 28 · Does saying Kaddish make it harder to let go? There is no way that you can get too busy and forget. Is that why men are obligated to say Kaddish and women aren't? Is it really about *minyan* or *zman grama* (fixed times)? Or did our Sages understand that a man would cleave to his wife and would need the daily reminder that his parent is no longer a part of his life? Did they know that a woman would not need that reminder?

WEEK 30 · In so much that I do there is my mother. On Chanukah I make *vikelach*, a rolled cookie with jelly, cinnamon and raisins that my grandmother and then my mother made. I always send them to Israel and this year I will bring them to my father. "Are there *vikelach* in *shamayim*, in heaven?" I wonder.

WEEK 32 · I am visiting my father and my son's family in Israel. This morning in *shul*, it was a solo. Despite my education and my thirty-one weeks of experience, I felt nervous. It was strange to hear my own voice aloud and alone in *shul*. Afterwards, my grandson complained that he could barely hear me. "I was scared that I would get the words wrong," I told him.

WEEK 35 · A new voice, a male, in our daily school *minyan*, is saying Kaddish today. I cannot see him. After davening, he comes over. Do I need him to go slowly, he asks. I reassure him that I can keep up.

WEEK 36 · I have been taking a weekly class on *tefillah*, and I have added something new. During the *Amidah*, before bowing at *Modim*, I pause and reflect and specifically give thanks to Hashem for what I have been given. I have come to realize that these last eight months have not only been about saying Kaddish but also about connecting to Hashem through *tefillah*.

I voice a growing concern to my husband: I am not the most disciplined person, and when Kaddish is over I am afraid that morning *tefillah* will fall by the wayside. Is it something I have needed since my mother died, to make sense, to come to terms with what is natural in the life cycle, to face my own mortality? Will I find the time to daven when it is not circumscribed by having to say Kaddish? Maybe a sign on my desk, "Have you davened today?" or "Thanked Hashem yet today?"

WEEK 37 · *Hakamat Matzeva* (the unveiling): My father, my brother, and I say Kaddish together once again. The monument bears witness to the fact that my mother died, but also to the fact that she lived. Harriet Sally Miller Weitz was my guiding light. A feminist long before the women of NOW, she was smart, clever, witty, sometimes sharp, and very capable. The words inscribed on the stone are a tribute to the vibrant and loving woman who was my mother.

WEEK 41 · Today I was really annoyed. We were one short for a *minyan* for the first Kaddish. The rabbi waited and then continued. Then another rabbi strolled in, eyes glued to whatever he was reading. Why can't he be on time? I wish him no ill, *ad meah v'esrim* for his parents – may they live to 120 – but I hope someday he will realize how important the *minyan* was for someone, even if she was a woman, even if he didn't approve of her saying Kaddish. I have given him the benefit of the doubt all these months as to why he is late but today my mood did not allow for it.

WEEK 44 · Almost to the finish line. I have "enjoyed" davening with a community, in a *shul* or *beit midrash*, from Seattle to White Plains, with Brooklyn in between. Although I know that Hashem can be any place, there is a growing appreciation in me this year of the value of davening *b'tzibbur*.

WEEK 45 · My daughter became engaged in far away Australia, Pesach takes its toll, and it's my last week of Kaddish. The worst day I ever had to leave the house to say Kaddish; the rain went down my neck and a UPS truck going down the road soaked me.

WEEK 46 · My last Kaddish. I am so tired, emotionally and physically. It has not been easy saying Kaddish. I was determined, and so I did it. I feel for the men who go three times a day but truth be told they do not have household responsibilities like a woman does. I do not have children at home, and I am fortunate to have a *minyan* at work and a husband whose love and support sustain me each day.

WEEK 50 · The last month has been weird. I no longer say Kaddish but when in *shul* the words are still on the tip of my tongue. Grief is a dull ache now, not the "I've been punched in the stomach and the wind has been knocked out of me" pain of a year ago.

WEEK 51 · The first *yahrzeit* of my mother, Chaya Zlata bat Aidell v'Shaul. If I could have stayed under my covers all day, I would have. I am glad to have my daughters with me. I had considered having a women's learning after *Maariv*, but I am glad I didn't. The support of my friends has been great this year but I need to be alone.

Today I sit behind my *mechitza*, saying the all too familiar words once again. Over the last few weeks, I had thought about this day but did not expect the heaviness I am experiencing in my heart. What will tomorrow and the next day be like? Does one slowly enter the world or jump right in?

I miss my mother. I need to believe that she is looking down and watching over us.

The very last *Kaddish D'Rabbanan*. Tears are streaming down my face. I weep – soundlessly, but soundly.

TOBA WEITZ GOLDBERG was born in Brooklyn, NY and has lived there her entire life. Educated at Yeshiva Rambam and Central High School (Yeshiva University High School for Girls), she received her BA and MS from Brooklyn College. Her professional career began in the NYC Public School System and after the birth of her children she began as a teacher at Yeshivah of Flatbush, eventually moving into administration and becoming Associate Principal. She is married, has three children (and three in-law children), and is a loving *savta* to her grandchildren in both the United States and Israel.

I Wasn't Trying to Make a Statement

ESTHER REED

WHEN I WAS FOUR MONTHS pregnant with my third child, my father died. He had Parkinson's disease and a heart condition, so it was not a complete shock. The doctors had informed the family that he'd have as much as six months to live . . . but he died only two weeks after that prognosis.

As a Conservative rabbi and an ideologically egalitarian Jew, I have taken on all the time-bound *mitzvot*, obligating myself to the same commandments as Jewish men. So I had no doubts that I'd say Kaddish one day for a parent. But I had no idea that I'd be doing so within the first five years of my rabbinate.

Whether my father believed in the power of Kaddish or not, I believed that it was a sign of respect to say Kaddish for him after he passed, and would play a role in my own healing process. I wanted to say Kaddish daily until the baby was born, and again after that, once I was able, for the full eleven months.

Going to daily evening *minyan* during the pregnancy wasn't terribly difficult. I made sure my husband would be home with our two small boys while I went to *minyan*. None of those logistical issues were particularly challenging or unusual in our lives.

Once the baby was born, though, I stayed home on maternity leave and didn't attend daily *minyan*. I felt lost trying to figure out when to go back to communal davening. Would I wait two weeks, until I was permitted by my doctor to drive a car? Would I wait six weeks, until after the post-partum check up? What was the proper amount of time to "take off" from a daily obligation? What if the baby got hungry during *minyan*?

Would I nurse in *shul?* These questions were really pressing to me at the time, but looking back, I honestly can't remember exactly how I resolved them. All I know is that I did my best to fulfill my obligation to say Kaddish during this time.

Then maternity leave ended. I needed to juggle a new baby, two other young boys, a demanding job, and getting to daily *minyan.* Because I work at a large Hillel, my job requires frequent evening commitments. So I decided to try for morning *minyan.* Hillel offered *minyan* at a great time – 8:15 a.m. I could drop off my three kids at daycare, drive to Hillel, make *minyan,* and be at my desk by 9 a.m. What could possibly keep me from doing that?

Well, a lot, actually.

The only morning *minyan* at our Hillel is an Orthodox prayer group, and I wear *tallit* (prayer shawl) and *tefillin* (phylacteries) for daily prayer. Women do not wear *tallit* and *tefillin* in that *minyan.* I was also concerned that if I were the only person saying Kaddish, then perhaps the group would skip Kaddish altogether, requiring a male to recite the prayer.

So I consulted the Orthodox rabbi at Hillel, to talk through these issues before I returned from leave. Fortunately, as colleagues, we had a relationship based on trust and we could talk through these issues rationally. As it turned out, a male student in the Orthodox community was saying Kaddish, so it would never be skipped. As for *tallit* and *tefillin,* that was more complicated.

I didn't want to create a stir within the Orthodox community at Hillel. As a Conservative rabbi, I have always respected their practices, though I disagree with them, and Orthodox students and staff alike have respected my practices, though they disagree with mine.

I proudly wear my *tallit* at Hillel's Conservative services, which take place on *Shabbat* and holidays. On Simchat Torah, when all the students dance together – Orthodox, Conservative, Reform, Just Jewish – I wear my *tallit,* as well. But I recognized that the morning *minyan* was an Orthodox service, where students were not used to seeing a woman in *tallit* and *tefillin.* I didn't want to threaten students who felt that the Orthodox community at Hillel was their "home." Moreover, if a new student came to the Orthodox service and saw me, would that student assume that the Orthodox rabbi was encouraging women to wear *tallit* and *tefillin?* That would certainly be false. Would that student think that I, as a Conservative rabbi, was trying to convince Orthodox students that women should wear *tallit* and *tefillin*? That would be false, too.

I wasn't trying to make a statement. I just wanted to say Kaddish. So we came up with a plan. I could come to Hillel, put on my *tallit* and *tefillin* in a staff member's office, and daven facing East, while looking directly across the lobby into the women's section of the *minyan*. Then, when I finished davening, I could take off my *tallit* and *tefillin* and join the *minyan* in time for Kaddish.

This worked well for everyone. I could be part of the community when I needed to, and also satisfy my own needs in a different prayer space. The students welcomed me into their prayer community and stood by my side as I said Kaddish for my father. I am grateful to the Orthodox community at Hillel for supporting me as I fulfilled my obligation to honor my father.

My experience showed me that different prayer services for different kinds of Jews are indeed important. But at the same time, *Kol Yisrael arevim zeh lazeh*, all Jews are responsible for one another. Saying Kaddish showed me that with open communication and mutual respect, Jews can still function as one unified people. Is there any better way to praise God?

ESTHER REED is the Senior Associate Director for Jewish Campus Life at Rutgers University Hillel. She attended Bryn Mawr College in Pennsylvania, graduating cum laude with a degree in Judaic Studies. She spent the following year working at Tufts University Hillel, where she fell in love with Hillel work and affirmed her decision to become a rabbi. She then began her studies at the Jewish Theological Seminary in New York. She received both rabbinic ordination and a Master's degree in Jewish women's studies from JTS in 2001. While at JTS, Esther Reed was a recipient of the prestigious Wexner Graduate Fellowship. She has been at Rutgers Hillel since 2001.

A Voluntary Mourner:
Kaddish for My Stepfather

DEBRA LUGER

M Y PARENTS DIVORCED when I was four years old, so I grew up in a home with my mother and stepfather. Looking back, I would venture to say that while my temperament may be more like my Dad's, the person I became is more reflective of my stepfather. His feelings of responsibility towards extended family, huge generosity to charitable causes and devotion to his Reform Jewish observance all helped to mold me into the person I am. With rare exception, I have always referred to him as "my father."

When my father had a relapse of prostate cancer and became increasingly ill, I began to think about what lay ahead. Neither of his biological daughters had any real interest in religious matters or were even members of a synagogue. Yet I knew that my father would want someone to say Kaddish for him.

I recalled incidents where I'd heard of people being told to NOT say Kaddish, for instance if their parent had been cremated, or if they were converts themselves. What about a "stepchild"? For a long time, I merely worried, afraid to voice the thoughts or ask the questions. If I wanted to say Kaddish, would I need to go to a Conservative *shul* where no one would know me? How would that make me feel? What rabbi should I ask and what if I didn't like the answers – then what?

Ultimately, I did ask the rabbi at our Young Israel, and was happily relieved to learn that while I was not obligated, neither was I *prohibited* from saying Kaddish. My status would be as a "voluntary mourner" with no obligations, only choices! Rabbi Brahm Weinberg further explained that the code of Jewish law (*Yoreh Deah* 374:6) says that if a person wishes to be stringent upon themselves and accept obligations of mourning for another relative (outside the obligatory – parent, child, sibling, spouse) no one should stop them. In his opinion, anyone you are connected to can gain merit from your actions, if their memory has triggered you to say Kaddish and to praise God's name.

Life unfolds in unexpected ways. My husband and I had spent a year or so alternating visits to ailing parents – his mother and my father. The emotional ups and downs, with repeated shuttling of grandchildren for "last visits," ended suddenly as they died only twelve days apart. Steven and I both became mourners.

Initially, I struggled with the words of Kaddish and the pace of both davening and Kaddish itself. Steven helped me go over the words and one of my daughters printed a larger size version of both the Hebrew and transliteration as an aid. Eventually, it became easier, although I will say, there is a phrase of about five words in the middle of the Rabbi's Kaddish that, despite *hundreds* of recitations, I still stumble over periodically. Perhaps, it's God's way of reminding me, that this is something I've not totally mastered.

Although I initially committed myself to the first thirty days, in the end, I said Kaddish at least once a day for all eleven months. I panicked occasionally, the last month or so, when it looked like there might not be a *minyan* or I ran late. Somehow I just didn't want to break the string of completeness.

Having my husband say Kaddish at the same time really eased a demanding endeavor. Anytime we traveled, he would do the legwork to find the times and the place for a *minyan*. I found there were times that my own thoughts drifted to his mother, whom I missed terribly, as well. It really was a combined effort that supported and consoled us both.

I've been asked whether it bothered me that I couldn't be "counted" as the tenth, to complete a *minyan*. In general, I would say not. If anything, I was occasionally amused when I would see hopeful looks on nine faces turn briefly to disappointment as I walked in. There were times when I, too, waited with anticipation, hearing cars roll down the driveway. I also knew that this tight-knit group worked just as hard, making calls or picking up extras, to complete the *minyan* for *me* as much as anyone else who needed to say Kaddish. I didn't feel "second class" in any way.

I attend a monthly women's *Tehillim* group. We have a lengthy list of those who are ill and in need of healing. Our intent is to help their recovery, with our prayers. We each read from booklets in English and Hebrew, and in this way the entire book of *Tehillim* (Psalms) is said at one sitting. Many times I read them, barely comprehending anything. Other times, there are verses or whole psalms that speak to me. But what moves me every time is that here is a small committed group of women, coming together with no motivation other than to try to help those in need. That is why I go; because for forty-five minutes, once a month, I am actively doing something totally outside myself that I hope is worthwhile.

Likewise, for me it was not the actual reciting of the words of Kaddish that was important. Frankly, the pace of Orthodox daily *minyan* davening is not conducive to thoughtful pondering or feeling the words being said. Rather, it was the carving out of a set time, in a group of like-minded people, for a valuable purpose, in remembrance of someone so important in my life.

On another level, perhaps it was simply replacing one habit with another. For the previous year, I would place a call to Florida: either first thing in the morning, over lunch, or driving home from work. Sometimes it was to a hospital, to talk to a caregiver, sometimes home. When life returned to "normal" after those few weeks following *shiva*, there was a hole in my daily routine. Setting aside that time to go to *minyan*, orienting life around that schedule helped to bridge the gap.

The *brachah* for health and healing in the *Amidah* was a bit of a challenge, as I changed my focus to someone *new* in need of healing, rather than the automatic insertion of those no longer able to heal. Even if my davening wasn't on target one day, there was always a moment of meaning somewhere: in a line of prayer, in opening my *siddur* with its dedication label in his memory, listening to something the rabbi might say . . . Most dear to me, however, was Psalm 91, recited in the *Psukei D'Zimra* of Shabbat. When my father had been most critically ill, I would read this Psalm – in hospital rooms, on airplanes, at home – it was to me, indelibly his:

> *You shall not be afraid of the terror of the night . . . For he has yearned for Me . . . I will elevate him because he knows My name . . . I am with him in distress . . . I will free him and will bring him honor.*

How startling it was, that first recitation of *Yizkor*, when I realized that this same Psalm had been in the *Yizkor* service all along, never noticed by me in all the previous years. It now seemed personally there for me.

Everyone mourns or remembers individuals in their own way. Torah study, taking on new *mitzvot*, visiting cemeteries, or caring for the remaining family are all actions with their own merits. For me, saying Kaddish was a pre-existing framework set up for me just to step into. It was a way for me to honor my relationship with my father – a bond extending beyond biological definitions of family – and to carry on a tradition that he greatly valued.

Brought up on Long Island in a Reform Jewish household, **Debra** attended afternoon Hebrew School through Confirmation Year at age 16. Graduated from the University of Rochester with a BS degree in Nursing, Debra met and married her husband Steven, a family physician with a traditional background, and moved to Connecticut, where they have lived ever since. They journeyed Judaically from no affiliation, to a Conservative synagogue in New London, to ultimately arrive at Orthodox observance at Young Israel of West Hartford. Their three daughters all graduated from local Orthodox day schools, and spent a year of study in Israel after high school. Debbie currently lives in West Hartford with her husband and works as a nurse at a local OB/ GYN office in Hartford.

Stones
we carry
in our pockets
finger throughout the day
when time permits
we take them out
every groove
every fissure
is familiar
every ragged point
that cuts
turn them over and over
until the surface is smoothed
our image reflected

still
they beckon
as if this time we might see
something
different
not finding
resolution, drop
them back in
oddly comforting
the weight

polished stones
some day that rains forgiveness
I will liberate these and
lay them on
your grave

לְעֵלָּא
מִן כָּל
בִּרְכָתָא
וְשִׁירָתָא
תֻּשְׁבְּחָתָא
וְנֶחֱמָתָא
דַּאֲמִירָן
בְּעָלְמָא
וְאִמְרוּ
אָמֵן

Trying to Go Home

GEELA R. R. NAIMAN

Listen, my child, to the teachings of your father. And do not abandon
the Torah of your mother.   *Proverbs 1:8*

M Y FATHER DIED SUDDENLY, and life became a blur with
bumps.

One moment in the U.S., the next on a plane to Israel, my
father's body boxed beneath. Numb days punctuated by my search for a
home, for connection, and flickers of peace as I found them. In the course
of eleven months, saying Kaddish changed my relationship with Hashem,
with the Jewish community, with my father, and even with myself.

At my father's funeral, the men and women were separated – the men
surrounding the grave. I can still remember being shunted aside, standing
on tiptoe with the other women, trying to see as they poured my father's
body into the earth. My brothers' Kaddish barely reached my ears. Surrounded as I was by the Orthodox Judaism that I had left years ago, I had
no choice but to follow the rules.

At the beginning of *shiva*, I did not say Kaddish. I stood on the stairs,
listening with the rest of the women. It never occurred to me to join in; I
did not even know women were allowed.

It was Erev Shabbat, only a few days since the funeral. The immediate
family was together, and finally, we could rest from *shiva*, that long stream
of "*HaMakom yenachems*," broken briefly by family meals and twice-a-day
prayers. My brother, Aharon, explained to me that according to many
opinions, it was custom, not *Halachah*, which stopped women from saying Kaddish. I could join in if I wanted; it was my choice.

My silence broken, that Shabbat I began a journey which has not stopped.

Returning to the *shiva* house, I still stood with the women, but now my brothers slowed the pace of Kaddish for me. I joined the men in chanting; I could feel the power of the "Amen" response.

At this time in my life, I was mostly estranged from the Jewish community. When my siblings and I came back to the U.S. after sitting *shiva* in Israel, they set up Sunday visiting hours for friends to come and be *menachem avel* (to comfort mourners). I realized that for me there was no point – there was almost no one who would come visit me.

I did not think I could belong to an Orthodox *shul*, let alone fit into an Orthodox community, not being *frum* myself. Yet I missed the warm support of belonging to a community. I also wanted to continue to say Kaddish, and I wanted to say it at an Orthodox *shul*. Why? I don't know; it just felt right.

At first, I tried *shul*s near where I lived. At one, I needed to come early to set up the *mechitza*. At another, a Sephardic *shul*, the *nusach* (tune) was so foreign I almost felt I was in another religion that happened to use Hebrew. In yet another *shul*, I was "allowed" to sit out in the hallway, like a schoolgirl being punished for talking too loudly.

Finally, I found a place that felt right. Unfortunately, it was forty-five minutes away. I began driving there twice a day, three hours travel a day. Living alone, this did not impact anyone else (other than my cats!), but the hours were wearing me out. Within a month of my father's death, I found myself moving to a new town to say Kaddish in his memory.

What was so special about my new *shul*? The name said it all: Ahavas Achim, Brotherly Love. No one turned me away when I mentioned that I wasn't Orthodox. No one looked askance about my wearing pants to *shul*. The rabbi told me I could even say Kaddish by myself, if no men were in mourning. I was accepted as I was.

I joined families for meals full of laughter and love. I especially loved the singing and learning, reminiscent of my childhood. Around town there were *shiurim* (classes) to challenge my intellect. As the year went on, more and more I felt a sense of belonging, of being valued as a member of this community.

I now faced prayer on a daily basis. At the beginning, barely able to keep up with the davening and nervous about saying Kaddish aloud, I scarcely thought about the prayers I was saying. After a while I got tired of this speed dating routine; I wanted a deeper relationship with prayer. On some days, I would ignore the fact I was lagging behind, concentrating instead on a specific prayer to further understand its meaning. Words in the second prayer before *Shema* in *Shacharit* tugged at my heart, the words written on my father's gravestone: "to learn and to teach, to observe and to perform, and to fulfill all the words of Hashem's Torah with love." My father epitomized this phrase, could I ever come close?

I began thinking about Hashem and spirituality – concepts that I once thought would have no place in my life. I wanted the surety that people surrounding me appeared to have; instead I found myself faced with questions. Does Hashem exist? Does Hashem listen to prayers? If so, do my prayers somehow affect Hashem's actions? If not, is praying still an important and positive action to take? What if I don't believe the words I am saying? I still grapple with these questions, and they are an important part of my life.

Kaddish brought a healing to my relationship with my father. At the time of his death, my father and I were having difficulties – I hadn't seen or spoken to him in several years. Yet I always believed we would become closer again. Now, with his sudden death, that opportunity was lost. Losing my father made me realize how deep my feelings were for him. I missed learning at his table, singing Shabbat songs, Pesach Seders until 4 a.m. Part of our separation had been due to my own estrangement from Orthodox Judaism. Continuing my father's traditions, doing what I believed he would approve of, became important to me. Kaddish was, in a sense, my way of saying to my father "I haven't forgotten your teachings, I haven't left Judaism." I felt a need to declare my feelings in a public manner, perhaps because there had been this time of separation. Kaddish was my way of telling the world "I love and miss my Abba."

Kaddish is a song of praise, a difficult song while experiencing grief, yet a helpful reminder that all is not bleak. It started as a rote recital of words, yet this prayer helped color the mundane world with highlights of holiness.

Saying Kaddish changed who I was and, perhaps more importantly, who I wanted to be. It made me realize how important Judaism was in my life and rekindled my love for Torah. My father's death showed me how much I had lost. Saying Kaddish made me realize how much there still was to gain.

Inspired by what I saw at Ahavas Achim, I now saw places for women to expand and develop within the Orthodox Jewish community. As a woman, I saw myself as important enough to be, if not counted in a *minyan*, at least *acknowledged* there. With newly found self-esteem, I began to stand up for these beliefs. Once, when visiting cousins, I was faced with men who had taken over the women's section on a Friday night. I entered the room and began my own prayers, despite the looks they gave me. Eventually, they left.

My father died suddenly and my life did a cartwheel – bringing me full circle while moving me forward.

I still have issues with faith and with Orthodoxy and do not consider myself Orthodox. Yet as I look to the future, I will continue trying to emulate the teachings of my father. Although our chosen paths differ, I think about the beauty of his ways: his words of wisdom, his strong silence while listening, and his comfort with people from all walks of life. I am still the little girl learning at the Shabbat table, looking for the perfect answer, or, better yet, the perfect question – just to see his eyes sparkle in a smile. I hope I have his acceptance. I hope I make him proud.

My father, My teacher –

Avee, Moree . . .

Born in Brookline, MA, **GEELA**'s family attended a *"chasidishe shteeble"* (the Bostoner Rebbe's). In addition, her father was a *"talmid muvhak,"* a student, of Rav Soloveitchik. She grew up seeing both the fervor of the Rebbe and the intellectualism of the Rav. Geela now lives in Highland Park, NJ and might be seen in any number of places on Shabbat: an Orthodox *shul*, a Women's Tefillah Group, a traditional Egalitarian Minyan, a Conservative Temple or a Havurah Minyan. Her work has ranged as well: computer programmer, assisting in special education classroom, tutor, preschool teacher and more. She has now started a business as a cat sitter, and is constantly trying to grow in all parts of her life, as a friend or family member, as an intellectual and as a poet, as a student of Judaism, as a student of the world.

Will the Place Comfort?

ANNE VENZE SENDOR

W HEN THE INTIFADA STARTED getting bad for Israel in 2001, my husband and I felt a strong urge to visit. It was the least we Americans could do. Many of our friends, though, tried to discourage us from going. My mother was already quite ill at that time, but still able to speak. When my father told her of our plans, she responded, "That's great. I want to go, too." That let me know that she knew better than all of us what was really important in the world.

My Mom died after a very long illness and a painfully slow decline. For years I made plans to do things, silently asking my mother to hold off so I could take care of this event or go on that trip. I think I asked her more often for permission to do things while she was in her coma than I did as a teenager living at home. But I was slipping more and more into sadness, which turned into a kind of inaction. Looking back, I realize that the fact that my mother lingered so long made me grieve before she died.

There is a flip in the mourning process the rabbis set up for relatives of the dead and for Yerushalayim. For Yerushalayim, there are three weeks of light mourning, then nine days of heavier sadness and restrictions, which culminate in Tisha B'Av, a full fast day commemorating the destruction of the Beit HaMikdash (Temple). For the mourner, in contrast, it starts out very stark, and then lets up step by step: burial, *shiva*, *shloshim*, the year. What was different for me, and I guess other people whose loved ones go through prolonged declines, was that I also was going deeper and deeper into a grieving.

When my mother died, I was relieved that the long nightmare of her illness was over. As the wife of a congregational rabbi for twenty-seven years, I've often had to figure out what to say to people at difficult times. But in this moment, I wasn't sure myself what I really wanted to hear.

I understood the reason for the *aninut* – not doing any *mitzvot* or saying any *brachot* from the time I found out that Mom had died until the burial. But I hated the sound of the dirt on the casket; it felt so cruel. Anything else would have been fine to do, just not hear the dirt falling. So saying Kaddish was just part and parcel of being in the cemetery. We were told to step up and say these things, the words that you don't say any other time. It seemed as surreal as every other part of the whole process.

In the Beit HaMikdash, mourners would leave through one gate, while everyone else would pass through a different gate. As they passed each other, people would utter to the mourners, "*HaMakom yinachem etchem b'toch sha'ar avlei Tziyon v'Yerushalayim*" usually translated as "May God comfort you among the rest of the mourners of Zion and Jerusalem." *Ha-Makom* means "the place" and functions as a name for God, based on the rabbinic formulation: "the world is not His place, rather He is the Place of the world." "*HaMakom yinachem etchem . . .*" is still the traditional verse to say when leaving mourners during *shiva*. It is not a phrase that rolls off the tongue; many people are uncomfortable saying it, and many don't know how. In many *shiva* houses, there is a sign with the sentence posted on it, often with the English translation.

When we were sitting *shiva* and people said that to me, it made me feel that Yerushalayim was with me and all the other mourners of the world. It was one of the only things that gave me comfort during that time. So many people apologized before they tried to read it, "I'm not really so good at saying this." And my answer was, "I'm glad you're not good, because that means you haven't had to say it that often," which turned it into me needing to comfort them. But that was okay, because Yerushalayim was comforting all of us.

There was no question my father would be going to *shul* daily to say Kaddish. My sister and I decided to go, too, in order to be with him. So saying Kaddish at that point was simply a matter of *kibbud av va'em*, or at least *av*. Being in *shul* was not natural; I felt like we were pretending or proving a point, being in the men's world. This is not something I wanted. I never felt comfortable in the whole feminist Jewish world, since I never felt that I had enough time to do what I needed or wanted to do without taking on more obligations. Did the fact that we *could* say Kaddish mean that we *should* say Kaddish? Were we doing something for Mom or were we doing something for ourselves? Would it ever feel right or were we in the wrong place? Would we find comfort among the mourners of the boys' club? Where was our place in all of this?

The words of the liturgy opened themselves up to me almost every day without fail; their wisdom coming through despite my frustration with the wordiness of it all. The prayers assert that transformation is built into life, and I saw that prayer would help me get through my grief and turn it into proper mourning. Even for parents, the recitation is only for eleven months and not a full year, since no one is supposed to be so wicked that s/he needs the prayer for redemption for a whole year. So is it wickedness that we are redeeming? Or mediocrity?

Finally, we stopped saying Kaddish. What was amazing was the first Kaddish after davening *Maariv*, when we didn't say anything; we just answered to Kaddish in the appropriate places. I felt pulled down to the earth in the oddest way; so very bound by gravity.

My sister and I both looked for signs that day of the change in our reality; of letting Mom go. I found mine in the camera shop, where I stopped on my way home from school because my camera had died that morning while trying to photograph students. The man at the shop told me that my camera wasn't broken, but the memory card needed to be reset.

Propitiously, that week's *parshah* was about fearing one's mother and father. I never feared my mother; I worry I never really honored her, either. And that's why I did this exercise in honor. I learned in that last week that the word "*nechemata*" in the Kaddish, which is usually translated as "comfort" (from the Hebrew word "*nechama*") actually comes from the word "*ne'ima*," or "pleasantness." So Hashem doesn't need comforting; He wants our praise. I don't know if I have praised Hashem enough; I certainly don't think I praised my mother enough. But for this exercise of the year, I am comforted.

ANNE SENDOR has worked in Jewish education for over twenty-five years, mostly in Early Childhood settings. She has recently started to work in Marriage Education, being trained through the PREP program. Having watched Rabbi Aryeh Klapper's Summer *Beit Midrash* program flourish over the last thirteen years in her *shul*, the Young Israel of Sharon, she was excited to help in a more substantial way as Program Director of the Center for Modern Torah Leadership. This entails overseeing the weekly *Dvar Torah*, the website, the annual professional rabbinic and teacher conference, and the Summer *Beit Midrash* program. Some of her former kindergarten students have become SBM fellows, which has given her almost as much *nachas* as her wonderful grandchildren.

Go to the Jews

DEBORAH GRENIMAN

Y MOTHER, DEAD on a relatively warm November day in 1972 at age 45, had two funerals. The first was a Reform ceremony held somewhere in Long Island. I say "somewhere," because I have no memory of where it was. Since our family had no synagogue affiliation and no rabbi, the ceremony was arranged through family friends. As I sat, shocked, in this unfamiliar place, surrounded by my mother's weeping friends and former patients, her coffin was swished in on a kind of rail that required no human hand. Everything about the place felt like that – as though covered by a hard patina through which no warm hand, no note of true connection, could pass.

The second funeral was held in a sweet green Jews' cemetery in Nottingham, England, where my grandmother lived and my grandfather had died just three years before, and where I, too, lived briefly as a child. Here, in the town that had received her small family when they arrived as refugees in 1938, my mother was finally interred near her beloved father. I remember rain, candles burning in the dark little chapel, Hebrew words, and the simple faces of the people around me, most of whom I had never met. It was my first contact with traditional Judaism.

It must have been on the way to or from the first funeral – I remember it was in a car – that my father turned to ask me, as the eldest daughter, to say Kaddish for my mother. Under the circumstances, this was a somewhat bizarre request; but everything about that time was bizarre. My father had never said a Kaddish for his own father, who died and was cremated in southern France when my father was just 11, during his family's flight from the Nazis. Apart from his wedding in London's largest Reform synagogue, my father had never observed anything Jewish at all. Every December, he took me and my sisters out with him in the frosty air to buy a big, solid Christmas tree, and we eagerly opened our presents beneath it on Christmas morning. On Easter, he hid chocolate eggs for us in the yard. He barely knew what the Kaddish was and couldn't read Hebrew. Yet he was sure that this was what my mother would have wanted.

Growing up, it seemed to me that my parents were a perfect match. They had a brilliance that made others pale beside them. Dad's family, assimilated German Jews – his mother was a scion of the Ullstein publishing house – had fled Berlin when the Nazis came to power in 1933. Mum's family of more traditional Polish Jews – *Ostjuden* – had fled Austria with the *Anschluss*. Arriving in England as teenagers just before World War II, they had both reaped the benefits of a fine British education (notwithstanding wartime military service for Dad), capped by medical degrees from Cambridge, where they met and where my mother, in 1948, was in the first class of women to receive degrees from the university.

My parents were humanists through and through, in the way that people were humanists in the 1950s and 1960s, with the liberal, universalistic, agnostic values that came with it. Lovers of literature and classical music, both of them were fluent in English, German and French, and Dad was versed in Latin and Greek as well. In our home, I never heard a word of hatred or condescension for any human group – not even the Germans.

Yet, as my mother grew older, these resemblances with my father began falling away before something more primal. She had distanced herself from both her parents and her Jewish consciousness by marrying my father and following him from England, where my younger sisters and I were born, to America. Increasingly alienated from the society into which she had been transplanted, she began trying to recover her roots.

It was my mother who sent me and my sisters off to Jewish summer camps and brought us to the occasional Passover Seder, so that we could get a little exposure to Jewish things. It was she who bought and played us records of Hebrew and Yiddish songs and dragged us backstage to shake hands with Theodore Bikel when he gave a concert in Long Island. For a time, she even paid for private lessons for us in Modern Hebrew, since Sunday-school indoctrination was not an option.

My mother, who danced in the streets when the State of Israel was declared and contemplated *aliyah* before her marriage, visited Israel in the early 1960s. She fell in love with the country, and in 1966 she sent me and one of my sisters – I was 12, and she had just turned 11 – to spend the summer with her friends in a secular, Hashomer Hatzair kibbutz. I spent a rather miserable, hot, lonely summer there; yet I also identified paradise in this place of flowers, flowing streams and olive trees.

Back in the U.S., home life was growing difficult as my mother's health declined. She suffered through several serious physical illnesses and sank into depression, even as she struggled to maintain her successful (and unusual, in those days) career as a psychiatrist. A decision was made for us girls to be sent away to school. So, at 13, I left home, never to live there again for any length of time.

I finished high school early. On my own at 16, I headed for Europe and eventually for London, the city of my birth, where most of my extended family still lived. When I landed on my German grandmother's doorstep, a scrawny, stringy-haired teenager without a plan or a place to live, it was her non-Jewish companion, a European academic woman, who said to me: "Go to the Jews. They will help you."

The Jews did help me. I was referred both to a kosher hostel where I could live with other young Jewish women and to a position as a "Junior Library Assistant" in the archives of the distinguished London *Jewish Chronicle*. My job, in those pre-electronic days in 1970/71, was to paste newspaper clippings into files according to the people named in them. Reading the clippings as I worked, I gained the beginnings of an education about the Jewish world. A veteran Czech Jewish journalist also worked in the archive. As he shared his painful memories and experiences, I felt like a window was opening upon the world my parents' families had to flee.

"Any visit to the land of your fathers," my mother had said before I departed, "will be paid in full." I had seen myself as going out to experience the wide world, yet, in doing so, I found myself recreating my past and my family ties. Now I felt the call of that other, Israeli root that I'd put down in the summer when I was 12. On the eve of Passover, I returned to Israel and to the same kibbutz, where my "family" there persuaded me, rather than volunteering, to join the kibbutz *ulpan* (an intensive language course). The knowledge of Hebrew that I gained there would impact the rest of my life.

Meanwhile, things at home were getting worse. My mother spent much of her time in bed. I returned to the U.S. to take the place awaiting me at Brown University, but some part of me was always tearing itself away from and returning to the morass at home; to the attraction of my mother's charismatic brilliance and the sinkhole of her illness, in which she inflicted pain on everyone around her.

And then, early in my second year at Brown, she died. That moment was a zero hour for me. There was nothing more to run from. I had to find whatever I needed to find in myself, in where I was.

It never occurred to me to refuse my father's request to say Kaddish, strange as it was. It didn't even seem especially problematic to carry it out, since I had yet to confront the strictures of Orthodoxy. The experiences of the previous two years had given me enough background – knowledge of Hebrew, and some rudimentary acquaintance with things Jewish – for the mechanics of reading the words from a prayer-book.

To carry out my promise, I began attending Friday night services at Hillel House. For the first few weeks, I sat there, stunned and angry, not praying, but when the time came at the end of the service, I stood up and recited the words. *Yitgadal v'yitkadash* – what was I saying? Nothing had prepared me spiritually for the task of praising God. I had no religious beliefs, no experience of prayer. If there was a God, I was angry at Him for taking my mother away before I'd had a chance to resolve things with her. Why did I have to intone these meaningless phrases, and why was I so alone?

Yet I kept coming. I appreciated the warmth of the service and the companionship of the dinners that followed. Getting dressed up on Friday nights and going to Hillel gave a shape to the week and to the world that had fallen apart around me. I began to feel at home.

Spiritually, though, my wounded heart had yet found no succor. My mother's death had left an emptiness, not only of her presence – vital to the end – but of anything that might have sustained her, or me, in a world devoid of spirit. Friday nights at Hillel were nice, but they were not profound. I knew that my Polish-born grandmother lit a *yahrzeit* candle for my grandfather on the anniversary of his death, and it irked me that I didn't know the Hebrew date of my mother's death. I sought out my Jewish Studies professor, who was a former communal rabbi. When I put my question to him, he heard the unspoken questions behind it and allowed me to pour out my heart.

My professor introduced me to Jewish texts and invited me to Shabbat meals with his family. From him I learned that there was a world in which my questions about good and evil, love and fear, hung in the air. That they were never really answered meant that they could be asked over and over, and be met again and again with words and images that touch the heart. It was precisely the contradictions that spoke to me, and drew me in.

At some point I started to attend off-campus Orthodox services, and before long I was invited to Shabbat meals in many homes. I learned the intimacy of observance and the "taste" of Shabbat. As I responded, orphaned soul that I was, to the kind people who reached out to "adopt" me, I came to know many sides of the community, a somewhat uneasy mix of teachers and students from the local Orthodox day school and academics. One sharply intelligent woman, widowed and living alone, showered me with maternal affection as she poured out her heart to me in an erudite, classical Hebrew. I saw how one could be critical of traditional Judaism and its sometimes small-minded practitioners, yet still feel bound to it at the core.

My Kaddish year ended. What it had revealed to me was not essential truths, but some kind of essential, spiritual and moral presence, a bedrock for the soul, made through texts and prayers, through living community and visceral human contact. My mother had deeply sensed the differentiation between good and evil, justice and injustice – yet she had lost her way. I was determined to keep mine, and survive.

Even as I hungered for the riches of traditional Judaism, I couldn't reject the humanistic and critical values on which I was raised. I changed my concentration to religious studies, which allowed me to study a hefty dose of Christian texts alongside Jewish ones. Judging the truth or falsehood of different faith claims seemed irrelevant. To me, the numinosity (a word I learned then) that I could feel emanating from these texts only confirmed the presence of the spiritual world, evident to non-Jews and Jews alike. That numinosity seemed to stand by itself, without demanding literal acceptance of every detail of the text.

In the early and mid-1970s, second-wave feminism had come into its own in both the academic and the Jewish world. There was a concentration of early Jewish feminist activists at Brown; among other things, my friends started one of the first women's *minyan*s, with a Torah reading, which I attended. Becoming observant and becoming a Jewish feminist happened to me at the same time; both seemed natural to me, and it seemed natural to be both.

And still it seemed that the place where my heart could sing and rise in prayer, the place where I could bring my darkest thoughts and offer them up, was the traditional, Orthodox Jewish service. Other, more "modern" services still had (and have), for me, the patina that I experienced at the first funeral – a sheath that stopped them reaching the depths of my soul.

When I went back to Israel for the summer of 1974, it was not to the kibbutz, but to Jerusalem, to study Hebrew amid the dust of reconstruction on Mt. Scopus. It was this root that finally claimed me. Returning to Jerusalem on the eve of Passover 1976, I ended up staying, marrying, raising a family, and developing a career in Jewish and Jewish feminist books. In Jerusalem, I found and helped to establish a community – Kehillat Yedidya, where women routinely say Kaddish – that has allowed my worlds to live, mostly, in harmony.

Would my mother really have wanted me to say Kaddish for her? Truthfully, I think not. She had tried religious observance in her youth and rejected it. She didn't fast on Yom Kippur, eat matzah on Pesach or light Shabbat candles. I think she, too, experienced that impassable sheath in the Reform temples of Long Island, but she had no patience for Orthodox mumbo-jumbo, either. I doubt that I could have made my religious journey in her lifetime. I would have been too fearful of her criticism. Yet I think her Israeli-born grandchildren, now consciously choosing their own paths as Jews, would have pleased her.

Perhaps a motivation for my father's request, conscious or not, was an understanding of what my mother had sacrificed in marrying him, the quintessential non-Jewish Jew, and following him to America. What will happen when he passes from this world? Two of his daughters are now observant Jews, yet that world remains foreign to him. His second wife is not Jewish, and if he has his way, he intends to be cremated like his father and mother before him. Yet I cannot imagine not saying Kaddish for the man who started me on this journey, and who, together with my mother, instilled in me many of the values and passions by which I live, and which I have tried to integrate into how I live as a Jew.

DEBORAH GRENIMAN, a Jerusalem-based editor, translator and writer, is Managing Editor of *Nashim: A Journal of Jewish Women's Studies and Gender Issues* and Senior Editor of English-language scholarly publications at the Israel Academy of Sciences and Humanities. Her writings and reviews have appeared in *Tikkun, Nashim,* and *Shabbat Shalom,* and her translation of Ada Rapoport-Albert's book, *Women and the Messianic Heresy of Sabbatai Zevi,* was recently published by the Littman Library. She and her spouse Rabbi Yehiel Grenimann helped establish Kehillat Yedidya in Jerusalem. They are the parents of four adults and are cradling their first grandson.

The Strength to Forgive

MICHAL SMART

MY MOTHER DIED SUDDENLY, when I was thirty-five. In those awful first weeks of loss, I clung to Kaddish in the maelstrom of my grief. Its rough edges sometimes cut my hands, but it kept me afloat.

I grieved mostly for the sadness of my mother's life; that she never received the love she so deeply craved, especially from me. I mourned the loss of my hope this would change. I'd stand in the *shul's* drab basement and say "Hashem, you are my only Mother now — please hold me." And I would feel embraced.

At that time, I had three children and the oldest was four. There was no way I could have left home for services each day for a year without constant anxiety and tears. This was not something my young family could sustain, or that my mother would have wanted. Yet I did not see Kaddish as an all-or-nothing proposition. So once *shloshim* was over, I did my best. The fact that I couldn't make it to *shul* every day did not undermine the value of my going when I could. In fact, it made each opportunity to say Kaddish more poignant.

There is something magic about the *siddur*. Sometimes a particular line or prayer is there, recited year after year without special attention, waiting for us to need it. In my experience, when we bring the truth of our lives into *shul* and open ourselves to the prayers, davening has the power to change us.

I remember at one point mulling over how unhealed my mother was. Despite years of therapy, she never recovered from the trauma of her childhood – not enough to protect us from her abusive father, not enough to be the mother she wanted to be and we so desperately needed. She tried to kill herself more than once and in some ways she had died for me long before the stroke that killed her.

Part of me was angry, not ready to forgive and reluctant to pray for her soul. She was not responsible for being hurt as a child, but she had the responsibility to do hard and courageous work to heal, and to protect her children. She failed us and I blamed her. I have always blamed her for not trying harder. For not succeeding.

Yet part of me pitied her. Terrified child, self-flagellating woman. My mother was smart, well-meaning, passionate and generous. Yet life was difficult for her and all those around her.

I wondered, and the possibility was new to me, what if she actually did try her best? Perhaps she brought every ounce of courage and strength she had to her therapy sessions, to her family each day, and it simply wasn't enough. Could I fault her for that?

Something inside me eased, for just a moment, to feel only sorry for how she suffered, perhaps beyond repair. But it scared me, too. What if, despite my efforts to write a different story, I lose the next battle and end up like her? Am I so sure we are different?

Immersed in these thoughts, I came to the *Amidah*. A line that I had uttered countless times jumped out at me from the pages of my *siddur*: "*Mi kamokhah, Baal gevurot*, Who is like You, Master of strengths?" I saw first that God is the master, the owner, the doler outer of *gevurah*. Perhaps Hashem does endow different people with different depths of strength. If so, it is beyond judgment, like intelligence or artistic talent. Perhaps, then, it was time for me to stop blaming my mother for having less. And maybe I did not need to second-guess my own endowment, I just needed to say thank you.

I also noticed that the prayer does not say *gevurah*, "strength" in the singular, but rather *gevurot*, "strengths" in the plural. So there are different kinds of strengths, perhaps an infinite array of them, and God is master of them all. I took comfort in this thought. If God created the world, and with it every kind of violence and pain, then God must also have created the particular kind of strength one needs to overcome each and every one.

I left, still pondering, but in a clearer place for having davened. Could it be that somewhere, my mother's soul was freer to move on, as well?

MICHAL SMART is the editor of *Kaddish, Women's Voices*.

Love Is Strong as Death
says Solomon
I begin to sense it's true
through tears that roll so freely
my relief when the children
remember
Yes, love is stronger

Standing in shul to say "Yizkor"
I see it
as those unmarked by death
gratefully, sheepishly, shuffle out
into bright sunlight
while the rest of us
who have tasted it
remain
to pray for our parents, spouses,
children, we pray for them now
as we prayed for them then
It is not only pain that we share
but also a quiet
and comforting knowing
that love is strong as death

Do we retain individual form
when we reach the next world?
Heaven would be too crowded
besides most lives do not merit
eternal distinction
No, unfettered the soul returns to
its source, droplet meets the sea

Yet as long as we reside in hearts
of the living, some part of us
remains
Maimonides said one gains eternal
life through knowledge but
I think it is the love

Someday when I pass on
to that world
– may it not be for awhile –
I trust Hashem will
resurrect your bodies, if
only for a moment, for my sake

Once again you will be there
to welcome me
and I, again a small child
in a strange, new world
will run to you
with open arms

"Pray for Me"

AVIVA EPHRAIM MALLER

THROUGHOUT MY ADULT LIFE, whenever I would leave for synagogue on Shabbat, Dad would be sitting at his usual spots; either at his desk or the kitchen counter – poring over *The New York Times* crossword puzzle. A deeply traditional man but one who preferred his communication with God to be one-on-one or with family, he rarely went to synagogue (at least in the US, claiming he was uninspired). So, as I would leave to go myself, he would look up at me, shake his head in an Indian manner and say "Bye . . . Pray for me."

Coming from a long line of Iraqi Jews in India dating all the way back to Babylonian times, religion and traditional customs have always been very important for me. My memories as a girl in the synagogue in India are sweet, bringing beauty and grace in our white flowing dresses on Rosh Hashanah and being splashed with rosewater on Yom Kippur, which filled the air with its sweet perfume. Spiritedly we ran to the Ark at the close of each Shabbat service to push behind the curtain and plant our kisses on the Torahs, to enjoy the same feelings of reverence and closeness as the men had experienced. Young and old, I remember all the women observing this custom and I can close my eyes and remember the smell in that sacred place.

Sadly, though, I grew up in a time and place where daughters, women, did not practice Judaism with the same depth that men did. Not only were we not formally taught to lead a service or to read from the Torah, we were not even encouraged to pray in any serious way other than to joyously sing along with the words and melodies that we recognized and knew by rote.

We observed rather than followed the services from our perches way up on the second floors of our magnificent synagogues. As such we never learned enough to uncover the mysteries of our sacred words or feel the intensity we would have were we as learned as the men.

So why, years later in America upon my father's death, did I feel at almost fifty years of age so compelled to come daily to a place that was mostly the domain of men, to learn the prayers more intimately and recite the Kaddish, a prayer that is *not* a prayer for the dead? Why, when I did not have to do this and I had so much else I had to do?

The answer lies in my soul: a deep connection to my father and a feeling that I had to keep this connection open to him for as long as I could, and a hope that perhaps this reciting of the Kaddish would delay the moment of him truly being gone from my life. Of course he was gone physically, but perhaps spiritually, we still had a little more time together. A little more time for me to have a daily talk with him as I sat in my seat, mostly alone in the women's section, as my mind wandered to my father in between and during different sections of the liturgy. Sometimes it was my father as I last saw him in his hospital bed surrounded by my mother, my brother and myself as his hand grasped around the *Tehillim* (Book of Psalms). Sometimes it was the image I had of him as I grazed past his seat and planted a kiss on his sweet forehead. Sometimes it went even further back to when he was young and virile, as he emerged from the waters of the Indian Ocean after a brisk swim. But mostly it was his voice, the dulcet sounds of his particular cadence as he spoke to me or to others. A sound that was at times comforting and at times heated and passionate depending on the message he had to convey.

There was one spot in the service where I practically heard my father's voice, and I looked forward to it every day. It was a section in the *Ashrei* prayer where we say, "*Pote'ach et yadecha u'masbia l'chol chai ratzon*" (You open Your hand, and satisfy the desire of every living thing). Every time I uttered this verse, I pictured how, in our Iraqi tradition, my Dad held up the challah bread in his two open hands and recited this line, sweetly, shyly, before the blessing of the *Hamotzi*. To me, this phrase epitomized my father's belief in God. It said God is good and will grant you all that you need. Then, while waiting for Mum and I to serve the soup, he would begin a rousing version of "*Zeh ha-yom asah Hashem nagila v'nismecha bo*," This is the day that God has made, let us celebrate and rejoice in it" (an excerpt from *Hallel*). In this special way, he set the tone for celebrating our being together every week.

Three years before he died, we had a scare that prompted us to call our Rabbi, Mark Dratch, to visit Dad in the hospital. Rabbi Dratch started reciting one of King David's most famous Psalms in English: "The Lord is my Shepherd; I shall not want . . ." To our amazement, through his respirator in a muffled voice, my father continued on: ". . . He maketh me to lie down in green pastures, he leadeth me beside the still waters . . ." In the quiet of that Shabbat night, Dad spoke stalwartly to God, telling Him he was not ready and pleading for more time, which God thankfully and graciously granted him.

As I recited the Kaddish with my feet firmly rooted on the ground, the words at first trembled but later fell easily from my mouth. The beauty about praying in a language other than your mother tongue is that you can recite it so accurately and yet think about something completely different while the words spill from your lips. You can think, "Dad, I am thinking of you with the sweetest thoughts" while you are saying, "May His great name be blessed forever and forever" and mean both.

"Pray for Me." What did my fathers charge to me really mean? I always took it to be twofold. "You know my prayers, Aviva, pray them for me"; and "Aviva, pray for your father's *neshama*." Why his soul? As if it needed redeeming? Well, sometimes it seemed like it. And so I did. I prayed for him when he was alive and I continued to pray for him now. I prayed that where he was, he could take full, deep breaths and inhale the memories of the love that he created here on earth, and that at last he could pray for himself as well as for all of us, as he would have an even closer connection to God.

Saying Kaddish enabled me to attend a whole year's worth of daily prayers, weekly *parshiot* and the cycle of festivals. It was as if I had a personal course in Judaism. By the end of eleven months, the prayer experience birthed in India blossomed into one of greater depth and understanding. I question whether saying Kaddish was a gift I gave to my father or one he gave to me!

I made the commitment to recite Kaddish to prolong our time together, and to pray for my father. In the end, however, the reason I continued to say Kaddish through the year was largely because I felt so connected to God Himself. He, most of all, knew that I was there not just to pray for my father, but indeed, to pray for me and all I loved, to pray for all that I had missed because I did not have to miss it anymore. I knew that I was richer for it and that the *neshama* of my Dad would fly higher and higher, as we both came closer and closer to God.

AVIVA EPHRAIM MALLER was born in India and is of Iraqi descent. As a young immigrant she has always tried to do what others before her might not have. She is a photographer and event planner. Her love of people drives her to reach out to her community, and she is known for creating events that are not only beautiful and enjoyable but also have depth and meaning. Her connection to her roots and history are her terra firma. She lives in Stamford, CT with her husband and two teenage sons, with her mother and mother-in-law very close by.

Why I Did Not Say Kaddish

SHIFRA AVIVA (POSNER) DEREN

F OR ME, IT WAS a positive and affirmative step *not* to say Kaddish for my mother, Risya bas HaRav Shlomo Aaron v'Chaya Fraida, ob"m. I'd like to explain why; to do so I need to share something of how I grew up and how I see my mother's impact on my life – and how I see the world and my place in it.

"It doesn't always pay to be ahead of your time – until people catch up, so much can be lost." My mother's tongue in cheek description of the frustration she felt in trying to bring the practice of *taharat hamishpacha* to her community in the 1950s speaks volumes – both about my mother and the Jewish world at that time.

My parents came to Nashville when they got married in November 1949; my father was the rabbi of the Orthodox *shul* there for over fifty years. People could not understand why a young man in his early twenties would "throw his life away to run a cemetery." Even among those who observed traditional Jewish practice, there was a given assumption that these were relics of the "*Alter Heim,*" the old country, soon to be a thing of the past.

My mother was even more of a mystery. Why would a talented, well-educated American-born young woman be content to be the Rabbi's wife? Growing up, as I became aware that most of my mother's school friends did not choose to practice the observant lifestyle in which they had been raised, I wondered what made her decide not to jump ship with so many others. There was no pressure to stay in the community, no fear of ostracism by one's peers. The wave of the future (or so it appeared in the 1940s) was full-fledged assimilation.

My mother was raised in a Chabad Chassidic home. One of her most cherished childhood memories was being at the pier when the previous Lubavitcher Rebbe, Rabbi Joseph Isaac Schneerson, arrived on these shores in March 1940. "America is no different," he declared, and those words set her imagination on fire, a fire that would glow for the rest of her life. It was her identity as a Chassid that shaped her life, an identity that she chose even more than she inherited it.

She was part of a small group of teenage girls who studied Chassidic philosophy with rabbis who took them seriously. There were not yet any Yeshiva high schools for girls, but later, as her daughters grew up and attended these schools she relished our every accomplishment. Throughout her life she built on the Jewish studies she had been tutored in as a child, and remained a focused student of Torah always.

Shortly after my parents came to Nashville, the previous Rebbe passed away and was succeeded by his son-in-law, Rabbi Menachem M. Schneerson. From the earliest years of his leadership the Rebbe emphasized the vital, critical position of Jewish women, throughout history and especially in contemporary Jewish life. My mother was thrilled.

GEOMETRY AND JEWISH LIFE – A CORE OF *KEDUSHAH*

In contrast to the typical perspective of seeing society divided into two distinct spheres – the public and the private – and the endless arguing over which sphere was properly the place of women, my mother embraced the idea that these two spheres are concentric, and therefore the center point of one is the center point of all.

What is that core, that center point?

At Sinai God spoke to us in the singular. Each individual person has been given the mandate of "*kadesh atzmekha* – sanctify yourself," which our Sages say is the first step, the foundation for the biblical mandate of "*kedoshim tihiyu*, You (plural) shall be Holy."

The core *kedushah*, the foundational holiness, the one that is the center of all surrounding spheres, is personal *kedushah*, personal holiness.

If the center point is weak, the rest is in danger of imploding. Everything, everything is based on the strength of that core.

Personal sanctity has its roots in the soul. Torah study, prayer and personal observance of *mitzvot* give expression to and nourish this *kedushah*.

Personal sanctity informs how we conduct our daily lives wherever we are – at work, in social settings, among family, and alone.

But *kedushah* also translates as "separate."

Judaism has a way of covering things that are precious to us. Take the Torah itself, for example. It is covered, and kept in a cabinet, and only taken out under very specific circumstances. We use fine fabrics – silks, linens, velvet, embroidery – for the mantle, and beautiful woods and carvings for the cabinet. And we take the Torah out with respect, with blessings.

Respect for our physical being is expressed in similar ways. This respect is an aspect of holiness. In a world of "if you've got it, flaunt it" (where the corollary often seems to be, "and if you're not flaunting it, probably you don't got it"), covering up raises eyebrows. Are you ashamed of something? What are you hiding? Yet *kedushah* requires boundaries: visual boundaries, boundaries of behavior, boundaries that set relationships apart. Boundaries that become holy.

And then what?

SPHERES OF *KEDUSHAH*

With holiness at the core – the holiness of each individual person, holiness that is both inherent and the fruit of intense and personal efforts – there are ripple effects. Circles emanate from this center point that influence all of society.

Judaism started with two Jews, Abraham and Sarah, a man and a woman who set about teaching others. Their students were not merely academic disciples but more like children to them, a part of their family, joining in that first Jewish journey, the journey of bringing Heaven down to Earth, a journey that continues in our own lives today.

One Big Idea of Judaism, from its very inception, is that the family is the prototype for how society should be organized. The key element of family is that it is a learning relationship. The family is the first circle, the circle immediately surrounding the core, the circle from which all of the others emanate. It did not evolve for economic reasons but was designed as the prime vehicle for transmitting other Big Ideas – that there is One God who cares deeply about Creation, that God's holiness can be emulated and is accessible to us, and that the ultimate purpose of Creation is that human beings join in partnership with God and draw down this holiness so as to permeate our world.

Torah describes many important social relationships in familial terms, and does not limit the family relationship to biology alone. To cite a few examples:

Devorah, who was a Judge and spiritual leader in addition to leading troops into battle, described herself as "*Em b'Yisrael* – a mother in Israel."

In the *Shema* prayer, recited daily, we are taught "*v'shinantam l'vanecha* – teach them [words of Torah] diligently to your children." Rashi, the foremost commentator on Torah, notes that "we find throughout [Torah] that students are called 'children' and the teacher is called 'father.'"

When Jacob and his family arrived in Egypt, the Torah teaches that they came "*ish u'beito,*" each man with his home (Exodus 1:1). This is clearly a reference to family, but also a harbinger of how family and home would be the signature for building Jewish life.

In fact, the word *bayit*, home, is found throughout Torah writings, in many different contexts. Whereas in English the word "home" connotes the domestic environment of a nuclear family, removed from the public sphere, in Hebrew this is not the case. For instance, the Jewish people as a whole are referred to as "*Beit Yisrael,*" the home of Israel. Likewise, an institution of Torah study is called a "*beit midrash,*" the home of study.

THE BEIT HAMIKDASH AS PROTOTYPE

Perhaps the most striking example of how the word "*bayit*" is used in Torah writings is the term "Beit HaMikdash." The Holy Temple is called Beit HaMikdash in Hebrew – (to me a far warmer and more intimate term than the grand and somewhat colder "Temple") – with the root words of "*bayit*" and "*kedushah.*"

The connection to God was more palpable in this Holy place. Coming to the Beit HaMikdash was meant to be a spiritual experience that would shine in the lives of the participants throughout the year, all through their lives.

Interestingly, the Beit HaMikdash was itself a reflection of a *bayit* that had come earlier. Sarah's tent was the first "Jewish place," and many *mitzvot* observed then and today had their roots in that first Jewish home. During the centuries that the Beit HaMikdash stood so gloriously in Jerusalem, those *mitzvot* flourished, both in individual Jewish homes as well as in

"My Home," God's Home, the Beit HaMikdash.

In the Beit HaMikdash itself, the place that most closely "contained" the *Shechinah*, the Holy of Holies, was by no means a public thorough-fare. Only the Kohen Gadol (High Priest) could enter, alone, only on Yom Kippur, and only after immersion in the *mikvah*. No one saw, no one was there, but the life of the nation was reflected in that experience.

It is such a Jewish idea that the very place that was the Holiest was the most hidden.

EVERY WOMAN A KOHEN GADOL

Most *mitzvot* are genderless and are incumbent upon both men and women – for example, Shabbat. One of the requirements of Shabbat is that candles be lit at the onset of this holy day. Although both men and women are obligated to keep Shabbat, in Jewish tradition and *Halachah* the mitzvah of lighting candles is preferably done by a woman. Why?

Shabbat itself has such a central role in Judaism, a sign to the whole world that there is a Creator to Whom every human being is accountable, and Shabbat is ushered in by candle lighting. Light symbolizes knowledge, Torah, holiness, kindness. The fact that Jewish law and tradition mandate that this is preferably done by a woman acknowledges the tremendous power that women have to bring light, in all of its dimensions, into the world. The whole world needs Shabbat, but women are the ones who first bring it in, who take the initiative.

Taking the initiative means being able to defy the status quo, to look at one's environment and to be the catalyst for transforming it into what it should be. The Torah entrusts women to take the initiative, and to make sure that certain key *mitzvot* remain at the center of Jewish life – individu-ally, in the family, in the community, and ultimately in the world.

The *mitzvot* that guide physical intimacy are among the most pow-erful, potentially drawing *kedushah* from Heaven down to Earth. Here, too, there is privacy, yet the impact is profoundly public. Here, as in the Beit HaMikdash itself, the *mikvah* is also integral to holiness. And this responsibility is primarily entrusted to women.

When the Talmud speaks about the woman being "*akeret habayit*," the main component of the home, this is no small thing. Similar to the Kohen Gadol in the Beit HaMikdash, each Jewish woman communes with God in ways that affect the nation as a whole. In her Torah, her *tefillah*, her *mitzvot* and in all of her relationships she infuses *kedushah* into her world. Not on center stage, not in public view, but crucial to each and every one of our people, our whole world.

We must further ask, to what "*bayit*" is the Talmud referring? The individual home, certainly. But not only that! If we understand home in the broader sense, what is the role of women then?

The Jewish home models how to make the world we live in a home, a home where each person feels that they are part of a family, where each one has a unique contribution to make, where respect and kindness are the building blocks for harmony and peace.

My husband once spoke at an event honoring his mother, a pioneering Jewish educator, a widely sought lecturer and an acclaimed community leader. "My mother did not go out of her home into the outside world to achieve success," he explained. "Instead, she pushed the walls of her home outward so as to bring the rest of the world inside."

As with the *kedushah* of the Beit HaMikdash, the ultimate purpose of that inner holiness is that it radiate outward and permeate the world. The Rebbe often affirmed the belief that Jewish women today have the ability to uplift society as a whole by taking the initiative in affirming personal *kedushah*, in all of its aspects. It is vital for both men and women, in every walk of life, at any stage of their lives.

After the destruction of the Beit HaMikdash nearly two thousand years ago, the Romans minted a coin with the legend, "*Judea capta* – Judea has been captured." It seemed that the Jewish people were fading off of history's stage. The Romans are long gone; that we continue to live and thrive two thousand years later is an accomplishment unmatched in history.

This was possible only because the *bayit yehudi*, the Jewish home, stood secure. The first circle remained intact, despite the incredible challenges it would face. Through the centuries, it was the constant foundation for building anew.

RECLAIMING OUR CORE

When I taught a college course on The Jewish Woman in the 1970s, questions about women's role in Judaism were first receiving widespread public attention. In one class, I covered the board with as many questions as the students could come up with. Almost all of them were connected to public prayer. When I asked them to list ten things that Judaism rated as more important than public prayer, they looked at me blankly. To make it easier, I posited the following: Three couples and their children are shipwrecked on an island. Is Jewish life possible? Obviously there is no minyan, no quorum for public prayer. So what do we have?

The *mikvah*, symbolic of personal *kedushah*, is bedrock. We start with that. I believe this is the idea behind the teaching that if necessary a community should sell its Torah scroll in order to build a *mikvah*. Those shipwrecked families might not have a *minyan* for public prayer, but they would certainly pray! Indeed, the obligation of prayer applies to every individual, women and men, every single day. They would study Torah, they would teach it to their children. They would have kosher food, and *mezuzot* on their doorposts. *Shabbat* and Jewish holidays would be celebrated. And before long there would be a *minyan*, as well. Strong individuals – men and women – build strong Jewish homes, and through them, strong Jewish communities.

The shipwrecks of history that we have survived happened this way. True, the richly textured *mitzvot* and the powerful *kedushah* of the Beit Knesset have sustained our people through the centuries. But true communal *kedushah* can only happen when the personal, intimate lives of individuals are based on *kedushah*.

We live in a world that values what happens in public over and above what happens in a person's personal life, in ways that are greatly disproportionate to the Jewish worldview, which sees the integrity of the individual, and then of home and family as foundational. We live at a time when the core of our existence is threatened; the notion of personal sanctity is under siege.

What are we doing to restore the balance? How do we make sure that our journey retains the integrity and authenticity of its own soul? Are we rising to meet the challenge? If so many are so unaware of the critical nature of personal *kedushah*, where do our priorities lie? Anyone who takes his or her Jewishness seriously needs to think about this, and take action.

My mother often told me about the study groups for women that she led in the 1950s, which focused on various elements of Jewish life. Shabbat was familiar to her students, *kashrut* was familiar. But *mikvah* and personal *kedushah* were a closed book. When she would broach the topic the women themselves were often intrigued. "But my husband would never go for it," they would say. And they were afraid to even bring up the issue. At a time when assimilation was prevalent and seemed inevitable to many, my mother stayed true to her own core, and taught about the power of Jewish women to infuse their marriages and homes, and ultimately the world, with *kedushah*.

Over half a century later there are positive changes to be noted. For example, the city where my family lives has just celebrated the opening of a beautiful, state of the art *mikvah* that is drawing serious interest in the community at large. Often, when people explore these "secrets," the impact is powerful and life changing.

FROM SAYING TO BEING

In recent years the Kaddish prayer has received much attention, and become the subject of books and studies. It is a prayer that often has a powerful emotional impact on those who say it and those who hear it. I am often moved when I hear Kaddish recited, especially for someone I knew and loved. I called California on the day of the last Kaddish at *Mincha* during the year of mourning for my mother, so I could answer "Amen" to my brother's Kaddish.

Yet I believe that Kaddish needs to be properly understood in the context in which it occurs: public prayer. Saying Kaddish may be public, but it is not core, it is not the center point and it is not first circle. It may be center stage, but it is not the central value.

"*Yitgadal v'yitkadash shmei rabba*, May God's name be exalted and sanctified." God's name is sanctified most when people bring that name into the details of their daily lives – how they do business, how they treat their neighbors, how they live the most intimate parts of their lives. The Kaddish is above all else a reminder to us, the living, to bring about *Kiddush Hashem*.

My *not* saying Kaddish is a reminder to me, and I hope to others, to actualize the words of Kaddish themselves, to draw the focus higher, to seek inward, to highlight the centrality of personal *kedushah*. As a Jewish woman, I have been entrusted to safeguard personal *kedushah* not only for myself, but also for my community, my world. That is first circle.

My mother showed me what *kedushah* in life means. To honor my mother's life, to continue to bring elevation to her *neshamah*, I must live my life with the same dedication to Hashem and the Torah that she showed, proud and confident and "ahead of her time."

By constantly striving to do as she did – by bringing more Torah and more *kedushah* into my life, by teaching Torah to others, by not limiting myself to what I did yesterday but instead trying to be brave enough to do more today and tomorrow, by lighting those candles of Torah, of Shabbat and of souls that will make our world warmer and brighter and truly a place where God feels at home – I hope that I will fulfill my lifelong obligation:

To *be* her Kaddish.

Yeah, Ma?

SHIFRA AVIVA DEREN is co-director of Chabad-Lubavitch of Connecticut and Western Massachusetts. With a passion for education, she is the founding director of the award-winning Gan Yeladim Early Childhood Center in Stamford, Connecticut. Shifra Aviva Deren is a sought-after speaker on the role of women in Jewish life, and a mentor to many.

Visions of My Dad

SANDI EHRLICH WALDSTREICHER

M Y FATHER, MURRAY EHRLICH, passed away in 2006, just before his 81st birthday. I thought I would never see him again. He was diagnosed with a brain tumor in January. We tried everything from surgery to radiation, chemotherapy and tube feedings, hoping to provide him with that last chance to be lucid and maintain a quality of life. It was futile. At the end, I sat at his bedside praying that he would die because I knew that he never wanted to live this way.

Despite Dad's illness, my very busy life continued. I was teaching at the JCC Sara Walker Nursery School, taking care of my family and volunteering for the JCC Summer Maccabi games. My commitment to chair four committees began eighteen months prior to the competition and ten months before I ever heard of the word "glioblastoma." In the end, Dad passed away the Friday night before Maccabi, and because of *shiva*, I couldn't attend the games. During his eulogy, the day of the opening ceremonies, Rabbi Daniel Cohen said to me "*lo alecha ha-melacha ligmor*, you don't have to finish all of the work that you started." With these words, I felt relief. I was ready to mourn.

During *shiva*, my mother, sister and I went to *shul* for *Shacharit. Mincha* and *Maariv* were in my house. This was my first encounter with reciting Kaddish and I found the *Kaddish D'Rabbanan* quite challenging. Since it was the summer, I asked the rabbi if we could daven outside on our patio, which felt so special and comforting. It reminded me of my days at Camp Massad Bet.

At the completion of *shiva*, reciting Kaddish came from guilt. I knew that other women felt the need to say Kaddish and thought that I should try, too. I decided to test it out during the *shloshim* to see if it would feel right to me, knowing very well that my Kaddish wouldn't fulfill the mitzvah. Because my father had no sons, I was told that I should pay a yeshiva student to say Kaddish for me, but could not get myself to do it because I felt it was my obligation as a child. Dad, if I sinned, please forgive me.

When the *shloshim* was over, I knew that saying Kaddish was the right thing to do. With the support of my husband, children, and friends, I decided to commit myself to the full year. This is when I became the newest member of the Kaddish club. It's like the old joke, it's a club that you never want to be a member of, but luckily it does exist and it was this group and our supportive rabbis that got me through the year. I went to *shul* twice a day and even managed to continue exercising in the morning before the 6:30 a.m. *minyan*! It was a mad rush. Our JCC gym opened at 5:30 and I devised a routine where I would work out until 6:10, take a quick shower, slip into my clothes (fake UGG boots from Costco with no socks worked very well) run out by 6:20, drive two miles to *shul* and be in the chapel just in time for *minyan*.

The Minyan Men, as I call them, are an amazing group of people. I will never forget how my friend Fred held the door open for me each morning as I raced into *shul* just in time for the first Kaddish. I always appreciated the fact that they were rooting for me. In return, I marveled at their commitment to daily *minyan*. They could just as easily daven at home, but instead they choose to participate each day as members of a *kehillah* (community), helping anyone who is in mourning.

The women who said Kaddish became my *minyan* buddies. They were with me when I cried and laughed. We understood each other so well, even though we were an eclectic bunch who for years had considered each other mere acquaintances. It was uncanny how quickly we developed a bond. The camaraderie of the men and women was something that I never expected to feel and did not even know existed. To this day I am thankful for each and every one and hope they know how much their friendship means to me. I must say that it was a strange feeling when each of my buddies was about to complete their *aveilut*. While I was happy for them, it felt like I was being left behind. But fortunately or unfortunately, there was always someone else coming up the pike who needed the help only we could offer, and the cycle continued.

Midway through my year of Kaddish, I had a vision of my Dad. It felt so real and came from nowhere. I was alone in my kitchen, preparing dinner, and while standing at the sink my Dad appeared across from me, sitting at the counter in his usual seat. No words were exchanged out loud but I envisioned a very casual conversation with him. I kept thinking that if anyone told me that they'd had a similar experience, I would have thought that they were out of their minds. I always think of myself as a very realistic person. Was all this Kaddish getting to me?

As my eleventh month approached, I had mixed feelings. On the one hand I could not wait for it to be over. I was tired of the running to *shul* twice a day and it was wearing on my family, too. On the flip side, I was wondering – now what? It was weighing heavily on me. With five days to go, I got to *shul* in my usual rushing fashion and found that I was the only woman present. During the last morning Kaddish, I felt a punch on my left arm. I looked around but did not see anyone next to me in *shul*. Then my Dad appeared. This time I actually felt him touch my arm with his usual "love tap" as he called it. Then I envisioned him rolling over in his grave as I heard his voice say to me, "Sandi, enough already." I was caught off guard and kept looking around to see if anyone was watching me or saw what I saw. As soon as *minyan* was over, I ran over to Rabbi Walk and told him what happened. I asked him if anyone else had ever told him a story like mine. He divulged to me that many people have visions of loved ones while saying Kaddish and then added, "But Sandi, usually the person says something more positive." I explained to the rabbi that he didn't know my Dad very well; the words were positive. I realized then that my Dad was trying to tell me "Sandi, it's time to get on with your life." His short visit helped me to get through that last week of Kaddish without guilt. I felt as if he appreciated my saying Kaddish for him and he was giving me permission to move on.

My first granddaughter, Meira, was born a year and a day after my Dad passed away. She was named for him on August 15th, which would have been his 82nd birthday. I marvel at the mysterious way God works, and appreciate the cycle of life.

Each year, as my Dad's *yahrzeit* approaches, I feel a heaviness come over me. Maybe it's because reality set in that my Dad is gone. I miss him and feel his spirit often, but I wonder if I will ever see him again, as I did while saying Kaddish.

SANDI WALDSTREICHER is the Educational Coordinator at the JCC Sara Walker Nursery School in Stamford, Connecticut. She resides in Stamford and has been an active volunteer in the Jewish Community for many years. Sandi grew up in Riverdale, New York, attended The Ramaz School in Manhattan for thirteen years and has a BA from Queens College in Early Childhood Education. Sandi is married to Stuart and together they have four sons Jonathan, Jeremy, Gregory and Bradley, three daughters-in-law, Shira, Talia and Rachel, and two granddaughters, Meira and Shayna.

Incantatory Comfort

AMY KOPLOW

MY MOTHER DIED LAST SUMMER, at the age of ninety. She was observant all her life, and despite many hardships and misfortunes, her faith in God and Judaism was rock solid. I regret that I never asked her why her faith was so strong.

Of course I knew that I could have opted out of saying Kaddish altogether. Yet I felt a strong need to sanctify my mother's memory. Wasn't I her child just as my two brothers? Hadn't I suffered her loss just as they did? I viewed Kaddish as a way of bringing my mother's soul to its eternal rest. I also knew it would help me accept her death and affirm my own belief in God. I feel it is an honor to recite it daily, and an honor to observe the laws of *aveilut*.

At certain synagogues, my experience has been very positive. On the first day after *shiva*, I arrived at my *shul* to a public welcome from one of the regulars, and the *tzedakah* box was made accessible to both sides of the *mechitza*. I had never noticed that the seats on the women's side of the *beit midrash* consists of folding chairs, while the men's section boasts upholstered chairs. One morning early on, I arrived to find a single upholstered chair on the women's side. During my first visit to a midtown Manhattan *shul* for *Mincha*, the rabbi wrote down my name and my mother's. Often, he remembers to mention my mother's name. I have become a loyal attendee at this *shul* because it means so much to hear my mother's name said out loud.

In contrast, my experience at another *shul*, where I had to rush through Kaddish to keep up with the men, felt so belittling. I felt like a little girl running on short legs after the big boys, so that I could be part of the group. Sometimes I could catch up, but when I couldn't, I was simply ignored. I had thought they might get used to me as time passed, but each time my schedule constraints lead me to daven there, I experience the same coldness. I've tried not to care, but in truth I am infuriated. I even wrote to the *shul's* rabbi. He was apologetic, even sympathetic, but ultimately the situation has remained the same.

I do not seek to beat down the walls of the *mechitza*. I grew up in the Modern Orthodox world and choose to remain in it. What I question are the *shuls* where women are not seen as equal members of the community. How much would it take to make a woman feel welcome at a daily *minyan*?

So much of being in *aveilut* involves restriction. You are conscious of all the things you cannot do. You cannot hear live music. You cannot attend parties or the theatre. You cannot wear new clothes. Saying Kaddish, however, is something I *can* do. It lets me believe that I am helping my mother's soul. And paradoxically, it helps me move away from the pain of her last days and her death.

It has been nine months since my mother's death. I can now say Kaddish without falling apart. I am grateful to the men at *shul* who have helped me learn how to honor my mother's memory with love and respect, while encouraging me to move forward. Most of all, I am grateful to the Kaddish, whose incantatory language takes me out of my suffering – one day at a time.

AMY KOPLOW was born and raised in Massachusetts and attended Brandeis University, where she earned two degrees. Since 2000 she has been the Executive Director of the Hebrew Free Burial Association in New York, a position she finds particularly rewarding. Amy lives in Riverdale, NY, and is the proud mother of two daughters.

On Rosh Hashanah
it is written
on Yom Kippur
it is sealed but
it is not read aloud

last year as we sat in shul
reciting these words, as we had before
I did not hear the decree
we went home for festive meals
challah round, for ongoing cycles
honey-dipped, that the
year should be sweet

next time we saw you
lunch tray propped on the bed
holding together gaps in the gown
blood pressure, oxygen, heart rate, temp
inputs, outputs, every detail
recorded on a chart

we watched the clock, awaiting
the doctor, sweeping into the room like
a king, flanked by attendants
silently, he reviewed what was written
we stood to hear
his pronouncement

At 10:06 it was written
in the basement of the morgue
it was sealed

Now I sit here
understanding for the first time, somehow
every one of us . . .
no goodness rails the margin
the bridge is too narrow
I have no recourse
save to beg

וחיים

עלינו

ועל

כל

ישראל

ואמרו

אמן

Remember us for life
King Who desires life
Inscribe us in the Book of Life
For Your sake, O Living God

Beneath My Father's Tallit

CHAYA ROSENFELD GORSETMAN

M Y FATHER, EZRIEL ROSENFELD, *z"l*, was a self-made, learned man with an amazing sense of humor. Life was always wonderful, even in moments when we didn't have enough money to buy *challot* for Shabbat. He walked around saying "*Hashem ya'azor*, God will help." My father was my nurturer. In my family they say that I am most like him; I consider it a compliment.

My parents lived in Israel from the 1930s to the 50s, and they always insisted that Israel was our true home. It never occurred to us that my father might be buried elsewhere. However, at the time of my father's death, my mother was unable to fly. My siblings proposed that I would stay back with my Mom, while my brother flew to Israel to join my sisters there for Dad's burial. Numbness is the word that best describes my feelings at that time. Although I didn't argue, I was internally angry and confused. No one thought to discuss *my* needs – myself included. I stayed behind.

Walking out of the funeral home, I saw them put the *aron* (casket) in the car and my brother, without saying goodbye, left to Israel. As I went home to begin sitting *shiva*, I kept thinking, where is my father? Listening by phone to the second funeral in Israel made me feel excluded, angry, and left out of the experience. I was missing a link in the process of mourning that didn't allow me to move to the next stage. This was the reality with which I would have to reconcile myself over the many months that followed.

Deciding to say Kaddish emerged naturally from the need to hold on to my father. In my mind I wasn't saying Kaddish for his sake. My brother took care of that obligation. Saying Kaddish was a way to find a space to think about him and how he shaped my life, and to take the time to mourn. It gave me pause in which to consider what happens after death. At the same time, it provided an opportunity to think about my mother and her future. The *shul* experience was a place to contemplate what was and what will be, and find solace in secluded moments to figure it all out.

I was lucky because I didn't have to face any personal family tragedy until the age of 62. I thought for sure that at my age losing a parent would be a natural event and therefore I would let go of my sadness after a month or two. After much reflection, it became clear to me that I was shocked at my father's sudden death. After all, he was present at the birth of my four children, and the *smachot* of my nine grandchildren. Moreover, I had several relationships with my father throughout my life: the early childhood years, the teens, as a young adult, as a mother and as a grandmother. The loss seemed even greater because of these many different relationships that we shared.

I went back to the days in Israel where my father would take me to soccer games and we sang *Hatikva*. It was in the early 1950s at the beginning of the establishment of the State of Israel. Life was adventurous and people were idealistic. I remember as a young child my father would say stand with your feet together, sing, and never talk when we sing *Hatikva*. It was a holy moment. I also remembered the many Sundays my father took my sisters and me ice-skating in Central Park, or to the opera, movies and shows. We could hardly afford tickets but sitting at the top row was not a shame for my father. It was important to him that we were cultured.

Saying Kaddish out loud was not only meaningful for me; I also knew that my father would have approved. He taught me Gemara, Chumash and Rashi when I was very young. He supported our Jewish education and encouraged my sisters and me to form a *zimmun* when my youngest sister became a bat mitzvah. In fact, he would have been proud of my commitment to say Kaddish, not so much for him as for my own growth in the process.

Until the age of twelve, I stood and prayed next to my father, who said every word out loud and often explained the prayers. My father taught me not only the words but who wrote them and the meaning behind them. He would wrap his *tallit* over both of us in a most protective way. Now, I imagine his *neshama* hovering over me when I am in *shul*.

Nonetheless, all is not well with women and the *shul* experience, even in Modern Orthodox synagogues. Routinely in one *shul*, for instance, men who came late thought it perfectly acceptable to walk into the women's section to pick up their *tallit*, reflecting a complete lack of respect and dignity for the women davening there. It is as if women are invisible. It also implies an unseemly unilateralism to the practice of *mechitza*, i.e., men need a *mechitza* to be "protected" from seeing women, but women aren't entitled to a consecrated, dignified prayer space of their own. In one particular *shul* where I prayed about once a month, I donated a *tzedakah* box to be placed in the women's section, so that I and other women could participate in the practice.

Fortunately, in my *shul*, women saying Kaddish is supported by both the rabbinical staff and the congregation. Hearing my own voice in *shul* was meaningful, when people responded by saying "Amen." I had a place to say something and others cared about my existence in that space; I made a communal difference. Two other women were saying Kaddish with me, and we formed a small community. They were my support with tissues in hand. We learned about each other's lost partners or parents and we mourned together.

And then, ready or not, we are asked to stop. Many questions arose for me at this time. How am I to behave? What will it feel like to go to a *simcha*? Will I forget my father?

After some thought and trying to make sense of the *neshama* making an *aliyah*, I concluded that whatever that *aliyah* is, it could only happen if I let go of the Kaddish, of the mourning. At my last Kaddish, I said another goodbye to my father, knowing that he would continue his journey to a better place and that I would keep his memory by repeating his jokes and retelling his Torah.

My father gave me the gift of appreciating prayer. The words my father taught me, their meaning, and the warmth under his *tallit* remain with me. Saying Kaddish added to my appreciation of praying with a *tzibbur*.

Yet it has been two months since I stopped saying Kaddish, and I can't seem to find a place in *shul* that gives me fulfillment. Prior to saying Kaddish, I was content to sit in the women's section. Now that my voice had a place, I feel a need to come closer to the ritual, and to continue to feel a full participant in communal prayer. I want acknowledgement that I count. I want the designated space for women in the synagogue to be as welcoming as the men's. I want women and men to use language of inclusion, and our rabbis to engage in a thoughtful halachic discussion regarding the importance of women's participation. The power of inclusion allowed me to find some peace while mourning. I am searching for that sense of inclusion and peace without the mourning.

————————

CHAYA GORSETMAN, Ed.D. is a Clinical Assistant Professor at Stern College for Women of Yeshiva University and coordinates the Early Childhood section of the Education Department. Her research has focused on mentoring which has more recently focused on mentoring educational leadership. She was the director and co-author of JOFA Gender and Orthodoxy *Bereshit* Curriculum. She has published several articles on gender in early childhood classroom and is currently researching gender in Jewish day schools. Chaya lives with her husband and son in Riverdale. She is grateful for the great joy of her children and grandchildren in Riverdale and Atlanta.

Kaddishes Lost and Found

JOYCE SOLOMON

SOME WOULD SAY that it takes a certain amount of determination, or even outright gumption, for a woman just to "show up" at an Orthodox *minyan*. Nonetheless, when my Father, *a"h*, was *niftar* in 1983, I was encouraged by Rabbi Reuven Bulka of Ottawa, Canada to say Kaddish for him. The *minyan*, made up mostly of older men, was welcoming. Perhaps I was like a daughter to them, and, at times they did fawn over me. Since I was pregnant with our first, their growing fondness equaled my increasing size. At a time when feelings of loneliness often pervade, I found warmth and a sense of belonging in a community.

On the day that I delivered, they all knew that "something was up" because I missed *Mincha/Maariv*. One member of that *minyan*, whose exterior self was usually coarse and crusty, actually came to visit me in the hospital. That day, I saw a side of him that I suspect few people were ever privileged to see.

From that point on, however, my opportunities to say Kaddish were quite diminished. How could I even think of going to *shul* when my daughter might need me in the interim? Giving final respect to my father conflicted with my sense of duty to my daughter. Did I dare even compare one need with the other? Yet there were times when I did. It was great when I could go to *shul* with her and say Kaddish, combining the two. But I sometimes felt cheated out of the opportunity to fulfill what I felt was also an obligation to my father. The exhaustion of caring for a new baby was ultimately the deciding factor.

When my Mother, *a"h*, was *niftara* in 2001, the experience was quite different. I had three older children now. With no babies to look after but a son to help "make the *minyan*," saying Kaddish became a focused event, three times a day. I would see images of my Mother, dressed in a familiar jacket and scarf, ready to travel. Indeed, this was her final journey, and I was comforted that I could, in some way, accompany her. At the end of *shloshim*, I also held a *siyum Mishnayot*. It was an unparalleled opportunity to share with those present, who were not at the funeral, who my Mother was.

One particularly unique time during this year was the day on which a different "*yahrzeit*" occurred. In 1985, I lost a daughter, whom I named Rachel, *a"h*, born unfortunately far too early. Her short life and death were unable to be marked with "typical" Jewish traditions of *shiva* and Kaddish because she did not live more than a few minutes. But because I was "already" saying Kaddish for my Mother I could, for the first and only time, also have her in mind on that day. Its poignancy remains with me forever.

JOYCE SOLOMON, BA, MA, is a Psychotherapist and Teacher of English as a Second Language who lives in Thornhill, Ontario, Canada. She also volunteers supporting breastfeeding mothers and working with seniors in her community. She enjoys photography, swimming, singing, writing poetry and prose, as well as playing Scrabble. She is grateful to Hashem and to the authors for the publishing of this essay. It is by far the most meaningful one she has ever written, and she hopes it will encourage other women to consider saying Kaddish for loved ones.

The Power of Women's Prayer

PAULA GANTZ

JUNE 15, 2010

"DOES ANYONE HAVE A *yahrzeit*?" Last night, while waiting for the *Mincha* service to begin, I was awakened from my reverie by this question, to which I automatically responded, "Yes." All the men started laughing, jokingly accusing me of being a rabble-rouser, which I suppose I am. Now recovered from my daze, I realized that the question was addressed to any man in the room who had an obligation to lead prayers, because of a relative's *yahrzeit*. Women don't and can't have this halachic obligation. Over the many years since my father's death, I have learned to be comfortable at many *minyan*s, and I'd like to think that most of the men feel comfortable with me there, as well.

MARCH 1986

During a call to my father before surgery for an aneurysm, I encourage him and wish him well. Towards the end of the conversation, he remarks: "And I have no one to say Kaddish for me if something happens." "I'll do it," I assure him.

He does not respond. I don't know if it is out of a disappointment that it should be me and not my brother who is completely non-observant, or if it is because he does not believe a woman saying Kaddish will count for him. He is in the middle of saying Kaddish for my mother's father. My mother, an only child, would never have been able to undertake such an obligation. In her day, women did not learn Hebrew or anything else of a religious nature.

My father's surgery is successful. I don't have to think about being his *"Kaddish macher"* (child who says Kaddish), as he sometimes called my brother.

JULY 9, 1986

In the middle of a departmental meeting, my secretary puts a call through: my father has just been rushed to the hospital. It does not look hopeful. His aorta has bifurcated and the only surgeons with the skill to perform such a repair are in Houston. My father is in Detroit.

JULY 17, 1986

My first hesitant Kaddish, at New York's Congregation Ramath Orah. Although not my regular davening spot, it is the closest and, therefore the most likely to ensure that I am actually able to attend daily. As I leave my husband with my four-year old son and 8-month old daughter, I tell him, "Watch, they'll never say a word to me." I learn very shortly that I am wrong; the environment is quite welcoming. Most of the men appear to be old-timers, but there is a smattering of Columbia University students. Although they never engage me in long discussions, they include me in rituals such as blessing the *lulav* and *etrog* (Sukkot palm and citron). I am almost always the only female, although one young woman does attend every Rosh Chodesh (first day of new month). I frequently miss saying the first two Kaddishes, sometimes because I am late, sometimes because the *minyan* is slow to assemble.

I learn the rhythms of daily davening, the cycle of prayer with a *minyan* throughout the year. Someone always says Kaddish with me. At the beginning, I stumble over words. It hurts to say them, but I also am not used to davening out loud. The pain is intense, but when I compare notes with my sister who is only saying Kaddish on Shabbat, I realize that unlike her, I do not have strange dreams about my father's actual death as she does. The time I spend reciting Kaddish seems to be my time to focus on his leaving this World.

NOVEMBER 1986

We have moved apartments and so I change to a *shul* closer to our new location: The Young Israel of the West Side. There is no *mechitza*, and I have to sit outside the *beit midrash* at the edge of a telephone booth. Nonetheless, I feel accepted, mostly. All but one of the *baalei tefillah* (prayer leaders) are comfortable saying Kaddish with me. A couple of the older men always make sure there is a chair for me and even greet me. I learn to bring my own *siddur* so I don't have to ask the men for one, especially if I arrive late. The rabbi never says a word as he passes me each morning. I take this as his tacit acceptance of my efforts. There are no other women davening during the week at this *shul*, but I am here to say Kaddish for my father, not to socialize. My focus is on my father and on my prayers for him, not on any political or ideological statements.

DECEMBER 1997

Eleven years later, my daughter Rachel's bat mitzvah takes place in a Women's Tefillah Group at the Jewish Center, where we now belong. Rachel *leyns* (chants) the entire *parsha*. She gives a beautiful *Dvar Torah* in the main sanctuary, and is self-confident and proud at the same time. She is so much more knowledgeable and comfortable with her spiritual side than I was at her age. In fact, I still have a ways to catch up to her. The effort to get her to this day was substantial. The Queens' *Vaad* (rabbinical authority) has recently ruled against women's *tefillah* services, and among other hurdles, we must borrow a Torah from another Orthodox synagogue rather than using one from our own.

3 TAMMUZ, EACH YEAR

Chicago, Madrid, Westhampton Beach, Manhattan, Jerusalem. I have always said Kaddish for my father on his *yahrzeit*. I bring the obligatory Entenmann's donut holes, a carton of orange juice and a bottle of schnapps, and I believe that my father's *neshama* does merit an *aliyah* from the prayers. At some point during the years, my son instructs me that if I am going to say Kaddish, I must say it loudly so that everyone can hear me. I do. There are a few more women joining me behind the *mechitza* in prayer in the mornings as the years go by. Very occasionally I help other women stumbling over the words of their own Kaddish. Rifka, a West African convert, is probably the most spiritual of them all. We should be encouraging women's spirituality so that everyone prays with the joy and intensity that she has.

Amazingly, no one has ever been even the least bit disturbed by my recitation of Kaddish, at least that I am aware. In fact, whenever I join a morning *minyan* in an unfamiliar place, the expectation is that I am there to say Kaddish. While this shows that Modern Orthodoxy has come a long way, it is also a disappointment. Do women only join the daily prayer community because of a parent's death? Where is the joyous spirituality of the female community?

MAY 2010 (ROSH CHODESH SIVAN)

As I stand at the back of the Kotel's women's plaza in the company of over a hundred women davening together, I realize how powerful women's prayer can be. Even having to hike around to Robinson's Arch to read from the Torah does not mar the spiritual nature of this experience. My new grandson's *brit milah* the prior day at the Shimon HaTzadik Synagogue in Katamon was no more powerful than this wonderful connection to Am Yisrael (the Jewish People) in Jerusalem's Old City.

JUNE 2010 (ROSH CHODESH TAMMUZ)

Our women's service is very inspiring, and held in Congregation Ramath Orah, where I first said Kaddish twenty-four years ago. For me, praying in a community of women creates a bond that elevates spirituality to a higher level than when men are present. My own spiritual development since that first Kaddish in 1986 is considerable. Many men find their spiritual core through saying Kaddish following the death of a parent. In the end, my journey may not have been that different.

PAULA GANTZ is a publishing consultant who specializes in scientific and medical publishing. She is a member of the Congregation Ramath Orah Women's Tefillah Group in New York City and the mother of four children. Paula has a BS degree from Cornell University and an MBA from The Wharton School.

God is Good

BARBARA BECKER

M̲y̲ ̲m̲o̲t̲h̲e̲r̲, Carol Mae Line, *z"l*, was my model for motherhood. I find myself saying things exactly the way she said them to me – little phrases like, "Don't sweat the small stuff" and "If this is the worst disappointment in life, you're lucky." She was young and vibrant and had just taken two of my children on the trip of their lives to Hawaii. It was inconceivable that she was gone. Friends told me that the depth of my grief was directly related to how close we were.

At the beginning when the pain was great, *tefillah* became a time that I could set aside to "be" with her and grieve her loss. Kaddish at that point was about me, not my mother. But as my daily trek to *minyan* continued, my focus started to change – now it became more about doing what I should do for my mother's *neshama*. Five weeks after my mother died, we celebrated my youngest son becoming a bar mitzvah. Saying Kaddish then kept her close and almost part of the celebration. I was reminded constantly of the mixing of joy and sorrow.

Saying Kaddish became a part of my being. I was incomplete each day if I didn't say it. At this point in my life, I had the flexibility to take on the daily commitment. My children were teenagers and could fend for themselves in the mornings, and I was working part-time. I began to look forward to my private audience with God each day as it became less about my mother's loss and more about my honoring her memory. I believe she would have understood my need to do this and would have welcomed being remembered each and every day. She had a very firm belief in the Almighty and would have seen the strength of my prayers as inspirational. The summer after she passed away, I spent time at her home in northern

Michigan with no daily *minyan* nearby, so I used this time to learn from some of the Judaic books in her library in lieu of saying Kaddish. I made a special point to rise early when the house was quiet to daven and study. My mother was always an early riser, so I felt that she was studying with me in those quiet hours in the mornings.

Attending daily *minyan*, I gained a new understanding and appreciation for the liturgy. One *brachah* in the *Amidah* praises God for maintaining the natural cycle of crops and rain in their seasons. Because my mother and I shared a passion for gardening, uttering this request for a fruitful growing season helped me bond with her. At the same time, when the pain was great, other prayers were difficult to say. I was almost too angry at first to mutter the prayer in the *Amidah* extolling God's ability to heal the sick. Eventually, I came around and saw that *my* healing was the healing for which I needed to praise. Likewise, I had a visceral reaction to the *Hashkivenu* prayer in the evening service, when I spoke the words "*U'fros aleinu sukkat shlomecha*, and spread over us a shelter of your peace." With my mother gone, where was my shelter? Where was my guidance? Of course this prayer refers to God, and with time I remembered that. It was God who worked with me all through the year, to help me use the liturgy for healing.

The regular *minyan* men at my synagogue were supportive of my participation from the start. They worked hard to make sure there were always ten, and apologized if we fell short. On my mother's first *yahrzeit*, I spoke about the journey that is the year of *aveilut* and thanked the men of the *minyan* for being my partners on that journey. Our rabbi occasionally calls upon me now to speak with other women, to share thoughts and help them decide if they want to take on this mitzvah. I am honored to be called upon in this way and I hope I can help others find a path through their grief.

One of my mother's favorite expressions was, "God is good." She said this after a tremendous experience like a trip to Israel or just after a very fulfilling day cross country skiing in the woods. She recognized God's hand in all the blessings in her life. Her connection with God inspired me to say Kaddish day after day. God is good for giving me the gift of Kaddish and the time to properly grieve and celebrate my mother's life.

BARBARA is married and has three children in varying stages of emerging adulthood. She has loved every minute of raising them and the increased involvement in Jewish learning that they have introduced to her and her husband. Her day job is as a Computer Literacy Facilitator for job seekers in a Hartford, CT job center. Working with this population carries on the tradition of giving to the wider community that she learned from her mother. She continues to feel enriched by the Kaddish year and to feel the peace that it brought her.

The One to Light the Candles

DINA ROEMER

I CHOSE TO BE MORE OBSERVANT as a teenager, and spent the next three decades of my life working to build a Jewish home and growing in my observances. However, *tefillah* and going to synagogue were somewhat left by the wayside as I was raising young children and building my career – working outside of the home more than full-time – let alone once we made *aliyah* in 1997 and I found myself in the grips of that daunting challenge to rebuild our lives. Nonetheless, I always knew I would say Kaddish for my parents.

My father, Mark Roemer, *z"l*, passed away in early July 2006. For days, weeks and months, I raced to make the initial Kaddish at our 6 a.m. *Shacharit minyan*. I scheduled work meetings around the 1:30 p.m. *Mincha minyan* at the offices of the Jewish Agency in Jerusalem, where I work. I got to know every synagogue in town and when the latest *Maariv minyanim* were, and ensured that I actually could say Kaddish either by bringing my husband or son along (to recite Kaddish with me) or by signaling my situation to someone in the *minyan*.

Although one of the less sentimental and superstitious people around, I found that as I said Kaddish I would feel a greater sense of my father's presence around me. Strangely, although he wasn't a Kohen, I frequently sensed my father "nearby" during the daily *Birchat Kohanim*, as if he were there blessing me at the same time.

For years, I have hovered on the "fringes" of feminism, keeping my own last name and pursuing higher education and a full-time career while raising a family. Yet my decision to say Kaddish was not motivated by a desire to make any type of "statement." In fact, I gained a greater appreciation of the hard work so many men put into going to *minyan* and davening three times a day. Nonetheless, I have been quick to realize that I am capable of doing that and more. I hope men can appreciate that there are those of us women who are managing to run religious households, work in serious careers and still go to *minyan*.

There are those people who, unfortunately, seem to feel upset by anything different, even when one explains to them the long history of women and minors saying Kaddish and the significant Rabbinic support for this practice. I have great appreciation for those men who aren't threatened by women who "encroach on their territory," but rather welcome and assist women who make the sincere effort to join the *minyan* and say Kaddish.

I have been shunned and admonished by women in Israel for saying Kaddish, and I have been drowned out by men who were afraid they might actually hear a woman's voice praising God. And then there are the men who believe saying Kaddish is a race against time. There were occasions on which I was compelled to raise my voice in order to bring the speed down. Worst of all, once the tenth man in a *Mincha minyan* – a personal acquaintance of mine – walked out just as Kaddish was starting, knowing I wouldn't be able to say Kaddish as a result. My internal struggle to be kind and understanding vs. feeling angry and resentful was a serious challenge, at times.

Since saying Kaddish, I have continued to get up early each morning to join our local *Shacharit minyan*. I also continue to say *Mincha* on a daily basis, and I generally make it to *shul* for every *minyan* on Shabbat and holidays – another gift my father has given me.

I find myself falling into the role my father took on in his later years – being the one in the family to keep track of the *yahrzeit*s, to light the candles and to say Kaddish for as many of our loved ones as I can trace back. I hope at least one of my children will decide they want to carry on this tradition, as well.

I have also learned that one must seek out happiness in life and truly celebrate the joyous events and occasions. Since being in *aveilut*, I have redoubled my efforts to attend weddings, bar and bat mitzvahs and other *smachot*. All of us are blessed with some happiness and success, often at the very same time that tragedies happen. We can't take the joys of life for granted while being devastated by our losses. Kaddish helped me appreciate that balance, and to reflect on the myriad happy memories I have of the loved ones I have lost.

DINA ROEMER was born in Brooklyn, NY and grew up on Long Island. She earned her BA from Stern College of Yeshiva University in 1977 where she majored in mathematics and holds two Master's degrees, one in social work from Yeshiva University and one in public administration from the City University of NY. She and her family made *aliyah* in 1997 from Cleveland, Ohio where they lived for fourteen years and where Dina worked at the Jewish Federation and served as campaign director for several years. After arriving in Israel, Dina spent nearly five years as director of operations for the Mandel Foundation-Israel and, since then, has worked at the Jewish Agency for Israel as a fund-raising executive based in Jerusalem. Dina and her husband, Dr. Shaya Wexler, live in Efrat and have four children (all of whom live in Israel) and three *sabra* grandchildren, one of whom is named for her beloved father.

עֹשֶׂה

שָׁלוֹם

בִּמְרוֹמָיו

הוּא

יַעֲשֶׂה

שָׁלוֹם

עָלֵינוּ

וְעַל כָּל

יִשְׂרָאֵל

Washing

batter bowl

inside, water-filled

instantly clean

rim, crusty

refused my hand

I put it back to

soak

So must it be

grief dissolves

with tears and time

A Child No Longer

BARBARA ASHKENAS

I N HIS BOOK, *Generation to Generation*, Rabbi Abraham Twerski asks the question: "How long is one a child?" His answer: "As long as one has a parent. An elderly parent may be thousands of miles away but as long as there is a parent, one can feel himself to be a child."

Fifteen years ago, my father died on a warm September day, about a week before the blowing of the *shofar* that would signal a new year. Like King David, he was 70. His reign as king of our home had come to a close, but his role as our home's spiritual leader and teacher would always be remembered.

Nearly ten years later, having suffered complications of a cerebral hemorrhage, my 57-year old brother died an untimely death. In May, 2007, I became the oldest child.

My mother died shortly after my brother, on the second of July. She was 80 years old and as her favorite crooner of the 1940s, Frank Sinatra, used to sing, she lived life "her way." Summer was her favorite season and everything was green and in full bloom that year. The Fourth of July was just around the corner and the 1812 Overture, cannonballs included, that she so fondly loved would play on without her. On that day I was no longer a child.

When I first whispered the words of Kaddish for my mother, as I would continue every day for the next eleven months, I realized I was no longer a daughter. I had lost a role. I was still a mother, wife, sister, and mother-in-law but through the loss of my mother, I had moved up a generational notch. Never again would I receive the unconditional love my Mom gave to me.

The decision to say Kaddish for my mother was partly a way of doing for her what she had done for all those she had loved. On all family *yahrzeits*, Mom would gather her friends to make a *minyan* at the Conservative *shul* in Akron. After saying Kaddish, she would then treat everyone to dinner and tenderly dust off and share the most heartfelt memories of those she loved. A year or so before she passed away, my Mom sent me, neatly handwritten, all the family *yahrzeit* dates. In her mind's eye, I was the *Kaddish'l* for the family, the one who would keep the memories.

But at the same time, my own memories of my mother were not all perfect. In fact, although we had a close emotional connection and unbreakable love, the reality is that for much of the previous thirty years, we had been at odds with each other. I was therefore faced with questions. How do you combine mourning with mixed memories? How do you combine responsibility to honor one's parents with honesty, sadness with optimism and hope? Perhaps through Kaddish I would find out.

During the eleven months I said Kaddish, the tri-color wheel of memory began to turn. Each day when I went to *shul* during those eleven precious months, I started to rediscover and come to terms with my mother. Our relationship was like a kaleidoscope, "a complex pattern of constantly changing colors and shapes," much like the beautiful stained glass windows in the chapel where I prayed. The different colors represented the real memories of my Mom and family, some light filled, and others opaque.

In his young adulthood, my father had rebelled against his own father's religious observance. By saying Kaddish for his father, my Dad returned to traditional Judaism. But my father's desire to weave tradition into our daily lives was not what my Mom had signed on for. As a result, the tension between her and my Dad was palpable; she pushed back against my father and what seemed to her to be his unbending ways. The seams of our family tapestry were unraveling, and a pattern of rebellion began.

Although I probably didn't realize it at the time, the struggle between my parents over religious observance was nothing short of guerilla warfare. My father would take us to *shul* on Shabbos morning, and then my mother would take us shopping in the afternoon. Dad insisted on a kosher home, while Mom took us out for ham sandwiches. Both agreed that being Jewish was important, but how that Judaism was expressed was a constant point of contention.

Ironically, being forced to attend a Catholic high school impacted my own decision to become more observant. Of course I was the only Jew and I hated it. However to reinforce my Jewish identity my father encouraged me, at the age of 16, to embark on the first youth group pilgrimage to Eastern Europe, with Israel our final destination.

Starting on July 2, 1969, our group's mission was to see our Soviet brethren and let them know they were not alone. We smuggled prayer books, *tallisim*, and *tefillin* past the KGB. While Neil Armstrong planted a flag on the moon's surface, we stepped onto the grey landscape of Russia and planted a garden of hope into the hearts of our Soviet and Eastern European brethren.

There are many types of journeys. Sometimes they are physical and public, and sometimes they are spiritual and private. Each can have an impact that stretches across generations. My trip that summer was both. In a bittersweet way, Mom felt that on the trip to Russia God had tapped me on the shoulder. Upon my return, I no longer wanted to be part of her fashionista ways or Emily Post world. Unlike our Russian brethren, we had religious freedom. The rules I wanted to follow were spiritual, and she couldn't understand them.

Later experiences in college and Israel further reinforced my commitment to a Modern Orthodox lifestyle. I wanted to raise a family that was wholly invested in the vibrant and colorful beauty of Jewish ritual. My life was going to be shades different than that of my mother.

Looking back, the spiritual transformation that was sparked by my trip to Russia on July 2, 1969 came full circle when I began to say Kaddish for my mother in 2007, also on July 2. There are no coincidences in the world of spirituality.

During the eleven months I fondly recalled the colors of Mom's life. I visualized her red, white and blue impatiens outside her home. Yellow roses gracing her elegantly set table along with navy linens and sparkling silver. I recalled the arrival of home made gefilte fish and kreplach, packed in dry ice, delivered by UPS in time for holidays. I remembered her love of roller coasters and the unique, affectionate relationships she nurtured with each of her seven grandchildren.

I also remembered my Mom's mid-life inclination to find her own spirituality. She became active in a small Reform Temple and became president! She invited guests into her home for Shabbat and holidays, visited the sick, and gave her time and compassionate ear to those who needed her wise counsel.

Yet it was in the last three months of her life that I saw a strength in my mother that I had never seen. Only a week after placing Mom in hospice, suffering from congestive heart failure and end-stage cancer, my brother had a car accident due to a cerebral hemorrhage. How could it be? My Mom in hospice. My brother, in the hospital ICU, hanging on to life by a thin mystical thread?

Six weeks later, upon hearing of my brother's death while sitting in her hospice chair, my mother was totally devastated. After a moment, she looked at me and said, I know . . . I have to be "big." As the matriarch of the family, she had to be strong and give everyone else strength. Wheelchair bound, with a miniature trowel, my mother tossed the requisite earth onto her only son's grave with grace, dignity and an abundance of strength. Six weeks later, she passed on to the next world.

Saying Kaddish enabled me to think about the more positive aspects of our relationship and to process my feelings, so that I could stop dwelling on what she was not, and finally accept and love my mother as she was. Though I grew up *not* sitting next to her in *shul*, while saying Kaddish she was by my side every day. We were finally on the "same page."

For me, to say Kaddish was to twirl the kaleidoscope and twist the tri-colored wheel of memory, to pick up long-forgotten strands and weave them back into the fabric of my life. Through the Kaddish, for the first time in my adult life, I saw my mother's reflection in my mirror. And it continues. I am no longer a daughter, but I am now a Bubbe! As I grow into this new role, I can blend the colors of my father's spirituality with the many shades and tints of the wisdom of my mother.

At the last line of Kaddish each day, I took three steps backward, chanting my Mom's favorite verse "*oseh sholom bim'romov.*" I bowed to the right and then to the left and then forward as I finished the prayer. Suddenly one day, I realized that is exactly what I have to do in life. First step back and remember the past. Second bow to Hashem and His infinite wisdom in giving me the exact tests that I needed to grow and develop. Finally, step forward into the future, and fulfill my purpose with love, passion and an open heart.

BARBARA ASHKENAS conceived the idea for *Kaddish, Women's Voices*.

Who Else?

JUDITH SCHWIMMER HESSING

I FELT LOST. I was standing in the vestibule of the office building at the cemetery, squeezed in with the other women to daven *Mincha* after burying my mother. I could not hear what the men were saying. I felt confused, harried, and all of a sudden they were saying Kaddish. I could not find the Kaddish. I had been going to *shul* for most of my life, and yet I did not know what I was doing. *Mincha* was over and I missed the first Kaddish.

After this experience, I gathered myself together, and got back into the car for the ride home, to the place that my mother infused with her personality for 47 years. Food was synonymous with love for my mother. No matter what my age, whenever I returned home, I felt like a child again, looking forward to my favorite meals, and to those baked goods that were my mother's specialty. Now, it occurred to me that I would never enter this house again and be met with the aromas of my childhood. My feelings of loss were overpowering.

For reasons I don't fully understand, my father refused to have a *shiva minyan* at the house. So twice a day, my father, sister and I trudged several blocks to my father's *shul*. There was no *mechitza*, so my sister and I stood outside the room, the door frequently opening as the men continued to stream in, and the cold air rushing in. We strained to hear the *shaliach tzibbur*. We were trying to pray and, at the same time, trying to listen, so we would not miss the Kaddish. I cannot say why neither of us thought to ask about putting a *mechitza* inside the sanctuary. Was it because we were so wrapped up in our grief? Or perhaps the idea that, as women, we were intruders and simply did not belong had become so ingrained in our minds that we passively accepted the situation. The men, for the most part, walked right by us, and not infrequently stood close by chatting with one another, with no awareness that their talking was disturbing us. We were invisible to them.

During those initial days of saying Kaddish, I felt very little that was positive about the experience other than the support my sister and I gave each other. In the two weeks prior to our mother's death, we had found ourselves once again sharing our childhood bedroom, where as children, we had argued incessantly about space. This was a very close time for us, as we would reminisce, cook together, and share stories about our families. All the while, quite aware that any day our mother would be leaving us.

A man is obligated to say Kaddish for his parents, and if there is no son, then some other man is designated to recite it. But I could not grasp the idea that someone else would be saying Kaddish for my mother. Who else could say Kaddish for the woman who gave birth to me? The woman who forced me to take cod liver oil, and gave her portion of meat to me because there was a shortage of food in Israel?

It seems to me that while one of the purposes of saying Kaddish is to honor the memory of the deceased, another serves to provide the living with an opportunity for consolation. How can someone without a direct emotional connection to the deceased perpetuate their memory or truly appreciate the experience? It was understood that my sister and I were both going to recite Kaddish for my mother over the next eleven months.

The weekday *minyan* at the Young Israel of West Hartford is held in one large basement room. There is no permanent *mechitza*, but rather, two accordion type partitions (initially purchased to designate a children's play area) are used to designate the women's section. When seated, I could not see through them. I was asked, on occasion, whether I felt insulted by the set up. In truth, I appreciated this secluded space that had been created especially for me. I wanted to be by myself, to turn inwards, and to be able to cry. I found myself reviewing images in my head, as if going through an old album. I could see my mother standing in front of the bathroom mirror, putting on her makeup to go to a wedding or bar mitzvah, and then when she was dressed and ready to go, my father would kiss her on the cheek and tell her how beautiful and young she looked. I was comforted to have a place where I could get in touch with my feelings, and think about my mother without interruption.

Taking care of her family was my mother's function, her very purpose and reason to live. I called her one Friday morning to say that I had started labor with our third child. My mother, without discussing it with anyone, decided that she was coming that very day. To make arrangements to fly out to Columbus, Ohio and to get herself to the airport, all within a few hours, may not sound like much nowadays, but it was a huge endeavor for my mother. There were no cell phones in those days. So, she left my father a note on the kitchen table telling him that the Shabbat meals she had prepared were in the refrigerator, and arrived before sundown. Each baby was welcomed with overflowing love, and held so tenderly, as if that child was the most precious possession in the world.

My mother was not an educated woman, but she was extremely intelligent and insightful. She maintained her faith in God even though she had experienced the horrors of the Shoah. What was most amazing about her was this inner strength and stubbornness that kept her going through the difficult times. The last time she saw her own mother as a teenager in Budapest, she promised her that she would always keep Shabbat and a kosher home, and she had always remained faithful to that promise.

And I remained faithful to Kaddish. Over time, the men accepted that the little corner in the back on the left was for women. No longer was there a question whether or not there should be a *mechitza* set up. When other individuals lost their parents, however, the *shiva minyan* was held in their homes. On occasion, it was a struggle to find even a little bit of space that did not intrude upon the men. I had to recognize, however, that I had every right to participate.

The prayers helped me get through the difficult days. The phrase "*Ha-Mechadesh b'tuvoh b'chol yom tamid ma'aseh bereishit,*" translated as "God perpetually renews the work of creation," filled me with hope. If God creates the world anew each day, then what an incredible opportunity exists for me to start fresh every day, and to create something magnificent for myself.

In the *Amidah*, there is a verse in which we thank God "*al nisecha sheb'chol yom imanu,* for Your miracles which are with us every day." So I started thinking of the miracles in my life, which is not an easy task for someone who tends to perceive the world negatively. On the way to *shul* each morning, I conversed with God, thanking Him for what went well the previous day. The more I did this, the more I found to be thankful for in my life.

When I had looked ahead, eleven months had seemed an interminable length of time. However, when my recitation of Kaddish was drawing to a close, I was surprised by my ambivalence. Kaddish felt like a worn-out, very comfortable sweater. The year began with a painful loss, but over time, there was healing, sharing, and growth.

Daily *minyan* was not something that I wanted to give up, even though it was no longer expected of me. I liked starting my day by speaking with God, and I liked being in *shul*. It framed the day differently for me, and I felt a connection there. I also found that other women, new to saying Kaddish, greatly appreciated my support and guidance. It seemed that having another woman in attendance was reassuring, and provided a camaraderie that is perhaps taken for granted by men. And there were instances, such as hearing the *shofar* blowing every day during the month of Elul, that I would miss. With some support, I gave myself permission to do what felt right for me at this point in my life.

It has been over two years since my mother passed away, and I have been going to *shul* regularly. Now two of us, and sometimes, three sit together in the back of the basement, in our little section on the left. And when I do not show up for one or two days, I get a phone call asking if all is okay. And it feels right.

JUDITH HESSING is married with four grown children and three grandchildren. She lives in West Hartford, CT with her husband. Recently, she has worked with the mentally ill as a clinical social worker. She has been an active member of the Young Israel of West Hartford and is most grateful for the support and encouragement of the synagogue community.

In Those Two Minutes

SUZANNE WOLF

M Y FATHER PASSED AWAY peacefully at home, in Melbourne, Australia, after a long illness. We were not particularly observant, yet even in the days before our father's death my sister, Evy, and I had taken comfort in Jewish customs and rituals in relation to death and dying. A rabbi had come that morning to perform the last rites and soon after he left, my father had lapsed into a coma. My sister and I both stayed at his bedside continuously after that. At about 8:00 that evening, two of my closest friends, who would have been at Israeli dancing with me in happier times, decided that they would instead come to spend some time with me at my parents' home. Evy called me away from my Dad's bedside to join them. She stayed a couple of moments to chat and then went into the bedroom. Dad had died. In those two minutes when neither of us was there with him, he was able to leave us.

One feels so helpless in the face of death, one looks for meaning, purpose and hope in different aspects of things. When our father died, taking on the role of saying Kaddish gave my sister and me a sense of purpose. Although it is not the practice for women to say Kaddish (usually a religious man is paid to do so), almost without discussion, we knew we would both say it.

The rabbi who conducted the funeral was a very quiet, gentle man, retired and well in his 70s. My husband let him know that my sister and I would be saying Kaddish. The rabbi was confused and uncomfortable. He had never heard of such a thing. It was not customary. Why did we want to do this? Eventually, he asked whether my husband could say it, too, and more loudly than us so we would not be heard.

The funeral was painful and sad and much of it is a blur to me, but it did feel good to have this role to perform, to know we were doing something important for our father. Although I can't be sure that my father, with his traditional background, would have been comfortable with this.

At one crowded *shiva minyan*, one of my friends overhead an elderly man ask his friend who was saying Kaddish. When told it was the daughters, he remarked in a surprised tone, in Yiddish: "They can say it better than most men!" I thought at least our father could feel proud that he had performed his duty – his daughters could read Hebrew (actually Aramaic) well enough.

As a feminist and a Jew, I have given considerable thought to the place of women in Judaism and have felt passionately angry about what I have seen as our exclusion and marginalization from many practices, as well as the obvious discrimination in areas such as divorce. In the 1980s, my activism created some opposition within the practicing community. Orthodox women I came into contact with were anxious to assure me how "equal but different" they were, and how happy they were with their status. As I was not Orthodox or observant, I felt it wasn't my right to fight for women who didn't want to change.

Nevertheless, my sister and I both felt we wanted to be observant at this time and not break Shabbat. Saying Kaddish was a spiritual act. The only *shul* close enough to walk to on Shabbat was the newly opened Chabad House in Malvern (the English word "synagogue" sounds so alien and cold). A friend's father who was at *shul* that day told me that he hoped his three daughters would do the same for him. I later passed on the message. To our pleasant surprise, Rabbi Shimshon Yurkevitch was very welcoming, and came to talk to us at the end of the service. He was intrigued by our choice, but said there was no law against a woman saying Kaddish, merely custom. He offered to look up some texts and have further discussion with us. So began our unexpected association with Chabad.

Rabbi Yurkevitch taught us that when a Jewish soul first goes to Heaven it is very far from God. In various different ways, the soul can eventually be elevated, particularly by any spiritual act performed in the name of the departed person. Saying Kaddish and giving charity are the most usual ways of honoring the soul. Finding out about the important purpose of Kaddish made it much more meaningful for us. We also accepted the rabbi's suggestion of forming a study group in his name, and ten of us came together with the rabbi on six successive Sunday evenings at our home to hear and discuss spiritual ideas that were not familiar to us.

Each weekday morning, we went to the second Caulfield Shul *minyan* in Melbourne. The "regulars" consisted mainly of elderly men, who did not know what to make of this new situation. At first they totally ignored us – no one addressed us, they didn't turn on the lights in the Ladies' Gallery upstairs and we sat in semi-darkness, and they didn't wait for us to finish our recital before continuing (we had difficulty finding the place and often didn't start 'til a few seconds after the other mourners). After about a week the rabbi's son (also a rabbi) came to the upstairs door and called to us. We had left the car headlights on. He took the opportunity to tell us that despite the attitude of the congregants, we were welcome there and that he admired what we were doing. This was extremely heartening and soon after there was a big change in their attitude, as if permission had been granted to acknowledge us. The lights were turned on and a great interest was shown in who we were and what we were doing. Some of the men had known our father and spoke warmly of him, some discovered that their children knew us. The grandfather of one of my nephew's classmates began to signal when it was time to say the Kaddish. Two old men, however, who always sat apart from the others, continued to ignore us and to speak loudly during our recital. Finally my sister told them how offended she was by the disrespect they showed our father. They said they hadn't meant disrespect, but were angry about what we were doing and therefore didn't want to listen. We didn't get into a debate or resolve the issue, but they didn't speak over us again.

My sister and I had never been to a *Shacharit* morning service before and found it a beautiful experience. It is a very quiet, meditative service, providing a peaceful opportunity for reflection. This service feels more spiritual for me than the more crowded Shabbat and Holiday services, which I have attended but never really participated in. Being upstairs without any specific role makes it difficult to feel included. Saying Kaddish made it different. My sister and I also felt closer to one another than ever sharing this experience.

Now on the morning of each *yahrzeit*, Evy and I engage in the same ritual we have followed for twenty-two years. First, we go to the morning service to say Kaddish for our father's soul. Now when we come to *shul*, the small remainder of this familiar group of men gathers around. I'm sure they secretly congratulate themselves on still being there, despite being well into their 90s. We then take our mother out for breakfast and together remember our father. Saying Kaddish remains very important to us, as it provides a significant and ritualized way of marking the anniversary each year. We've been fortunate in being able to access rituals that brought us closer to our Jewish heritage.

———

SUZANNE WOLF has lived in Australia all her life, her parents having escaped Vienna after the Nazi invasion, not without their trials. The Holocaust has, in many ways, informed her Judaism and her way of life. She has a beautiful supportive family – her husband Johnny of 42 years, her daughter Gaby, her son Josh and her grandchildren Leo and Saskia; and of course her sister Evy who says Kaddish together with her every year. She is a Counseling Psychologist in private practice and a committed feminist. It was her Jewish feminist readings in the 1980s that encouraged her to say Kaddish when her father died in 1990.

Ten Plus One, Two, Three . . .

CHANA REIFMAN ZWEITER

I AM SAYING KADDISH for the second year in a row. Just three months separated my last Kaddish for my mother and my first Kaddish for my father. My mother always said, "We will live together and we will go together," and she was right. We played tug of war for a year: We pulled my father one way and she pulled him the other. She won.

My father passed away at 2:30 p.m. on a Friday afternoon, and we sent him Home at 6 p.m., only an hour before Shabbat. We could only do that here in Israel. I came back to *shul* Friday evening, soon after I returned my father to her and to Him. I stood up at the end of *Mincha* as I had done so many times not so long before, and once again, in the same spot, I started a new cycle. My voice quivered the way it did the first time I said Kaddish for my mother. But unlike the first time, I said it loud and clear. The men looked up and the women looked from side to side. "But she finished saying Kaddish. It's too soon for another *yahrzeit*." And then, those who knew how ill my father was understood. When Rav Benny Lau walked me back into *shul* as they said "*HaMakom yinachem etchem*, God should comfort," the words that are said to the mourner during Friday night services, I couldn't believe that this was happening to me, that I had lost both of my parents so quickly. I felt alone. Yet, I was enveloped by those who had enveloped me for so long not so long before. I felt my solitude and community joining forces. Like Kaddish – a personal reflection that must be said in the presence of community. This time, I had the advantage of knowing the importance of that joining.

I have been asked, "Is there a difference in the Kaddish experience now than before?" "Doesn't it get repetitive?" The Mishna in Tractate *Brachot* deals with the challenge that we face when we repeat the same words over and over again in our *tefillah*, day after day. The Mishna says that a person should renew her prayer and should add something – a thought? a feeling? – to it in different ways. In his reflections, Rav Kook, the first Chief Rabbi of Israel, suggests that to find meaning in *tefillah* we need to relate it to our day-to-day lives. This is the way my Kaddish experience has been. I go to *shul* three times a day. I say Kaddish a minimum of seven times a day. Yet I am not robotic. I work on finding meaning in each Kaddish (well, maybe not *each*). And then the Kaddish speaks to me in different ways. And its meaningfulness transcends that moment and becomes part of me.

For instance, three weeks ago on Friday night, as we sang "*Lecha dodi likrat kalla, p'nei Shabbat nikabela* – Go my beloved to your bride, We will welcome the Shabbat," I began to cry. I saw us giving my father back to his bride, my mother, just an hour before we all entered Shabbat. The *tefillah* spoke to me in a personal way. And now I speak to that *tefillah* in a personal way. *Kabbalat Shabbat* has a new meaning for me. The *tefillah* has become connected to my life, and I have become connected to my *tefillah*.

Recently, when I said Kaddish, I understood as I never have before the essence of "letting go" and not being in control. And maybe for the first time in my life, I welcomed that lack of control. "I am angry at God." "Why me?" "I don't understand it." "I should have . . ." These are phrases that I have heard myself and others say. That day when I said the words of Kaddish, *Yitgadal v'yitkadash*, I realized in a new way – cognitively, viscerally and spiritually – that there is a power much greater than me. This realization brought me much comfort. About not understanding where my parents are and what is going on. About not understanding how and why this could happen. *Yitgadal v'yitkadash*, God is great and God is Holy – I began to let go of the need to understand. It was not an epiphany. It was an internalization that resulted from repeating and reflecting.

I don't have any stories to tell about how my saying Kaddish was rejected or how I was made to feel secondary. Not that it was self-understood. Not that it was always simple. I inherited a situation of it not being typical for women to say Kaddish. I knew that. But I did what I knew was correct and have been a player in our community's change. People ask me if I asked the rabbi before I began to say Kaddish. It never dawned on me to ask. When I came that first morning after my mother's *shiva* I stood alone in the women's section and started to say Kaddish. I still could not pronounce the words. I still could not hear myself. The gentleman leading the prayers kept going until Rav Benny put his hand on his shoulder and swiveled him around to see me. From then on, Yosef would turn around and nod before he started Kaddish. And Chaim who had lost a child would look and we would nod to one another as if to say, "Ready." It is all about awareness and community.

My father had been so proud that I said Kaddish for my mother. He understood that by saying Kaddish, I was giving the utmost of respect to my mother. It is now about giving respect to him. I have a saying that I use often: "Anger nurtures anger. Calm nurtures calm." Over the years I have added, "Respect nurtures respect." I know that certain men changed the way they feel about women saying Kaddish, because what they have seen and heard is respect. Respect for my parents and respect for others.

I believe that I can say Kaddish without the accompaniment of a man. And I have in my *shul*. But others do not. I do not feel secondary when someone joins in. I want others to feel comfortable just as I want to feel comfortable; it is *our shul*. The halachic understanding that I can say Kaddish alone must be joined with the halachic imperative to respect. That is the Judaism I choose to practice.

People say that I can only think and live as I do because of the nature of my *shul*. And I answer that I did not land here, I chose to be here. During *aveilut*, I davened wherever I had to, but for the most part, I chose where to say my Kaddish where I knew I would find support. And we have brought success.

When I first started saying Kaddish for my mother almost two years ago, I was *the* woman saying Kaddish. Come to *shul* now for *Mincha* on any given day and there are several women saying Kaddish. We are now ten plus three, four, five . . .

I believe that success in one place is a catalyst for success in other places, as well. And I very humbly share this as the founder of the international Yachad program, which fosters inclusion of individuals with special needs. We chose the community for our first Yachad Shabbaton (the Young Israel of West Hempstead, NY) because we "knew" we would succeed. And success brought success. Change fostered change.

I have just completed the eleven months of Kaddish for my father. The challenge is now mine to create a new structure that will enable me to grow and to respect my parents in a proactive way. I believe that this is what *olam haba*, the after-life, is all about. I no longer dwell on what goes on with them up above. I think about what goes on with them here below.

CHANA REIFMAN ZWEITER is Founding Director of Kaleidoscope and its mother organization, The Rosh Pina Mainstreaming Network: an Israeli-based organization dedicated to promoting caring learning environments and the social and emotional competencies that they are made up of. Before making *aliyah* in 1991 to Jerusalem, Chana founded and directed the Yachad program, integrating children and youth with special needs into the American Jewish community. She has earned a BA from Yeshiva University and an MA from New York University.

Eleven
months since
anyone was born or died
I carry the number
around in my hands
like something fragile and precious
breathe into my body
growing safety

To wake in the morning
not with a heart
pounding with anxiety
nor unwilling eyes
too exhausted to see day
only a lazy desire to linger
in the comfort of sheets while
children giggle
This is joy

I go down to breakfast
browse over the news
drop kids at school
go about errands that
keep us clothed and fed
pausing briefly
to offer a song
of thanksgiving
in praise of ordinary days

Women and Kaddish: The Halachah

MARK DRATCH

The question of women reciting of the Mourners' Kaddish has a long history and much ink has been spilled both in favor of and in opposition. Contemporary Orthodox communities have established varying policies that encourage, accommodate or restrict its recital. Many contemporary authorities not only find support for this practice, but actively support it on religious and moral grounds. This chapter will discuss the highlights of the debate and show the substantial and authoritative sources which support the recitation of Mourners' Kaddish by women who wish to do so.

Originally, Kaddish was recited by the prayer leader in order to conclude various sections of the service, as a recitation following the learning of *aggadeta,* and following burial. The recitation of Kaddish on behalf of the deceased is found in early rabbinic sources, the earliest being *Masekhet Sofrim* 19:12 (c. eighth century c.e.). The primary literary source to which authorities trace this practice speaks of a dead man's request that his son be taught by Rabbi Akiva to lead the prayers and recite the Kaddish; acts that would be meritorious for the father's soul and that would consequently release him from eternal punishment. Over time, the practice of mourners reciting *Kaddish Yatom* (literally, orphan's Kaddish) evolved to accommodate those who could not lead the prayers because they did not possess the fluency to do so. The influential halachic compendium *Or Zarua,* written by R. Yitzchak ben R. Moshe of Vienna (1180–1250), a student of the Tosafists in Ashkenaz and teacher of Maharam of Rothenburg, noted that it was customary in the Rhineland and in Canaan for orphans to recite Kaddish following the *Ein Ke-Eloheinu* prayer. Since that time, it has become a vehicle for children to fulfill their obligation of *kibbud av va'em*, honoring parents after their deaths, and, as attested to by many, a form of comfort to the mourners themselves.

Initially, only one mourner at a time would recite Kaddish and a system was developed to divide the opportunities for recitation among various mourners. In more recent times, so as to prevent conflict, Kaddish is recited by all mourners in unison. As *Kaddish Yatom* is not an essential part of the liturgy, most authorities, even those who restrict women from reciting Kaddish, do not consider a women's traditional disqualification from leading public prayer to be an issue.

The earliest record of a woman's desire to recite *Kaddish Yatom* is found in the seventeenth century responsa of Rabbi Ya'ir Hayyim Bachrach (*Teshuvot Havot Ya'ir*, no. 222). In his responsum, Rabbi Bachrach presents arguments both for and against the daughter's recitation, thus setting the stage for halachic debate that continues until today.

Rabbi Bachrach, reacting to a father's request that his only child, a daughter, recite the Kaddish on his behalf responded that, in theory, it should be an efficacious way to bring comfort to the soul. After all, a daughter, like the son in the Rabbi Akiva account, is also a child, and a woman is also included in the general obligation of *Kiddush Hashem* (sanctification of God's Name), the general obligation of which the recitation of the *Kaddish Yatom* is an expression. However, the daughter was requested to recite Kaddish for her father every day in the presence of a *minyan* convened especially for this purpose, in her home. Rabbi Bachrach therefore opposes the practice as a breach of longstanding Jewish custom that will lead to a weakening of respect for Jewish practice.

Nonetheless, several early rabbinic writings make it evident that women did, in fact, recite the *Kaddish Yatom* in a number of Jewish communities, and in a variety of ways. For instance, Rabbi Yaakov Reicher, author of Responsa *Shevut Ya'akov* (Germany, 1670–1733) took for granted that daughters may recite the Kaddish in the presence of a *minyan* in the privacy of a home. Rabbi Elazar Feckeles (Prague, 1754–1826) in his *Teshuvah me-Ahavah* permitted daughters of five or six years of age to recite the Kaddish in gathering places specially designated for informal prayers, the *kloize* in which the elderly and infirm spent their days reciting Psalms, but not in a formal synagogue used for prayer.

Permissive authorities include Rabbi Yosef Henkin (Russia, New York, 1881–1973) who rules that daughters may recite Kaddish in the women's section of a synagogue when the men are reciting it in the men's section. He records having seen this done during his youth. He feels that the community should not impose the same prerequisites on one reciting Kaddish as it expects from one serving as prayer leader. As a matter of public policy, he argues that Kaddish has served as an impetus for teaching children how to read Hebrew and pray and a catalyst for increased Jewish observance; no less should be done for women. Responding to those who cite concerns of breaches of modesty should women recite Kaddish publicly, Rabbi Yehudah Herzl Henkin argues that in communities in which more than one person recites Kaddish in unison, modesty is not an issue. Others suggest that since women's public presence and engagement is much more ubiquitous than it was generations ago, public recitation of Kaddish by a woman is not immodest and does not illicit improper thoughts by the men in the community. In fact, Rabbi Joseph Soloveitchik is reported to have permitted a woman to recite Kaddish in a synagogue by herself. In his book, *Women, Jewish Law and Modernity*, Rabbi Joel Wolowelsky records a conversation he had with Rabbi Ezra Bick concerning Rabbi Joseph Soloveitchik's position of this matter. He quotes Rabbi Bick:

> I spoke to the Rav about the question you asked concerning a girl saying Kaddish. He told me that he remembered being in Vilna in the "Gaon's Kloiz" – which wasn't one of your Modern Orthodox *shuls* – and a woman came into the back (there was no *ezrat nashim* [ladies section]) and said Kaddish after *Maariv*. I asked him whether it would make a difference if someone was saying Kaddish along with her or not, and he replied that he could see no objections in either case – it's perfectly alright. Coincidentally, checking around, I came across a number of people who remember such incidents from Europe, including my father (in my grandfather's *minyan* – he was the *rav* in the town).

Another argument made on behalf of women saying Kaddish in Orthodox *shuls* comes from Rabbi Aaron Soloveitchik. He writes:

> Nowadays, when there are Jews fighting for equality for men and women in matters such as *aliyot*, if Orthodox rabbis prevent women from saying Kaddish when there is a possibility for allowing it, it

will strengthen the influence of Reform and Conservative rabbis. It is therefore forbidden to prevent daughters from saying Kaddish.

Rabbis who oppose the practice do so on a variety of grounds. Some cite concerns such as *kevod ha-tzibbur* (the dignity of the community), the prohibition of *kol be-isha ervah* (the licentious nature of women's singing voices), the prohibition of *hirhur aveirah* (illicit thoughts), the prohibition to derive benefit from the service of women, and the possibility of mistakenly counting women as part of the *minyan*.

Chief Sephardic Rabbi Ben Zion Uziel ruled that we are not permitted to deviate from the parameters of the original rabbinic enactment that instituted the recitation of Kaddish by sons only; "one should not innovate the practice of the recitation of Kaddish by daughters." The restriction is not because daughters cannot bring merit to their parents' souls, he explained; it is just that Kaddish is not the vehicle by which they can achieve this goal.

Considering the permissibility and desirability of allowing, accommodating, or encouraging women to recite Kaddish in our synagogues is not only a halachic decision, but requires meta-halachic and community policy considerations, as well. There are those who object to any innovation or expansion of ritual and religious practice, arguing for the preservation of the *mesorah* (Jewish tradition). They adopt that position of Hatam Sofer who decreed "*hadash asur min ha-Torah*, new is forbidden by the Torah," and argue for increased stringencies in Jewish practice in light of the perceived challenges posed by changing sociology, technologies, and opportunities to morality and the continuity of Jewish practice. They are also suspicious and dismissive of any innovation that may be motivated or influenced by, or even gives the appearance of support to feminist ideology since the 1960s. Many rabbinic authorities dealt dismissively with anything that hinted of feminism or Women's Liberation, defining it as a heretical movement which denies God, Revelation, and the halachic system. Their arguments and depictions are the framework in which many contemporary Orthodox rabbis still view many initiatives that impact on creating greater opportunities for women within Orthodox life and the Orthodox community. Even if technically within the framework of halachic possibility, and regardless of the motives and loyalties of the women who express such desires, proposals for increased participation of women are often dismissed as insincere, heterodox, deviant, and out to undermine Torah.

I feel that such perceptions are most often undeserved and unfair and do not accurately reflect the feelings and motivations of most women in the Orthodox community. They and their mothers and daughters have benefited from many of the achievements of the feminist movement, even if they deny that they are feminists. And their motivations are most often rooted in longings of *devekut* (spiritual yearning), *ahavat Hashem* (love of God), *ahavat Torah* (love of Torah), and *yirat Shamayim* (reverence). Perhaps the legacy of feminism has enabled these pious women to see the possibilities of new opportunities and to advocate for them, but their motivation is to increase Torah observance, not to chip away at it. Such motivation has led, to cite just one example, to increased opportunities for Torah study, sometimes on the most advanced of levels, for women. Despite possible halachic concerns in this area, the benefits that accrued to these women as individuals, as well as to their families and communities, have proven the innovations to be meaningful and worthwhile. Even in Temple times, accommodations were made for women to participate in certain aspects of the Temple ritual despite serious legal objections "in order to bring spiritual pleasure and benefit" (*Hagigah* 16b). Just read the essays that make up this book in order to get an inkling of the various and sincere spiritual, personal, and halachic motivations of some of the women in our community.

In addition, *Kaddish Yatom* is an expression of honoring parents, an obligation shared equally in most respects by women and men. *Kaddish Yatom* is also an expression of honoring God, an obligation shared equally in most respects by women and men. And from personal anecdotes by children of both genders, the recitation of Kaddish is a great cathartic mechanism for the bereaved to find comfort, healing, a sense of community, and spiritual support during the most vulnerable, alienating times of their lives. Why should women be deprived of this important tool? To those who say that innovation in ritual is dangerous to the future of Torah, I say that the lack of innovation and accommodation when it is halachically valid is even more dangerous.

Moreover, what we are advocating today is not really an innovation. There is precedent for women saying Kaddish from previous generations. There are great halachic authorities who permitted it. And many Orthodox synagogues today have created opportunities and space for women to recite it.

We have the opportunity in this book to appreciate the impact that these opportunities have had on individuals, their families, and their communities. We have the challenge, through this book, to become even more supportive, sensitive, and helpful by encouraging those women who desire to recite Kaddish to be able to do so and by creating spaces and opportunities for them that are more welcoming and sympathetic. The recitation of Kaddish is, by definition, an act of *Kiddush Hashem* (sanctification of God's Name). Responding to the call of women to recite Kaddish is a *Kiddush Hashem*, as well.

MARK DRATCH is the Founder and Director of Jsafe: The Jewish Institute Supporting an Abuse Free Environment. He is an Instructor of Judaic Studies and Philosophy at Yeshiva University. Mark Dratch received *Semikha* at the Rabbi Isaac Elchanan Theological Seminary of Yeshiva University and served as a pulpit rabbi for 22 years.

One Kind Gesture

DANIEL COHEN

HOW DID ONE KIND GESTURE change the course of Jewish history? When our ancestor Joseph was thrown into jail after being accused of assaulting the wife of Potiphar, he could have wallowed in his own misery. Yet, the Torah records that he reached out to his fellow inmates, the butler and the baker. Joseph asked, "Why do you look so despondent today?" (Genesis 40:7). In response, the butler and the baker shared their anguish about not knowing the interpretation of their dreams. We all know the rest of the story. Joseph's simple caring gesture serves as the catalyst for his liberation from jail in Egypt, his rise to power and the subsequent rescue of his family during the famine in Canaan. In Egypt, the family of Jacob transforms into the nation of Israel. One sensitive question, one choice to reach out to someone in a time of need, changed the course of history.

We are living in a generation of greater connectedness among people, but ironically people feel lonely and less connected. A synagogue is not merely a loosely connected group of people who share a place of prayer. Rather, a *shul* should comprise a conscious community, ideally an extension of family. People long for the sense of belonging that a *shul* can provide, and often look for it at key moments in their lives. When a baby is born to a member of our *shul*, we all rejoice. At a bar or bat mitzvah or a wedding, the *shul* embodies the expression of communal *simcha*. Likewise, when a person experiences a loss, the community, in emulation of the Almighty, shares their sorrow and supports them.

The creation of true community stems from an appreciation of each person being uniquely created in God's image, yet all united as one. We

245

are not merely members of an organization, but children of God bound by a transcendent vision of *Knesset Yisrael*. In the absence of the Beit Ha-Mikdash, the synagogue serves as the foundation of sacred community.

An environment conducive to a woman's recitation of Kaddish emerges from a community of consciousness. It is derived from a realization that every encounter in a *shul* may be a moment of truth. From the greeting one receives on the phone to the *shiva minyanim* or meals provided at home, from the time a person enters the parking lot to their experience in the sanctuary, each moment possesses the possibility of forging an emotional connection to the *shul*, and to Am Yisrael. This connection may then carry over well beyond the period of mourning. As King David writes in Psalms, people who sow in tears will harvest in joy. When we share sorrow together, we will merit celebrating together as a community, as well.

As the largest synagogue in Fairfield County CT, with multiple daily *minyanim*, at Congregation Agudath Sholom we often find not only female members joining for Kaddish, but women from other communities, as well. There are a number of practical steps a rabbi can take to create an inviting environment for these women. The place of prayer should foster engagement by all participants by having a comfortable place for women to sit and ideally orienting the *mechitza* side by side, rather than relegating women to the back of the *shul*. Kaddish should be recited slowly, so everyone can keep pace with the recitation. In addition, the *tzedakah* box should be passed to the women. Most essentially, women present should be acknowledged and made to feel that although they are not counted in the *minyan*, their presence is welcome and they count. Announcing pages in user-friendly *siddurim* that offer transliteration makes Kaddish accessible, while personally welcoming people fosters an environment that emotionally offers comfort and consolation.

In reflecting on my own mother's passing, the most difficult time for me was when *shiva* ended. I was forced to confront the world after my own world was turned upside down. In the days immediately following *shiva*, welcoming a woman (as well as a man) to say Kaddish offers a unique opportunity for communal support and friendship. If other women are present, daily attendance at *minyan* establishes a sorority of people who have experienced personal loss, and the sounds of Kaddish provide a link with one another that is lasting.

Although a woman's recitation of Kaddish is one path to honor a loved one and many find this expression meaningful, there are multiple ways to elevate a *neshama* and to find strength in a time of sadness. These also include *tefillah*, acts of *chesed*, and the study of Torah. The possibility of a woman reciting Kaddish should be offered, but not with the implication that a woman who chooses not to follow this path in any way gives less honor to her loved one.

My hope and prayer is that the experiences of female mourners in our *shul*s will inspire them to become more involved in Jewish life, and also serve as a catalyst for developing the synagogue even further as a conscious community. Every encounter may bring people closer or farther away from God, Torah and the Jewish people. Let us not forget that one effort to welcome a person or inquire about their well-being may alter her life, and be a trigger for events in the future that may well change the course of Jewish history forever.

DANIEL COHEN began serving as spiritual leader of Congregation Agudath Sholom of Stamford, CT in 2005. He is a graduate of Yeshiva University in New York and its Azrieli Graduate School. He received his rabbinic ordination from Yeshiva University's Rabbi Isaac Elchanan Theological Seminary. Daniel Cohen also launched a webite for personal growth www.40daystoabetteryou. com where you can read more of his writings. He and his wife, Diane, are the proud parents of six daughters: Sara Malka, Michal, Adina, Elisheva, Tamar and Shalhevet.

The Laws of Aveilut

DAVID WALK

THE RECITATION OF KADDISH must be seen in the larger context of *aveilut*, the Jewish systematic process of mourning. According to *Halachah*, the mourner is required to go through a schedule which both demands proper observance of mourning and sadness while also insisting that the bereaved re-enter the world of normalcy. According to Rav Joseph Dov Soloveitchik (the Rav, 1903–1993), when the mourner declares, "*Yitgadal v'yitkadash shmei rabba*, glorified and sanctified be the Great Name," one is stating that however powerful death is, how terrifying the grave is, and how black is one's despair, we profess both publicly and solemnly that we are not giving up. We commit ourselves to carry on the work of our ancestors "as if nothing happened." This isn't easy, and is only accomplished through a series of steps.

There is a fundamental argument about these practices. Are we going through this program of grief for the mysterious benefit of the deceased or for the psychological therapy of the bereaved? Even though the correct answer may be both, I believe that most of the customs surrounding *aveilut* are for the mourner. The system is designed to help the healing and binding of our shattered psyche. As it says in our morning prayers, "(God) heals the broken hearted and binds up their sorrow" (Psalms 147:3).

According to Jewish law, one becomes a formal mourner upon the loss of one of seven close relatives: mother, father, sister, brother, son, daughter, and spouse. There is an initial period, brief but profound, between the death of one of the seven close relatives and the burial, called *aninut*. During this period, grief is so uncontrolled that the bereaved isn't required to fulfill any *mitzvot* obligations. However, the Rav pointed out that with the commencement of *aveilut* at the graveside, "Halacha commands the mourner to undertake a heroic task: to start picking up the debris of his own shattered personality and to reestablish himself as a human, restoring lost glory, dignity, and uniqueness" (in "Aninut and Aveilut" in *Out of the Whirlwind: Essays on Mourning, Suffering and the Human Condition* by Rabbi Joseph B. Soloveitchik [edited by David Shatz, Joel B. Wolowelsky and Reuven Ziegler, published by Ktav]).

During this time, returning to *shul* each day to say Kaddish gives an otherwise functioning person the opportunity to don the mantle of mourner again, and to focus on grieving. Traditionally, mourners also absent themselves from large festive gatherings, and live music.

Halachah expects the mourner to go though three distinct steps before re-entering society. We call these steps: *shiva* (the seven days), *shloshim* (the thirty days), and *yud beit chodesh* (the twelve months). The Talmud in Tractate *Moed Katan* (23a) states: A mourner the first week does not leave the home, the second period one leaves home but doesn't sit in their normal place, the third period one sits in the normal place, but doesn't talk and by the fourth the mourner is like everyone else." The clear goal is to achieve a return to the normal beat of life.

This process of re-entering the realm of the normal begins with the custom we call sitting *shiva*. For this initial seven days, the re-composition of the individual is achieved through visits from the community. These visits contain three parts. First the comforter enters in silence, without greeting or comment. Then the visitor awaits the lead of the mourner. It is always appropriate to praise the deceased, but we patiently remain silent until the mourner breaks the ice, or we linger in silence. I have experienced the most profound emotions in a *shiva* home, when the bereaved share their memories of the deceased with the visitors. The guests are enlightened, and the mourners are validated. The final act of the visit is the recitation of the formal formula of comfort: "*HaMakom yinachem etchem b'toch sha'ar aveilei Tzion v'Yerushalayim*, May the Omnipresent comfort you among all the mourners of Zion and Jerusalem." We are all in mourning for something – either personal or national – and therefore in a small way share your pain. Our attempts at consolation may be feeble, but they are needed and appreciated, nonetheless.

As mourners, *shiva* includes many restrictions on our behavior. We wear a garment which was torn at the funeral for the entire week. This custom dates from the behavior of our biblical Patriarchs, and represents that our hearts and souls are broken. We sit on low stools and don't wear leather shoes. We cover mirrors throughout our house, because of our temporary lack of concern for our appearance and also to show that death has temporarily removed us from society and its normal concerns, along with the deceased. Even the most natural of behavior is modified. We limit bathing and the use of cosmetics. We don't greet people, engage in Torah study or even have intimacy with our spouse.

This stage of *shiva* ends with the courageous stepping out into the world, typically a ritualized walk around the block. In some communities the mourner is sent off with the recitation of the following two verses: "Your sun shall no more go down; neither shall your moon withdraw itself: for the Lord shall be your everlasting light, and the days of your mourning shall be ended" (Isaiah 60:20), and "As one whom his mother comforts, so I will comfort you; you shall be comforted in Jerusalem" (66:13). This is perhaps the most critical juncture of the mourning process. The mourner is perched precariously between the very private domain of sitting *shiva* and the wide open spaces of the vast world beyond, and must begin to re-enter the realm of the normal. It's scary, and many mourners need support of family, friends and community during the first days following this critical transition.

The mourner now enters a psychological territory called *shloshim*, or the thirty days. Most of the restrictions of the *shiva* period are lifted, most importantly leaving the home, but also working, greeting, sitting on regular chairs. Certain very private acts which represent the regularity of life are resumed, such as marital relations and Torah study. But we remain careful not to attend parties or joyous public occasions, because happiness is still curtailed. There are debates about the appropriateness of music. Most authorities ban live music, but many are lenient about recorded material. We refrain from haircuts and shaving. We neither buy new things nor accept gifts. This period can often be seen as a halfway house. One public demonstration of our status within Jewish custom is that the mourner doesn't sit in their normal seat in synagogue during this period, an outward expression of the fact that, although we are once again physically present, we remain dislocated. Since we count the seven days of *shiva* as part of this thirty-day period, it only lasts twenty-three days. For all relatives except parents, formal mourning ends at the conclusion of *shloshim*.

For a mother or father, *aveilut* extends for twelve months. This long period, spanning the cycle of a whole year, is marked mostly by refraining from attendance at public celebrations of joy, but often also contains many private moments of reflection about life without one who bestowed upon me life. Although this is clearly a fulfillment of the precept of respecting parents, I've heard speculation that this full year of sadness is based on that first year of life for us, when parents sacrificed so much while we were totally incapable of taking care of ourselves.

Outside of Israel, it has become common for mourners to mark the end of the full year since the death with the unveiling or the erection of a monument over the grave. In Israel, generally this is done at the end of *shloshim*. The grave marker reminds us that the deceased will never be forgotten, even as we go back to "life as usual."

Kaddish is one component of this comprehensive program of mourning. It is important and stands out as a declaration and constant reminder that we still glorify God and life in spite of our depressed state. We recite Kaddish for only eleven months of the twelve months of parental mourning, and that's because mystical sources claim that the judgment process in heaven is completed within eleven for the righteous. Kaddish, like the other laws of *aveilut*, is a tool that helps us climb out of our suffering, one recitation and one day at a time.

Ultimately, by the end of the year we have gone through a large number of moods and psychological steps which hopefully bring us to the conclusion that Maimonides pointed out in his Laws of Mourning (13:11): death is part of the way of the world. We must be able to accept this fact to again be part of this world, which can be so cold and cruel as well as beautiful and fulfilling.

I don't know if Kaddish and mourning are for us or for the deceased, but I hope that we can all agree with the analysis of Rabbi Shlomo Ganzfried (1806–1886) in his *Kitzur Shulchan Aruch* (Concise Code of Jewish Law): "Though saying Kaddish and prayers are helpful to the departed, they are not of primary importance. Rather it is essential that the children proceed in the path of righteousness as paved by their parents, for by this, they bring merit to their parents. . . . The greatest honor to our beloved departed ones is how we live our lives, not any of the rituals connected to mourning."

DAVID WALK is a Jewish educator who has taught Torah on the elementary and high school level in the United States and in post-high school Yeshiva in Israel. He also teaches many informal education classes, and writes a weekly *parsha* article. He is presently teaching at Bi-cultural Day School and is Educational Director at Congregation Agudath Sholom both in Stamford, Ct.

Kaddish and Kabbalah

PENNY COHEN

A S A SPIRITUALLY ORIENTED PSYCHOTHERAPIST, I have come
to believe that all problems are psychologically rooted, while
solutions come through God. While saying Kaddish and praying,
we can work through our afflictions by becoming aware of what they are
and asking God to free us of these burdens, and we can do the psychological work to help us open to receiving God's love and to feel supported,
guided, and blessed.

Rabbi Isaac Luria, "the Ari" and the greatest of Kabbalists, described a
great river with parents going upstream, while children go downstream.
We are mirror images for each other. He believed children inherit un-
resolved issues from their parents, and that healing these issues frees both
souls of each other's burdens. The departed soul is then free to move on,
while the remaining soul is free to be who he/she is meant to be. Abraham
was told, "Leave the land of thy fathers . . . and go to the place that I will
show you." We must each leave behind the internal voices and conditioned
behavior patterns we may be carrying from our parents or ancestors, in
order to actualize our purpose.

Traditionally, Kaddish is about affirming God's greatness through
prayer. It's a way of helping to bring a person's soul into his or her resting
place. Psychologically we take into account what that soul has left behind
and shed light upon it. That means the negative as well as the positive
aspects of our relationship, and how we were affected by it. It's noticing
the thoughts and behavior patterns regarding our parents and possible
repressed or reactive emotional charges towards our parents that have kept
us from feeling love and being loving. This includes anger, resentments,

need for revenge, feelings of abandonment, rejection, dependencies and excessive attachment, etc. It's also dealing with shame, guilt, sadness, hopelessness, fear, and forgiving them and ourselves. It's resolving unfinished business.

For example, your mother may have always had a pattern of putting herself down. "It's all my fault!" Perhaps you hear yourself saying the same thing. We may treat our children the same way we were treated, or we may act just the opposite of the way our parents treated us, which means we're still reacting to our parents rather than having come to terms with what we believe is right. To resolve unfinished business we have to sort out what we are carrying from our parents that repeats or opposes their patterns.

Yet we may find ourselves holding onto patterns, even negative ones, in order to feel connected. For example, a client, Craig, was angry at his father for having beaten him until age 17, when he was able to move out of the house. When I asked Craig how willing he was to let go of his anger – measuring it on a scale of 0 to 10 – he said, "10." However, when I asked the same question during meditation he said, "I can't. He's a part of me. If I let go of him it would be like I'm abandoning him." These internal voices allow us unconsciously to feel close to our loved ones. However, true closeness comes when we resolve the old ways of how we stay connected. To make the repair we have to open our hearts to our parents, deceased siblings, loved ones and God.

As for the deceased, Kabbalists believe that after we die we review our lives and we experience the impact of our actions, both the happiness and pain we imposed on others. It's important to note that souls who have passed on may have as much of a difficult time moving on as the living, because they have the same attachment issues with us, even though they are now out of body. They may feel guilty for causing hurt or for not being a good enough parent, or want to help and protect their loved ones. So what is healing for us heals them, as well.

The goal of this process is to help all of us, the deceased and the living, to be who we are truly meant to be, rather than mirrors of each other. It's breaking the old patterns so we can all move on to reach our true destiny – to love and emulate God and claim our rightful place in the World to Come. To that, I wish us all blessings and joy on our continuing journeys.

PENNY COHEN, LCSW is a groundbreaking transformational psychotherapist, relationship expert, life coach, speaker and author. She earned her Master's degree from Columbia University. Penny is the author of *Personal Kabbalah: 32 Paths To Inner Peace And Life Purpose* and she conducts Professional Training workshops on integrating spirituality and psychotherapy using the Kabbalistic Tree of Life. Her practice is in Pound Ridge, NY and she works with individuals and groups onsite, and on the phone.

A Chorus of Praise:
Reflections on the Meaning of Kaddish

MICHAL SMART

A**CCORDING TO TRADITION**, the recitation of Kaddish by a mourner can elevate the soul of the deceased. In addition, the rabbis teach elsewhere that the world itself is sustained by the recitation of this prayer.

Why? What is the unique power of Kaddish? While volumes can and have been written on this subject, I want to share a few insights I gained while editing this book.

To the surprise of many new mourners, Kaddish makes no mention of death. Rather, it is a prayer of praise to God. It is also Judaism's paradigmatic responsive prayer, in which the prayer leader addresses the congregation, and the congregation responds, in turn. So Kaddish is simultaneously an expression of praise to God and an invitation to all those assembled to praise God, as well. Its power lies not in the leader's recitation of Kaddish per se, but in eliciting the response from the assembled community.

Grammatically, Kaddish is formulated in the future tense. For example, it does not say "*gadol v'kadosh*," but rather "*yitgadal v'yitkadash*." The words do not simply invite one to praise God in the present, then, but to look towards a future in which the world will praise its Creator in a fuller way.

When we praise God as a community, we participate in something larger than ourselves. The Psalmist perceived that "the soul of every living thing praises [God's] name." Biblical prophets and traditional liturgy describe the existence of entirely spiritual beings that likewise praise God by virtue of their very existence.

In all of creation, it seems, only the human being – uniquely self-conscious, articulate, and blessed with the gift and burden of free will – has the choice to deny, defy, or praise our Creator. Only when we choose to stand together consciously in the presence of God and lend our voices, as we do when we recite Kaddish, is the world's chorus of praise complete.

The central phrase in Kaddish declares: "*Yehei shmei rabba mevorach l'olam ul'olmei olmaya*, May God's great Name be blessed. . . ." The end part is usually translated in temporal terms, something like "forever and ever." Yet it is literally more akin to a spatial reference: "in this world, and in all worlds of this world." The cosmic chorus of praise links all realms of existence: the human and the non-human, the temporarily physical and the wholly spiritual, the living and perhaps the dead.

There are twenty-eight words from the start of this key refrain "*Yehei shmei rabba mevorach* . . ." until the end of the half-Kaddish. The rabbis likened these to the twenty-eight phrases in Ecclesiastes that poetically depict the vicissitudes of human life: "To everything there is a season . . . A time to be born and a time to die. . . . A time to kill and a time to heal, a time to wreck and a time to build, a time to weep and a time to laugh, a time to mourn and a time to dance . . ." In fact, the rabbis considered the connection between Kaddish and this section of Ecclesiastes to be so essential that during the ten days between Rosh Hashanah and Yom Kippur, when a repetition of the word "*l'eilah*" ("*Beyond* any blessing and song . . .") is inserted into Kaddish, two other words of the prayer are contracted into one (*min kol* becomes *m'kol*) in order to keep the parallel intact.

It is the mortal human who stands to praise God with the words of Kaddish, despite the apparent imperfection of the world and the tragedies of human existence. This is underscored by the absence of God's name itself, as well as the prayer's use of Aramaic: the everyday language (in its time) of human society, not the holy tongue of Scripture. Through Kaddish, we affirm that notwithstanding our pain and the hiddenness of God, the universal endeavor is nonetheless worthwhile. We remain willing participants and extol the divine vision that underlies our existence. And who can do so more poignantly than the recently bereaved?

The rabbis formulated the central verse, "*Yehei shmei rabba mevorach l'olam ul'olmei olmaya*," to mirror the structure of two key verses in the Torah, thereby linking them, as well. This core proclamation contains precisely seven words and twenty-eight letters, just like Genesis 1:1, the verse which begins the Creation narrative ("*Breisheet bara Elokim et hashamayim v'et ha'aretz*, In the beginning God created Heaven and Earth") and Exodus 20:1, the prelude to the Ten Commandments ("*Vayidaber Elokim et kol hadevarim ha'eileh laimor*, And God spoke all of these words, saying").

Thus, when we declare as a congregation "*Yehei shmei rabba mevorach l'olam ul'olmei olmaya*," we not only praise God, thereby joining our voices to a transworldly chorus and surmounting the limitations of human existence, anticipating a better and ultimately messianic future, we also affirm our faith in Hashem as Creator, in the revelation at Sinai, and Israel's mission in bringing the created world to the fulfillment of its spiritual purpose.

And so the world is sustained, and the individuals who inspired the living generation to carry on this task and vision are judged favorably.

The multifaceted meaning of the Kaddish prayer is arcane, yet profound. One who prompts the congregation to recite these powerful words performs an act not only of personal value but perhaps of cosmic significance, as well.

The Kaddish envisions a time when God's Name will become even greater, even more widely sanctified: *yitgadal v'yitkadash shmei rabbah*. By saying Kaddish, women add our voices to the community of Jews praising God. In so doing, perhaps, we help in some small way to actualize the meaning of the Kaddish itself.

קדיש יתום

יִתְגַּדַּל וְיִתְקַדַּשׁ שְׁמֵהּ רַבָּא

בְּעָלְמָא דִּי בְרָא כִרְעוּתֵהּ וְיַמְלִיךְ מַלְכוּתֵהּ

בְּחַיֵּיכוֹן וּבְיוֹמֵיכוֹן וּבְחַיֵּי דְכָל בֵּית יִשְׂרָאֵל

בַּעֲגָלָא וּבִזְמַן קָרִיב וְאִמְרוּ אָמֵן.

יְהֵא שְׁמֵהּ רַבָּא מְבָרַךְ לְעָלַם וּלְעָלְמֵי עָלְמַיָּא

יִתְבָּרַךְ וְיִשְׁתַּבַּח וְיִתְפָּאַר וְיִתְרוֹמַם וְיִתְנַשֵּׂא

וְיִתְהַדָּר וְיִתְעַלֶּה וְיִתְהַלָּל שְׁמֵהּ דְּקֻדְשָׁא בְּרִיךְ הוּא

לְעֵלָּא מִן כָּל בִּרְכָתָא וְשִׁירָתָא תֻּשְׁבְּחָתָא וְנֶחֱמָתָא דַּאֲמִירָן בְּעָלְמָא

וְאִמְרוּ אָמֵן.

יְהֵא שְׁלָמָא רַבָּא מִן שְׁמַיָּא

וְחַיִּים עָלֵינוּ וְעַל כָּל יִשְׂרָאֵל וְאִמְרוּ אָמֵן.

עוֹשֶׂה שָׁלוֹם בִּמְרוֹמָיו הוּא יַעֲשֶׂה שָׁלוֹם עָלֵינוּ וְעַל כָּל יִשְׂרָאֵל

וְאִמְרוּ אָמֵן.

Mourner's Kaddish

Magnified and sanctified may His great name be in the world that He created by His will, and may God give reign to His kingship in your lifetimes and in your days, and in the lifetime of the entire house of Israel, swiftly and soon. And say: Amen.

May His great Name be blessed forever and ever.

Blessed and praised, glorified and exalted, raised and honored, elevated and lauded be the Name of the Holy One, Blessed be He, beyond any blessings, songs, praises and consolations that are uttered in the world. And say: Amen.

May there be abundant peace from heaven, and life for us and for all Israel. And say: Amen.

May He who makes peace in His high places make peace for us and for all Israel. And say: Amen.

In Loving Memory
לעילוי נשמת

Ken Weinberger   יהודה בער בן אליעזר ורבקה
by Barbara Ashkenas

רייזל בת סימה
by Nechama Goldman Barash

Carol Mae Line   קילא משה בת צבי הרשל ובשא
by Barbara Becker, Rebecca E. Starr

אלישבע בת פסח הכהן   פסח בן אברהם הכהן
by Ellen Copeland Buchine

Sandra Cohen   שרה מלכה בת אהרון אברהם הלוי
by Daniel Cohen

Mollie Levenberg Lotto   מלכה בת רבקה
Sam Lotto   שמואל בן שרה
by Penny Cohen

George Kaplan   גרשון בן חיים הכהן
by Rachel Cohen

NATHANIEL RICHMAN COHEN נפתלי צבי בן ראובן נחום הכהן
ורחל לאה

by Shelley Richman Cohen

ריסיה בת הרב שלמה אהרון וחיה פריידה

by Shifra Aviva (Posner) Deren

BARBARA DRATCH ברכה בת חיים לייב וחיה שרה

by Mark Dratch

SUSAN FAY FINEBLUM SCHARF שפרה פריידה בת שניאור זלמן
וחסנה רייזה חיה
TOBI SHARON FINEBLUM טובה רוחה בת שניאור זלמן
WEISMAN וחסנה רייזה חיה

by Deborah Fineblum

DR. GEORGE GANTZ גרשון בן ישראל

by Paula Gantz

HARRIET SALLY MILLER WEITZ חיה זלטא בת איידֿעל ושאול

by Toba Weitz Goldberg

HERBERT GOLDMAN חיים בן שמואל
BEATRICE SCHECTER ברכה בת משה יהודה

by Jeralyn Goldman

ALVIN GOODMAN אברהם בן שמואל

by Laila Goodman

Paul Greenwald   פרץ בן משה יענקל ומרים

by Meryl Greenwald Gordon

עזריאל בן משה וחוה

by Chaya Rosenfeld Gorsetman

Dr. Hanna French, née Adler   חנה בת עדה ומאיר
Ada Adler   עדה בת נפתלי הערץ הכהן ובלומע

by Deborah Greniman

Samuel Hallegua   שמואל בן חיים

by Fiona Hallegua

Sarah Schwimmer   שרה רבקה בת חנוך הינך

by Judith Schwimmer Hessing

Susan Fast Bloch   שרה ריבה בת וולף וחנה לאה

by Marlyn Bloch Jaffe

Irv Yatzkan   יצחק פסח בן חנוך וחוה גיטל

by Debbie Yatzkan Jonas

אברהם עזריאל בן חסיה ויצחק

by Rachel Goldstein Jubas

Leon Kahn   אריה לייב בן שאול הכהן

by Hodie Kahn

Steven Gil Ellison   שלמה גיל בן גבריאל וחיה הודל
by Abby Ellison Kanarek

Dorothy Koplow   חיה דאבא בת מאיר ובריינדל
Milton Koplow   מיכאל בן יהושע זעליג
by Amy Koplow

הרב עזריאל בן יוסף טוביה ובלומה
רחל בת שבתאי יהושע יצחק חיים ונחה
by Deb Kram

Paul Braunstein   פנחס בן צבי ראובן
by Leah Braunstein Levy

Rita Skidelsky Kaufman   רבקה בת בנימין והניה דינה
Benjamin Kaufman   זאב דב בן מרדכי ואסתר
by Belda Kaufman Lindenbaum

Maurice Goldstein   משה בן שמואל ואיטקה
Jerome Kleinberg   יעקב יוסף בן אברהם קלמן
by Debra Luger

Mordecai Rahamim Ephraim ben Emanuel Eskell Yadida
מרדכי רחמים אפרים בן עמנואל אסקל ידידה
by Aviva Ephraim Maller

Karen Tendler   בלימה נחמה בת בריינדל ודוד
by Pearl Tendler Mattenson

CARYL MESCH   חיה בת מאיר ורבקה

by Rachel Mesch

~~~~~~

IRVING MARKOWITZ   יצחק בן יוסף חיים וחיה שרה
MILDRED MARKOWITZ   מלכה רחל בת משה יהודה ומינדל

by Karen Markowitz Michaels

~~~~~~

DR. CHARLES S. NAIMAN   יחיאל שמחה בן אסתר חנה ומשה צבי

by Geela R. R. Naiman

~~~~~~

BENJAMIN KERSHENBAUM   בנימין בן אהרון ושושנה
HELEN KERSHENBAUM   חיה שרה בת בנימין הכהן וחוה

by Joni Nathanson

~~~~~~

RABBI JOSEPH H. WISE   הרב יוסף חיים בן הרב מיכאל ושרה

by Sara Wise Prager

~~~~~~

DR. ABRAHAM RAPOPORT   אברהם אבא בן ישראל הכהן ונעשע
נין ונכד לנשר הגדול הש"ך דצ"ל

by Nessa Rapoport

~~~~~~

DR. ALLEN H. REED   חיים אהרון בן פנחס ואסתר

by Esther Reed

~~~~~~

MARK J. ROEMER   מרדכי יוסף בן מרדכי מאיר ואסתר
JANE S. ROEMER   יוכבד שרה בת מרדכי יוסף וחיינה

by Dina Roemer

~~~~~~

Dr. Norman S. Rosenfeld   נטע שמואל בן יוסף חיים
by Jennie Rosenfeld

Ilene Rita Shaffer   חיה רבקה בת אברהם ורייזל זיסל
David Evan Shaffer   חיים דוד בן אפרים נחום וחיה רבקה
by Debra Shaffer Seeman

Charlotte Venze   שרה בת שמעון וחיה
by Anne Venze Sendor

Albert H. Barouh   אברהם בן יוסף
Miriam L. Barouch   מרים בת ישעיהו
by Rochelle Barouh Senker

Edward Ritten   אברהם בן יעקב
Lorraine Ritten   לאה בת דוד
Rachel bat Yocheved   רחל בת יוכבד
by Joyce Solomon

ייטה בת צבי הרש   אליהו בן צבי
by Vera Schwarcz

Murray Ehrlich   מנחם מנדל בן יצחק
by Sandi Ehrlich Waldstreicher

Jacob Walk   יעקב בן דוד אליה
Lilian Dobrow Walk   רוסה לאה בת שמחה
by David Walk

ESTHER JOYCE REIFMAN   אסתר יוחא בת שרה לאה ונח
YOSEF REIFMAN   יוסף בן שמואל וסעשא
by Chana Reifman Zweiter

ARTHUR WEISINGER   אהרון יהודה בן יהושע
by Suzanne Wolf

Glossary of Hebrew and Yiddish Terms

Abba — Father

Aliyah — lit., ascension; refers to moving to the Land of Israel, or being called up to the Torah reading in synagogue

Am Yisrael — the People of Israel

Amidah — central prayer, recited silently while standing

Asarah B'Tevet — the Tenth of Tevet, a minor fast day marking the beginning of the siege of Jerusalem leading to the destruction of the First Temple

Aveilut — mourning

Baal/Baalei tefillah — prayer leader(s)

Baalat/Baal teshuvah — Jew who returns to Jewish observance

Bar/Bat mitzvah — coming of age celebration

Beit HaMikdash — the Holy Temple

Beit midrash — room or place devoted to Torah study

Brachah (pl. brachot) — blessing(s)

Bris/Brit milah — ceremonial circumcision of a male child (often on the eighth day after birth)

B'tzibbur — publicly, in a congregation

Chag (pl. chagim) — holiday(s)

Challah — bread traditionally eaten on Shabbat

Chazzan — prayer leader

Chesed — kindness

Chevra Kaddisha — Burial Society

Chiyuv — religious obligation

Daven — pray

269

Dvar Torah — lit., word of Torah; a teaching

Frumkeit — religious observance (adj. frum)

Gabbai (pl. gabbaim) — person who organizes the prayer service

Halachah (pl. halachot) — Jewish law(s)

Halachic — in accordance with Jewish law

Hamotzi — blessing recited before eating bread

Hashem — traditional name for God; lit., "the Name"

Hesped — eulogy

Kaddish — Kaddish prayer

Kaddish D'Rabbanan — Rabbi's Kaddish, also recited by mourners

Kaddish Yatom — Mourner's Kaddish; lit., Orphan's Kaddish

Kavana — intention, concentration

Kedushah — holiness

Kibbud av va'em — honoring one's father and mother

Kotel — Jerusalem's Western wall

Maariv — evening prayer service

Makom — place; HaMakom is a name for God

Makom kavua — permanent place, e.g., designated for a set purpose

Mechitza — divider between the men's and women's sections in synagogue

Megillah — Scroll of Esther, read on Purim

Mikvah — ritual bath for purification

Mincha — afternoon prayer service

Minhag — custom

Minyan (pl. minyanim) — a quorum of ten that is needed to conduct formal prayer services; Orthodox *minyan*s count only men, egalitarian *minyan*s include women

Mitzvah (pl. mitzvot) — religious commandment(s)

Neshama — soul

Niftar(a) — died; lit., released from religious obligation

Pesach — Passover holiday

Sabra — native-born Israeli Jew

Shabbat (alt. Shabbos) — Sabbath

Shacharit — morning prayer service

Shaliach tzibbur — prayer leader

Shamayim — Heaven

Shiva — seven; the first week of the mourning period

Shloshim — thirty; the first month of the mourning period

Shul — synagogue
Siddur (pl. siddurim) — prayer book
Simcha (pl. smachot) — celebration(s), happiness
Siyum — The conclusion of a set portion of Torah study
Taharat hamishpacha — laws of family purity
Tefillah (pl. tefillot) — prayer
Tefillah b'tzibbur — public prayer
Tallit — prayer shawl
Tzedakah (box) — charity; a box used to collect charity
Tzibbur — congregation
Yahrzeit — anniversary of someone's death
Yishuv — lit., settlement; rural community in Israel
Yizkor — memorial service, held on certain holidays

MICHAL SMART teaches widely on Jewish texts and philosophy, with a focus on Jewish women. A Fulbright scholar in Jewish Thought, Michal received her A.B. from Princeton University in Religion and an M.S. from Cornell. She is also an alumna of the Wexner Graduate Fellowship, the Melton Senior Educators Program at Hebrew University, and Machon Pardes. Earlier, Michal pioneered Jewish outdoor and environmental education in the U.S. She is a founder of the TEVA Learning Center and co-author of Spirit in Nature: Teaching Judaism and Ecology on the Trail (Behrman House, 2000). Michal lives in Stamford, Connecticut with her husband, James, and their five children.

BARBARA ASHKENAS received her BA in early childhood education from the Ohio State University, and a Masters in Art Education from Manhattanville College. She has been professionally involved in the Arts for over thirty years. Earlier in her career, as a freelance calligrapher, she crafted Ketubot, logos and invitations. More recently, as an Arts educator, she conducts seminars for staff development on the integration of the Arts into Jewish educational settings. Barbara has served as the Educational Outreach Coordinator at the Stamford Center for the Arts, and as an Adjunct Professor of Art Education at Housatonic Community College. Barbara also participated in the Drisha Arts Fellowship program in New York City. Barbara is an active member of Congregation Agudath Sholom in Stamford, Connecticut where she is a founding member of the Women's Tefillah Group. She and her husband, Ron, are blessed with three adult children Eli, Shira and Ari, daughter-in-law Rebecca and son-in-law Elie as well as three adorable grandchildren, Noam, Mori and Eitan.